\THE

ANTISLAVERY STRUGGLE

AND

TRIUMPH

IN THE

METHODIST EPISCOPAL CHURCH. /

By REV. L. C. MATLACK, D.D.

WITH AN INTRODUCTION BY REV. D. D. WHEDON, D.D.

NEGRO UNIVERSITIES PRESS
NEW YORK

Originally published in 1881
by Phillips & Hunt

Reprinted from a copy in the collections
of the Brooklyn Public Library

Reprinted 1969 by
Negro Universities Press
A DIVISION OF GREENWOOD PRESS, INC.
NEW YORK

SBN 8371-2738-6

PRINTED IN UNITED STATES OF AMERICA

To the Memory of

JOHN WESLEY,

WHO DECLARED "AMERICAN SLAVERY
THE VILEST THAT EVER SAW THE SUN;" TO
THE FATHERS OF THE METHODIST EPISCOPAL
CHURCH, WHOSE PRAYER, WITH BISHOP ASBURY, WAS,
"O LORD, BANISH THE INFERNAL SPIRIT OF SLAVERY FROM THY
DEAR ZION;" TO THE ANTISLAVERY HEROES OF OUR CHURCH, WHOSE
FAITHFUL TESTIMONY AND ZEALOUS ACTION WERE NECESSARY
TO THE EXTIRPATION OF SLAVERY; AND, FINALLY,
TO ALL WHO CHERISH THESE MEMORIES, AND
NOW HAVE CONFIDED TO THEM THE
VINDICATION OF ALL RIGHTS
FOR ALL MEN, IS THIS
VOLUME DEDI-
CATED BY

THE AUTHOR.

PREFACE.

D URING the session of the General Conference of the Methodist Episcopal Church, held in Baltimore, Md., May, 1876, the following communication was placed in my hand, which was the immediate occasion for writing this volume. The purpose had not been contemplated. The responsibility belongs to those whose words are given below.

REV. L. C. MATLACK, D.D.:

DEAR BROTHER: A full and impartial history of the antislavery struggle in the Methodist Episcopal Church has never been written. We believe that such a work would be of great interest and permanent value ; and that you have peculiar facilities for writing it. The interest we feel in this matter, and our desire that justice may be done to the Abolitionists of our Church, prompt us to express the hope that you may be able to prepare such a work at an early day.

> R. M. HATFIELD,
> R. S. RUST,
> WILLIAM RICE,
> GILBERT HAVEN,
> DANIEL CURRY,
> C. H. FOWLER,
> THOMAS W. PRICE.

GENERAL CONFERENCE ROOM,
  BALTIMORE, Md., *May* 23, 1876.

After a few days' deliberation upon the matter, I replied, consenting to undertake the task thus assigned to me. The duties of the pastorate and the preparation for pulpit services have allowed only occasional hours of leisure in which to prepare the manuscript for the press. Being in no haste, and desiring to do justice to the subject — if practicable for me at all — it was necessary to prolong the time of its accomplishment. Now to my task.

The subject of slavery has ceased to be an exciting question. A general agreement has succeeded the former dissensions attendant upon its discussion, only a few years ago, in both civil and ecclesiastical bodies. And this is so, because in America slavery has ceased to be a fact. It is now only a memory, kept painfully vivid with its victims by the spirit of caste which remains in both Church and State.

The relations which American slavery sustained with the Churches, as well as with the government, of the United States, during and preceding the century just closed, were so friendly and so controlling, that the record of it must ever be an essential feature of current history. American Church history, with no record pertaining to slavery, is necessarily incomplete. And to have made no antislavery history is a positive reproach upon the Christian integrity of any Church in the United States.

This is not the case with the Methodist Episcopal Church. Hitherto her history in connection with slavery has had no adequate record. The necessary facts lie spread over the pages of numerous volumes of history, minutes, and periodicals. A single volume is needed, which shall contain satisfactory answers to the questionings of those who shall follow us in the coming years.

It is not, however, required that all the facts from every source should be gathered into one huge volume. It is only necessary that these facts pass under careful review for classification and generalized statement; and that a narration thereof should be framed, if possible, which shall be fully authenticated, condensed, clear, and sufficiently attractive to invite and hold attention.

For such a narrative there is abundant material at command. How well it has been combined in this work the reader has now an opportunity to determine. The scope, or field of observation embraced, covers four periods in the order now indicated: A preliminary period, anterior to American Methodism, when slavery was rooted and grounded in our land by the agency of European and American Christians; a primary period, during which the fathers of Methodism unsparingly denounced and prohibited slavery; the period of toleration, in which their sons, however illegally, allowed and practiced slavery; and, finally, the period of extirpation, when, for almost thirty years, the grandsons of our fathers warred with slavery until a glorious victory crowned their efforts.

The many years covered by this history, the ample record of facts included, the extended discussion involved, might have warranted the production of a large quarto volume. But a concise statement of essential facts in a smaller number of pages, with the hope of a larger circulation, was deemed preferable.

To tell the story of this struggle with slavery, which continued during the first century of American Methodism; to supplement the history of our Church with a chapter from the antislavery records of those times; and to honor both the heroic defenders of primitive Methodism and the people who accepted so heartily the platform of 1774, as laid down in "Wesley's Thoughts on Slavery," is the ambition of the writer of "THE ANTISLAVERY STRUGGLE AND TRIUMPH."

INTRODUCTION.

A HISTORY of the relations of the Methodist
Episcopal Church to the origin, existence, and
destruction of slavery will generally be considered as
a required part of our Church literature. It seemed
quite proper that the writer should be one versed in
all that might be esteemed wrong in the connection
of the Church therewith, and yet morally competent
to treat the whole subject with Christian candor. An
"original abolitionist," excluded from our ministerial
orders on account of his persistence, Dr. Matlack had
about as good a right to complain and reproach us as
any body, and when he is selected as the historian by
the Church, a readiness is shown to have the severer
view fairly presented. All will concede that he nar-
rates with unflinching explicitness, yet with passion-
less calmness and candor. He does not find it necessary, as did an Albert Barnes or a Judge Jay, in
the heat of the battle, to vituperate the Church
in order to correct and deter her from wrong; nor
like later maligners, after the battle is over, to avail
himself of the occasion to serve the cause of skepti-
cism and irreligion. He seeks to present the views of
both sides fairly; he shows that antislaveryism arose
from the religious consciousness of men, that Methodist antislaveryism in its latest form was the true offspring of her early and permanent record, and that

Methodism, in spite of many an unhappy concession to slavery, has an antislavery history of her own of which she may be justly proud.

But while we cheerfully concede to an "original abolitionist" the office of historiographer, it seems right (as no one will more cordially concede than himself) that the counter side should also be allowed to state its apology and justification. The writer of this Introduction was an original opposer of the Garrisonian movement, and of Mr. Garrison himself. Looking back from the pedestal of the present to that distant period of more than half a century, he approves that opposition. Fully appreciating the martyr-like heroism of Mr. Garrison and his followers, fully acknowledging their royal adherence to their views of truth and duty, and never reading their story, as usually narrated by themselves, without a very ready sympathy, we think now, as we thought then, that the wisdom of the movement, in the style in which it was conducted, was more than questionable. At the start of that movement, while there was a general quietude on the subject of slavery, there was little conscious pro-slaveryism North or South. "Slavery in the abstract," as it was called, was universally condemned. Especially with the conscientious Christian community, and most especially with Methodism, there was underlying all this quietude and quandary as to what could be done a protest against its existence, and an assumption that it was but temporary. When Garrisonism rung out its "fire-bell in the night" there were millions unprepared for its peal and doubting the certainty of its sounds. The movement was started by men who had little at stake in the existing order of society, and the alarm was felt by the great body of those who had much to lose in a coming convulsion. The great aggregate of the weighty, wise, and good, stood in the opposition. They believed that slavery was a moral and political evil; but they also believed that somehow it was temporary, and that rash measures would both perpetuate the evil and produce other evils of incalculable magnitude. But as the battle waxed warm, and the slave-power, in self-defense, became bold and announced a claim to perpetuity and even supremacy, thousands after thousands felt compelled to join the antislavery ranks, and to demand, first, the limitation of slavery, and finally to claim its immediate extirpation.

It is of the first importance for us fully to realize that the abolition movement was, in fact, an utter moral failure. It is a signal, popular illusion that original abolitionism was a great, successful moral reform. This error is propagated with much magniloquence by Mr. Garrison's latest biographer. You would think from the ordinary story that slavery was abolished by moral suasion, and that essentially by the Garrisonian programme. Quite the reverse. All Mr. Garrison did was to madden the slave-holders and bring on a war. The war might have created a slave empire and have perpetuated the system forever. The abolition was not a moral achievement but a war measure. Had the slave-power stood solid yet calm, maintaining its silent position and making no aggressions, slavery would, to all appearance, be standing at this hour, perhaps the stronger for the opposition.

Nor did the alternative then before the conscientious inquirer lie between Garrisonism and nothing. Before his movement the Colonization Society existed, claiming to be, though a slow, yet a hopeful remedy for slavery. To it, we are told by Mr. G.'s biographer, " every rill of antislavery feeling flowed." Organically, indeed, it did not claim to interfere with slavery. It assumed that there was no practicable hope for the elevation of the negro in America. But it pointed to his ancestral home in Africa, and maintained that, restored to the land of his fathers, a new civilization might there be by him built up, which would vindicate the negro character and equalize him ultimately with the Caucasian. This would react to elevate the negro in America. Meanwhile the society proposed to render emancipation easy by furnishing a desirable home for the emancipated. Government aid might give a stupendous magnitude to the movement. And all the while the agents and friends of colonization were able to freely discuss the subject throughout the South, interesting the Southern people in plans for emancipation. It was the owners of the slave who were expected, even by Southerners, to surrender the slave by deliberate, peaceful, and ultimately advantageous process. The vacancies of population were to be filled up by a Caucasian immigration; and thus, by a happy but slow and conservative series of measures, slavery was to fade away, Africa be civilized, America be harmonized, and the millennium be approximated. We freely affirm that we were more fascinated by this picture than by any product of Mr. Garrison's artistic pencil. And even now in the retrospect we prefer the peaceful to the bloody way. Could half the expenditure laid out upon our late civil war, and half the heroism and self-sacrifice on both sides displayed—to say nothing of devastations and desolations committed, fierce and

diabolic passions aroused, and historic scars inflicted
— have been exerted in colonization and peaceful
emancipation, we calmly believe that 1950 would
have found a happier situation of both races and both
continents than will now be presented. This, however, is a problem too vast for human solution. The
actual result is indeed worth all it cost. It may be that
the bloody way alone had victory and freedom at its
end. It is sufficient for our present purpose to make
clear the fact that there were two sides to the question, before which the Christian, the humanitarian,
and the Church might well pause; and that the poet-
ico - rhetorical denunciations poured by such writers
as Mr. Oliver Johnson on those whom he calls "the
leaders of the popular Christianity of the day," are
written in the interests of semi-infidelity.

Had Mr. Garrison and his followers manifested a due
degree of wisdom, these two ways need not have been
antagonistic. Such, as we learn by the late biography
of Dr. Channing, was his view. Such certainly was
the view of the writer of these lines, expressed in an
address delivered before a colonization society at Middletown, July 4, 1834. "In brief, the proposition of
the emancipationist is, to induce the Southerner to
immediately free his slaves. The proposition of the
colonizationist is, to offer to all who are freed the
opportunity and facilities of a spontaneous voluntary
emigration to the land from which the slave has been
stolen. Now, upon the first flush one is inclined to
ask, What is there incompatible in these two plans?
If the emancipationist has any means of peaceably inducing the Southerner to manumit the slave, why not
apply himself to it, and allow the colonizationist, in his
own sphere, to complete the benefaction by restoring

every manumited slave, who desires it, to the land of
his ancestry? Will the emancipationist reiterate the
stale objection, that colonization timidly leaves the
relation of master and slave undisturbed, and so aban-
dons the poor negro to the cruelty of his oppressor?
Then let him apply himself, not to destroy the benefit
of colonization, but to supply the field of benevolence
which it leaves untouched. What should we say,
were the Bible Society to denounce the missionary
scheme, because it impiously supported the plan of
evangelizing the world by mere fallible men, and left
the benighted heathen to perish for the want of the
volume of inspiration? In both cases, each society
has, and should have, without impeding the other, its
own sphere of operation."

It was Mr. Garrison who opened the war between
the two methods by a public onslaught upon the Colonization Society. "He pronounced the society a
'conspiracy against human rights;' he asserted that
'the superstructure of the society rests upon the following pillars : 1. Persecution ; 2. Falsehood ; 3. Cow-
ardice ; 4. Infidelity.' 'If,' said he, 'I do not prove
the Colonization Society to be a creature without
brains, eyeless, unnatural, hypocritical, relentless, and
unjust, let me be covered with confusion of face.'"
Such is a fair specimen of Mr. Garrison's fervid rhetoric. His spirit breathed an exasperation into the
whole contest which auspicated strife and bloodshed
from the beginning. As the plan and purpose of
colonizationism were comprehensive, enabling it to
unite in one organic enterprise both Northerners and
Southerners, men of various shades of opinion, so
many of the utterances in the speeches and other
documents of the society were truly objectionable,

and on these utterances most of Mr. G.'s assaults were grounded. The real value of the objective enterprise it proposed was never disproved. Yet in the course of the contest that society became a rallying point of the most violent pro-slavery men, men who cared nothing for its real principles, but availed themselves of the respectability of its flag to cover their own inhuman baseness. In the convulsive strifes that ensued the way of colonization and peace receded to the background, and was forgotten. Reluctantly, yet surely, both sides were marching to the final arbitrament of the sword. The refusal of the Churches to put themselves under the dubious leadership of Mr. G., happily retarded this arbitrament; and, what is an all-important point, retarded the crisis until the North had become powerful enough to meet it triumphantly.

About 1834 we put the question to Dr. Wilbur Fisk, who had resided in the South: "Suppose the entire ministry and Churches and people of the North had at once become Garrisonian with perfect unanimity, what would have been the result?" He promptly replied in substance: "The result would be that the South would be equally unanimous on the other side; war would ensue and an independent slave empire would be established." We could hardly believe it. But we think from our now past experience our every reader will respond that Dr. Fisk foretold the "Solid South." *Had the whole North in 1834 become Garrisonian, a Southern slave nation would now be our neighbor at the South.* For at that time the South was far nearer equality in fighting power with the North, and could easily, at any rate, have defended herself and maintained her own territory. The refusal, therefore, of the Churches to hear Mr. Garrison in truth prevented the perpetuity of slavery in its worst form, and so postponed the conflict that slavery was finally destroyed. Nay, we can put a stronger case. Whatever the Churches may have done, the Democratic party, true to its historical instincts, would have solidly united with the Solid South. It has been often said by our Abolition friends that "if the ministers would only come right all would come right." It is a most idiotic proposition. The Democratic party has ever gloried in not being priest-governed; and its antagonism against a solid antislavery clergy would have been as violent as solid. In the consequent war there then would have been a Solid South against a divided North. In the contest of arms the South would have conquered. The limitations of slavery would have been abolished, and Boston would have been as completely under the slave-power as Charleston.

Alarmed at the progress and infuriated by the boldness of the Abolitionists, the slave-power became menacing and fatally aggressive. To maintain one great despotism it became necessary to threaten every other liberty North and South, and it grew gradually evident that the rights, not only of the southern slave but of the northern freeman, were at stake. As this grew clear the ranks of antislaveryism grew thicker and stronger. Our General Conference of 1844 disclosed to us the fact that complete surrender was demanded by the South. All barriers were to be broken down and slavery was to become perpetual and supreme. Old opponents of "abolitionism," (like the writer of these lines,) who were nevertheless opponents of slavery, in increasing numbers took their stand; at first in favor of limiting its territory, and finally for driving it out of existence, at whatever cost.

From these views it will be seen that while we accord all praise to the original Abolitionists in the Methodist Episcopal Church, we award quite as much praise to those who at first manfully opposed the early movement. Mr. Garrison's admirers largely expatiate on the supposed fact that no clergyman would officiate at the first meeting of the Abolitionists in Boston; and we have elsewhere declared, and here repeat the declaration, that we would have refused so to officiate, and would now indorse that refusal. Not only did the Christian ministry show a proper self-respect in declining such a leadership, but their reserve delayed the contest which the movement would have precipitated until the North was powerful enough to secure the victory of freedom.

The relations and dealings of the Protestant Churches with slavery would be very likely to depend very much upon the strength of their organic connection with the South. The Congregational and Unitarian communions being Northern only, could readily without fracture become antislavery. The Episcopal Church, on the other hand, was practically indifferent to the existence of the oppressive system. While Dr. Matlack well shows that in spite of every concession made to slavery, the Methodist Episcopal Church, the most massily organic Protestant Church in America, has the most pronounced record of all. From the very earliest period she had been avowedly hostile to the existence of slavery. Her disciplinary declarations, though modified and minified, ever remained, pronouncing slavery a great "evil" destined to "EX-TIRPATION," placing a ban upon the ministerial slave-holder, and denouncing the "buying and selling" as a mortal sin, were never removed until emancipation evacuated their significance. Nor were they a dead letter. The argument of freedom in 1844 was based upon our old and permanent antislavery platform. And Dr. Matlack and other original Methodist Abolitionists, whether remaining in the Church or seceding from it, grounded themselves upon the old traditions and entire history of the Church. Underlying all the yieldings to the slave-power during the concessive period, there was a powerful protest that forbade us to concede the right or the perpetuity of slavery. And that protest, though often overridden, was never dead or powerless.

It is easy for the present generation to condemn without jury the good and holy men who made those concessions. The leaders of Methodism truly believed they were securing all the good possible without incurring an overbalancing evil. They had quadrennially met their southern brethren in General Conference discussion, and believed they most truly understood both sides of the subject, and had made a platform on which alone the Church could rest without danger to both the unity of the Church and the peace of the country. On that platform the South conceded that slavery was "evil" and destined to "extirpation," and the North was to wait some peaceful method by which, under a gracious Providence and the law of humanitarian progress, the "evil" should disappear. Neither side defended slavery as right or to be perpetual. The authorities of northern Methodism, including the General Conference men, the episcopacy, and the press, were, therefore, unanimous for a common concurrence on the agreed platform. The *old* antislavery doctrine was to be retained, but the *new* "modern abolitionism," as it was called, was to be rejected. We believe that all this was justifiable so long as the agreement remained that slavery was to be temporary, and so long as the churchly authorities confined themselves to the use of only persuasions. But when they concurred so far with the anti-abolition violences of the hour as to withhold ordination and inflict ministerial suspension upon ministerial Abolitionists, their course was despotic and suicidal. The arraignments of the Abolitionists before the Conference clothed them with the sacredness of martyrdom, and awakened misgivings, spoken and unspoken, that this crushing of the freedom of speech was a very serious concession to such a system as American slavery. Every such movement was a generator of new abolitionism.

But to enter more fully into the consciousness of these venerated men we must realize the advancement of the slave-power produced by the cotton monopoly. That singular potentate, the cotton-power, began to fancy itself holding the world at its feet. It had growing visions of a great southern slave empire, chivalrous, aristocratic, and warlike, which could in time show to the world a right royal history. It was growing to hold the bonds of "the Union" as of far less value than the fetters of slavedom. It was beginning to feel that only so long as it could rule the Union was it worth while to be in the Union. Hence it could menace the North in the lordliest tone, and impose conditions of the most despotic nature. But with the North the dissolution of the Union was viewed as a national death. It was the breaking up of old historic ties. Patriotism, politics, commerce, social influence, churchly ties, all united in condemning not the menacing slave-power but the Northern resistant to its despotism. The lamb and not the wolf was guilty of the disturbance. It was firmly held by all these various interests that the man who rebelled against the agreed terms of "Union" and peace was a genuine disturber, an enemy of public peace, a destroyer of the institutions of the country, to be rightly and thoroughly silenced.

Whether the future result was to be perpetual slavery, or even a predominant slave-power, or an extension of slavery into all the States, a large secular majority never troubled itself to inquire. And the moralist and religionist now realized that slavery, from having been a creeping interloper, had now become so inwrought into the social and political fabric as to require that palliative treatment which we are ever obliged to accord to irremediable organic evils. It was under this view that ecclesiastical discipline was fatally inflicted upon the candidates for orders, to the indelible dishonor of our own Church.

But the slave-power in its madness committed unintentional suicide. It is the peculiar treachery of slavery that while it stimulates the pride and war-spirit of the slave-holders it weakens their common strength for war. Modern war requires those vast resources which free industrial enterprise alone creates and which slavery excludes from existence. As the slave-power grew prouder and madder its strength grew unconsciously fainter. Insensible of its weakness, it rushed into the battle with fierceness and bravery; but the slow, relentless "anaconda" of Northern science, resources, and stalwart courage, wound around it and crushed it into non-existence.

So may the foes of truth, righteousness, progress, and freedom, fall!

Before the commencement of the war the great body of the moral worth, including the ethical and the literary classes, with the ministry and membership of the evangelical Churches, had passed over to the antislavery side. Yet, of these, a so-called conservative residuum remained, demanding silence and quietude even after it became transparent that the policy of silence would soon secure the fixed and final perpetuity and supremacy of the slave-power. To this class belonged in our Methodist Conferences a large share of the old leaders. It became a fight between "the young generals and the old generals." We are entirely unable so to enter into the consciousness of these pseudo-conservative men as to understand what at last they meant. Our impression is that such had been their self-commitment that they refused to yield from sheer unreasoning persistence, until commencing war enabled them to become antislavery on patriotic grounds. But it must be confessed that the large majority of the ante-bellum secular North never became antislavery upon principle. Down to the eve before the war even the Republican leaders offered securities for the perpetuity of slavery as the price of peace. Down to that final moment there were the most violent mobs raised against antislavery men to propitiate the Southern autocrats. And be it remembered that through near the whole preceding period it required as much moral courage, it cost as much ostracism, to become an antislavery man as it did the original Abolitionist. The writer of these lines has an ample personal experience of this sort, and speaks therefore with authority on this point.

The pro-slaveryism of the Northern secular majority lasted far into the war, postponing the emancipation act, incurring for us many a defeat, and forfeiting our antislavery prestige with foreign nations, thereby prolonging and endangering the entire success of the war. The abolition of slavery thus loses the claim of being a great moral reform. The slave-holder nearly up to the proclamation of liberty could have purchased the life of slavery by re-assuming his place in the Union, and resuming his dictatorship over the whole. Happily for the world he maintained a proud refusal. The slave-power, like the fire-girt scorpion, died of its own venom.

CONTENTS.

24 CONTENTS.

THE

ANTISLAVERY STRUGGLE AND TRIUMPH

IN THE

METHODIST EPISCOPAL CHURCH.

CHAPTER I.

EUROPE AND THE AMERICAN COLONIES. 1492–1776.

ALL American institutions, directly or indirectly, are of transatlantic origin. This is especially true of slavery. American responsibility does not reach back to the beginning of its own "peculiar institution." That was born in other lands.

"Slavery and the slave-trade antedate the history of human society. Every portion of the globe has suffered and supported both, except Australasia. The Saxon race carried the most repulsive forms of slavery into England. There the price of a man was but four times the price of an ox. Slaves were exported from England to Ireland. Early in the twelfth century a national Synod of the Irish decreed the emancipation of all English slaves in the island. The long wars between German and Sclavonic tribes filled France with such numbers of Sclavons, that the name of that nation became the name of the institution of servitude every-where. Rome was a mart where Christian slaves were sold to Mohammedan masters." —*Bancroft.*

About the time of the discovery of America the

moral sentiment of Christian nations abolished the traffic in Christian slaves. But the traffic of Europeans in negro slaves, which had existed before the discovery of America, became fully established before the colonization of the United States.

The aborigines of America were early made to feel the cruelty of European Christians. Even Columbus stained his glorious record by enslaving five hundred Indians, whom he sent to be publicly sold at Seville. And Isabella reserved for herself and Ferdinand a fourth part of the slaves which the new kingdoms in America might furnish during their life-time. This traffic in Indians at the foreign marts continued nearly two hundred years.

These "heathen round about" the early Puritans thought were not ill used by being held as slaves. The excellent Winthrop enumerates Indian slaves among his bequests. And the articles of the first New England Confederacy class persons among the spoils of war.

An unexampled benevolence toward the Indians whom Spanish cruelty oppressed was awakened in Las Casas, a Dominican missionary to St. Domingo, in 1510. As Bishop of Chiapa, Mexico, in 1544, he refused to administer the sacraments to those of the colonists who reduced the Indians to slavery, and drew upon himself the hostility of the planters and disapproval of the Church. Opposed to him was one Sepulveda, a canon of Salamanco, who published an infamous work, justifying oppression, cruelty, and murder, even saying it was the duty of the Church to "exterminate those who refused to embrace the Christian faith." To him they adhered who rejected Las Casas; and it is alleged that the mortality fol-

lowing enslavement, and massacres of Indians who
resisted their oppressors, caused fifteen millions of
these innocent victims to perish in ten years. This
must be an exaggeration; yet the minimum total
must have been a fearful destruction of human life
in the Spanish possessions of America. The current
history of that period attributes the introduction of
negro slavery to the efforts of Las Casas to alleviate
thereby the suffering of the Indians. This is on the
testimony only of one writer of no authority, Herara
by name, whose slander, as it is called, has been fully
refuted by later writers of the first rank. Moreover,
one historic fact demonstrates the impossibility of its
being true. Spain had authorized negro slavery in
America by royal ordinance in 1501; this was nine
years before Las Casas was an ordained ecclesiastic,
and thirty-four years before he became a resident of
St. Domingo. Before he died, in 1566, the English
royal family were arranging for a private speculation
by the introduction of negro slaves to America.

Bancroft, the historian, is authority for most of
the preceding statements, as well as for those which
follow. He says: "Queen Elizabeth, in 1567, protected Sir John Hawkins in an illicit traffic in negro
slaves, and by contract shared the profit thereof;"
and she became at once a smuggler and a slave-trader.
The depravity of morals indicated by this corruption
of English society had its legitimate sequence in the
horrible atrocity of this Hawkins, who relates, as a
specimen of his method, that he set fire to a city of
huts in Africa, with dry palm-leaf roofs, where dwelt
eight thousand people, two hundred and fifty of
whose strong men and women he seized and sold.
The other thousands were left in nakedness and mis-

erable destitution. The Protestantism of England was not unlike the Popery of Spain in its inhumanity.

By a strange misapprehension of justice, joined to a stranger perversion of religious truth, men of the best reputation seemed blinded by their surroundings, or by the god of this world, so that they did "call evil good, and good evil—put darkness for light, and light for darkness—put bitter for sweet, and sweet for bitter." Luther, the German reformer, wrote in the sixteenth century: "He that says slavery is opposed to Christianity is a liar!" And Bossuet, the great pulpit orator of the French Catholics, joined his words with Luther's, the following century, by declaring that "the laws of all nations sanction slavery. To condemn it is to condemn the Holy Ghost."

Among the colonies of North America during the seventeenth century negro slavery had generally obtained. A Dutch man-of-war brought twenty slaves to the shore of the James River, Virginia, in August of 1620. Sir John Yeomans, one of the Carolina "landgrave," brought slaves from Barbadoes to South Carolina in 1671, the very next year after its organization as a province. New York in 1664 had imported as many Africans for its population as Virginia, although five years later in commencing that commerce, which Stuyvesant used every exertion to promote. The Friends, who controlled Pennsylvania in 1668, held slaves. William Penn sought without success to secure the mental and moral culture of Pennsylvania slaves, with the rights and happiness of domestic life. And he died a slave-holder.

At the Treaty of Peace at Utrecht, in 1713, between Great Britain, France, and Spain, a monopoly

of the traffic in negro slaves was granted to Queen
Anne, who stipulated to bring to the West Indies one
hundred and forty-four thousand within thirty years,
at $33 33⅓ per head duty.   If she brought over "by
persons whom she shall appoint " · more than four
thousand yearly, the duty would be one half this sum
for the excess.   Thereby her Britannic majesty became the exclusive slave-trader for the Spanish possessions in the Gulf of Mexico, on the Atlantic and
Pacific Oceans, as well as for the English colonies.

Slave ships from Africa entered nearly every considerable harbor south of Newport.   The slave-trade
party in England dictated the laws as early as 1695.
These laws declared the trade "highly beneficial and
advantageous to the kingdom and the colonies," which
"ought to be supplied with negroes at reasonable
rates."   In 1702 Queen Anne instructed the Governor
of New York "to give due encouragement to the
Royal African Company of England."

The Provincial Legislature of Virginia in 1726
checked this importation by a law taxing the traffic
heavily, which law the home government had repealed.   Madison, in after years, said : "The British
Government constantly checked the attempts of Virginia to put a stop to this infernal traffic."   The bare-
faced reason for this interference is expressed in a
statutory provision of 1749, declaring that "the slave-
trade is very advantageous to Great Britain."   Sir
Horace Walpole is responsible for the statement, in
1750, that "six and forty thousand of these wretches
are sold every year to our plantations alone."   And
therefore it was that the Earl of Dartmouth said on
behalf of the government, "We cannot allow the
colonies to check or discourage, in any degree, a

traffic so beneficial to the nation." This pecuniary benefit is thus summed up by Bancroft: "For the century prior to 1776 the number imported by the English into the West India and Continental colonies we assume to have been nearly three millions, to which are to be added a quarter of a million thrown into the Atlantic on the passage. The gross returns to English merchants for the whole traffic may have been not more than four hundred millions of dollars. This estimate is by far the lowest ever made by any inquirer into the statistics of human wickedness."

The Commonwealth of Georgia, the youngest colonial enterprise of England, in 1734, two years after its organization, forbade the introduction of slaves. Said Governor Oglethorpe: "Slavery is against the Gospel, as well as the fundamental law of England. We refused, as trustees, to make a law permitting such a horrid crime." Four years after that a request was made to allow slaves to be admitted to Georgia, and repeated for years following, but the governor, as its civil and military head, persisted in denying the colonists the use of negro slaves. The trustees in England applauded the decision, although many settlers threatened to leave the colony. Thirteen years afterward, in 1751, George Whitefield, then resident in Georgia, went to England, and pleaded with the trustees of the colony to allow the introduction of slaves. Tyerman is authority for the statement that Mr. Whitefield said: "As to the lawfulness of keeping slaves I have no doubt. What a flourishing country might Georgia have been had the use of them been permitted years ago. I should think myself highly favored if I could purchase a good number of them in order to make their lives

comfortable, and lay a foundation for breeding up
their posterity in the nurture and admonition of the
Lord." Twenty years afterward he died, owning
seventy-five slaves in connection with his Orphan
House plantation in Georgia. For, without repealing
the law of 1734, the colony had allowed slave-traders
to sail direct from Africa to Savannah from 1751
onward, and sell their heathen victims to the highest
Christian bidder. A slight resistance was kept up
for a few years by the Moravians; but they yielded
finally to the conviction that African slaves might be
employed in a Christian spirit, and that their treatment in a Christian manner would prove their change
of country to be a great benefit to them. This conviction was largely promoted by a message from the
Moravians of Germany, which declared: "If you
take slaves in faith, with the intent of conducting
them to Christ, the action will not be a sin, but may
prove a benediction." An argument, this, which em-
bodies the entire logic of volumes of after-thought
and speech uttered during the ensuing century of
slavery in America.

The triple alliance of Protestant England with
Catholic France and Spain in support of the slave-
trade; the cupidity and avarice of English merchants,
fed as they were on a profit of hundreds of millions;
the reckless utterances of Luther and Bossuet; the
insinuating sophistry of Whitefield and the Moravians, are so many indices, and sources, as well of the
ultimate foothold secured in America by this fearful
European invasion. Add to these exterior forces the
innate desire for gain, love of ease, and lack of conscience on the question of human rights, and it was
not strange, although unjustifiable, that there was

awakened in the Colonies a similar feeling in favor of making haste to be rich by ungodly gains. So that the slave-trade and slavery were accepted, and in after generations cursed the country and crushed millions of Americans of African descent.

A singular fact, and prophetic as well, stands upon the record of a hundred years ago. A voice was uplifted, antagonizing, denying, denouncing, in clear, shrill tones, the popular pro-slavery sentiment of the times in Europe and America. Hear it: "I strike at the root of this complicated villainy. I absolutely deny all slave-holding to be consistent with any degree of natural justice. Much less is it possible that any child of man should ever be born a slave. Liberty is the right of every human creature as soon as he breathes the vital air, and no human law can deprive him of that right."—*John Wesley.*

Finally, and fully confirmatory of the fact that the slave-trade in America was the creature of European speculators, and especially of British royal interference, there is that paragraph in the original draft of the Declaration of Independence, by Thomas Jefferson, which was omitted because, although true to history, it was not palatable to the Southerners who loved slavery. It reads thus:

"The present king of Great Britain has waged cruel war against human nature itself; violating its most sacred rights of life and liberty in the persons of a distant people who never offended him; captivating and carrying them into slavery in another hemisphere, or to incur miserable death in their transportation thither. This piratical warfare, the opprobrium of infidel power, is the warfare of the Christian king of Great Britain. Determined to keep an open market where men should be bought and sold, he has prostituted his negative for suppressing every legislative attempt to prohibit or restrain this execrable commerce." Such is the testimony of Jefferson, and such would have been the language of the immortal Declaration, but for the corruption of public sentiment already taking sides with the enemies of African liberty while clamorous for the freedom of white colonists.

CHAPTER II.

SLAVERY AN OUTLAW SYSTEM.

THE assumed legal relation of master and slave was a cunning fabrication. The fact of slavery in America was a fearful reality. The law creating it cannot be found; it does not exist. Laws recognizing the fact exist, but they are always found to have been enacted subsequent to the fact. The fact of the relation of master and slave is one thing; the legality of that relation is quite another matter. The definition by statute of the condition of a slave does not constitute the being so described a slave. Behind the definition, and behind the recognition, there remains the bold usurpation of a claim to ownership in men, without the shadow or pretext of law antecedent thereto which created the right of ownership. As slavery did not originate in law, the whole process of enslaving men was, and ever has been, illegal from beginning to end. What, then, was the origin of slavery—the so-called legal relation between master and slave as it existed in the United States?

The fact is unchallenged, that the claim to ownership of negroes in America originated in the African slave-trade. That trade, by the laws of the United States and of Europe, was declared to be piracy. How much legality can be given to a pirate's claim? Just that much and no more belonged to the slave-buyer. And this gave to John Wesley's words their pungency and power when he said, " All men-buyers are exactly on a level with men-stealers." This is equally a judicial and a historic truth.

" The legal-relation fiction existed for centuries in England, because not tested before the courts until 1772. Then Granville Sharp brought forward the case of James Somerset against his master, Charles Stewart, of Virginia, at the Court of the King's Bench, Lord Chief-Justice Mansfield presiding. After labored argument, and a continuance of the case over two terms, the decision was rendered June 22, 1772, and the principle established that the whole process and tenure were illegal; that there was not and never had been any legal slavery in England. His words were : ' Immemorial usage preserves the memory of positive law ; and, in a case so odious as the condition of slaves, must be taken strictly. Tracing the subject to natural principles, the claim of slavery never can be supported ! The power claimed by this return never was in use here. We cannot say the cause set forth by this return is allowed or approved of by the laws of this kingdom, and therefore the man must be discharged ! ' "

" The laws of this kingdom " extended over the Colonies of Great Britain in 1772, and the decision of Lord Mansfield covered the case of every slave in our land. But there was no Granville Sharp to bring their case into court; and the separation of the Colonies occurring soon afterward would have prevented the application of this decision in America. What secret force the interest of slavery gave to the movements for independence, as a guarantee against universal emancipation by judicial decision, if any, can now never be known. Less threatening, but equally feared, antislavery influences, ninety years afterward,

were deemed a justification for rebellion and a san-
guinary war, greatly exceeding in magnitude the
struggle of 1776. Upon how slight a tenure American slavery continued and flourished, until 1863, will
now be stated from historic and judicial authority.

Judge Matthews, of Louisiana, (5 Martin's Report,
275,) affirms "the absence of any legislative act of the
European powers for the introduction of slavery into
their American dominions," adding, "If the record
of any such act exists we have not been able to find
any trace of it." He also declares, "It is an admitted
principle, that slavery has been permitted and tolerated in all the Colonies established in America by the
mother country. No legislative act of the Colonies
can be found in relation to it." Let us hear Judge
Matthews further: "On turning our attention to the
first settlement of the British Colonies in America
we find that the introduction of negro slaves into one
of the most important was accidental, (to Virginia,
1620.) About twenty years afterward slaves were
introduced into New England, where Indians were
then held in bondage. The absence of any act or
instrument of government under which their slavery
originated is not a matter of greater surprise than
that there should have been none found authorizing
the slavery of the blacks."—"*American Slave Code*,"
Goodell, p. 260.

"Messrs. Sumner and Palfrey have declared that
slavery never existed by law in Massachusetts. Sumner's words are : 'If in point of fact the issue of
slaves was sometimes held in bondage, it was never
sanctioned by any statute law of Colony or Commonwealth.' Palfrey confirms this by the assertion, in
his history, that no person was ever born into legal

slavery in Massachusetts. Against these Mr. Moore
('History of Slavery in Massachusetts') takes issue.
He proves that slavery existed—which they concede
—and was recognized by courts, but does not cite the
statute that decreed it. He quotes from the 'Body
of Liberties,' which declared, 'There never shall be
any bond-slavery, or villanage, or captivity among us,
unless it be lawful captives taken in just wars, or
such as shall willingly sell themselves, or are willingly sold to us.' This recognizes two kinds of slavery
as allowable—lawful capture, and those who enter it
voluntarily. These expressly exclude negroes stolen
from Africa and brought here as merchandise. That
slavery of negroes crept in under the shadow of the
captivity of Indians is true, and that this species of
property was recognized by the courts; but that it
had legislative enactments for its support he does not
show. Statute law never protected nor legalized the
iniquity."—*Dr. Curry, Book Notices, Christian Advocate, May* 24, 1866.

"The first introduction of slaves into Georgia was
in direct violation of law. Into the other colonies
slaves were introduced a long time before there was
any colonial enactment authorizing it. When statutes were enacted they did not pretend to create or
originate the relation. They did not define with ex-
actness who were slaves and who were not. They
only assumed, or took for granted, the existence of
slave property, and made laws for its security and
regulation. The consequence was that no slave-holder
could prove that the particular slaves claimed by him
were ever made slaves according to law, or that their
ancestors were thus enslaved. And there were no
statute laws in either of the States by which it could

be legally proved, by the common rules and usages
of courts as applied to other subjects, that slavery
legally existed there. This was avowed by Mr.
Mason, of Virginia, in the Senate of the United
States, when the Fugitive Slave Bill of 1850 was
pending. He objected to the 'trial by jury,' as proposed in that bill, that it would bring up the question
of the legality of slavery in the States, which, said he,
it would be impossible to prove. Mr. Bayly, of Virginia, took the same ground. So Congress struck out
the jury trial because slave-holders avowed, in 1850,
their inability to prove the legality of slavery in a
court of law!"— "*American Slave Code,*" *Goodell*,
p. 260.

Under the fugitive law of 1793 a New York slave-
holder pursued and claimed a runaway in Vermont.
Two justices of the peace at Middlebury decided to
surrender him. The slave's counsel, Loyal Coxe,
Esq., brought him up to the Supreme Court on a
writ of habeas corpus, asking his liberation. The
master brought forth documentary and other evidence
to show his title to the slave. Judge Harrington
gave the opinion of the court. He said that the evidence of the title was good as far as it went, but the
chain had some of its links broken. The evidence
did not go far enough. If the master could show
a bill of sale or grant from the Almighty, then
his title to him would be complete; otherwise not.
And as he had not shown such evidence the court
refused to surrender the slave, and he was discharged.

This transaction was in 1807. It was related by
Hon. Horatio Seymour, formerly senator from Vermont for twelve years, who was present at the court.

Hon. D. Wooster, of Middlebury, to whom Mr. Seymour told the facts, gave them to Hon. S. E. Sewall,
of Massachusetts, by whom they were published. In
later years Col. J. P. Miller, of Vermont, often related at antislavery conventions that on his return
from the war for Grecian independence, when in
Paris, he was delighted to find in a public literary institution, among great words from great men, this
saying, credited to Judge Harrington, of the United
States of America: "A bill of sale from Almighty
God is needed to render valid the claim set up to a
human being as a slave." With these words Judge
Harrington touched bottom, where Lord Mansfield
only leveled the ocean of human rights. And Vermont soil was never after pressed by the steps of the
hunters of men. A second claim was never set up in
that State.

CHAPTER III.

WESLEY AND SLAVERY.

AMERICAN slavery, not being the legitimate offspring of law, must be accepted as one of a
class of bastard institutions of evil origin, which deserved and had the unqualified condemnation of the
best men of their times, whose epithets were none
too strong when most emphatic.

The opposition of John Wesley to slavery, which
originated when he was a missionary to the colonies
of Georgia and South Carolina, in 1736, was closed,
after fifty-five years' continuance, with his dying exhortation to Wilberforce, who had just then, 1791,
offered a resolution in the British Parliament for the
abolition of slavery in the West India Islands. A
brief quotation from several of his publications on the
general subject will demonstrate this opposition.

"But, waiving for the present all other considerations, I strike at the root of this complicated villainy.
I absolutely deny all slave-holding to be consistent
with any degree of natural justice, mercy, and truth.
No circumstances can make it necessary for a man to
burst in sunder all the ties of humanity. It can
never be necessary for a rational being to sink himself
below a brute. A man can be under no necessity of
degrading himself into a wolf.

"You first acted the villain in making them slaves,
whether you stole them or bought them. And this
equally concerns every gentleman that has an estate

in our American plantations; yea, all slave-holders of whatever rank or degree — seeing men-buyers are exactly on a level with men-stealers.

"Have you, has any man living, a right to use another as a slave? It cannot be, even setting Revelation aside. Liberty is the right of every human creature as soon as he breathes the vital air, and no human being can deprive him of that right which he derives from the law of nature."—"*Thoughts on Slavery*," *Wesley*, 1774.

Thirteen years afterward he wrote to Mr. Thomas Funnel:

"MY DEAR BROTHER: Whatever assistance I can give those generous men who join to oppose that execrable trade, I certainly shall give. I have printed a large edition of the 'Thoughts on Slavery,' and dispersed them to every part of England. But there will be vehement opposition made by both slave-merchants and slave-holders, and they are mighty men; but our comfort is, 'He that dwelleth on high is mightier.' I am your affectionate brother,

"JOHN WESLEY."

Finally, only four days before his death, February 25, 1791, he wrote to Mr. Wilberforce, saying:

"Unless the divine power has raised you up to be Athanasius against the world, I see not how you can go through your glorious enterprise in opposing that execrable villainy [the slave-trade] which is the scandal of religion, of England, and of human nature. Unless God has raised you up for this very thing, you will be worn out by the opposition of men and devils. But if God be for you, who can be against you? Are all of them together stronger than God? O, be not weary in well doing! Go on in the name of God, and in the power of his might, till even American slavery, the vilest that ever saw the sun, shall vanish away before it.

"Your affectionate servant,
"JOHN WESLEY."

Mr. Wesley's opposition to the slave-trade antedated the organization for its overthrow fifteen years. His "Thoughts on Slavery" were published sixty years before the abolition of slavery in the West Indies, and his rebukes of American slavery anticipated Lincoln's proclamation three quarters of a century. His influence became a fountain of multiplied forces, and originated a vast ecclesiastical system in Europe and America which had much to do with the overthrow of slavery on both sides of the Atlantic.

His followers in opinion, and his associates in labor, were among the most active of those who inaugurated the great conflict. The antislavery force was as the little stone at first cut out of the mountain without hands, but it became an overwhelming power against oppression, and lifted high up in the scale of being redeemed millions of the sons of Africa. Less than one hundred years had elapsed after the spoken thoughts of Wesley on slavery when all the slaves of every island of the sea controlled by Europeans, and the millions more held on the American continent, were free.

But the antiquity of the institution of servitude, the European combinations in favor of establishing slavery in America, the special patronage extended over it by the English government, and the ultimate selfishness and avarice of the colonists, combined to root and ground slavery on the continent, with the prospect and hope, to its friends, of universal extension and perpetual existence. It was comparatively an easy task for the European authorities afterward to legislate against slavery, at a distance from the home government, on their islands, and abolish it. While, to grapple with slavery at our own doors, in our own American homes, sanctioned and sanctified by law and religion as it was, and representing twelve hundred millions of dollars, as Henry Clay in 1839, estimated it to be; to correct the false religious sentiment of a nation, to repeal the unjust laws of a hundred years, to annihilate their property claim in four millions of human beings — involved mountainous difficulties to be removed, and fierce discussions to be maintained, through long years of strife, which made the task appear an absolute impossibility with man. Those who entertained the thought of its practicability, and hoped to see the end of slavery in America, were deemed visionary enthusiasts, were laughed to scorn, and were compelled to rest their confidence wholly on the truth that with God all things are possible. Nor was this scorning strange —this unbelief. Look at the facts.

The distinctive features of American slavery, after it attained to the monstrous enormity of 1850, when the climax of "mischief framed by law" was reached by the enactment of the Fugitive Slave Law, may be thus portrayed. Slaves were goods and chattels; being property, they could not own property, nor make a contract, nor enjoy marital rights, nor parental authority, nor be a party to any civil suit whatever. They could not be witnesses against any white person, but were personally subject to the will, and were liable to become the helpless victims, of all white persons. Their offspring, like mere domestic animals, were the property of those who claimed to be the owners of the mothers. To teach slaves to read or write was made a crime by the law of the slave States generally. Emancipation was discouraged, obstructed, and prevented in most of these States, except by legislative action. And in some cases the State constitutions prohibited legislative action. All discussion in favor of emancipation, by voice or pen or press, was suppressed as incendiary, and punished as crime. Free people of color were, by the laws of slave States, made liable, upon various flimsy pretexts, to be sold into slavery. The American domestic slave-trade grew to be a commerce in "the bodies and souls of men," rivaling in dimensions and enormities the African piratical slave-trade. Dr. Elliott, on "Slavery," (vol. i, p. 47,) well and truly said : " As the African slave-trade constantly reduces innocent free persons to slavery, and assumes its piratical and felonious character from this act, so the system of American slavery, by enslaving the children of slaves and free persons of color, and by re-enslaving manumitted persons, must also be piratical and felonious. And he or she who voluntarily enslaves innocent children must rank with the man-stealer ! "

The enormous revenue derived from this commerce, and the influence of this great money-power to prevent the earlier success of antislavery men and measures, will be appreciated by brief statements from Southern sources. Hon. J. M. Randolph, of Virginia, before the Legislature, in 1832, said : " The

exportation of slaves from Virginia has averaged
8,500 annually for the last twenty years;" "an exportation of nearly 260,000 since 1790." The editor
of the "Virginia Times," Wheeling, said in 1836:
"Intelligent men estimate the number of slaves exported from Virginia alone within the last twelve
months at 120,000, whose average value was $600
each, a total of $72,000,000. Two thirds of these
were removed with their masters; one third were
sold, leaving behind them $24,000,000 revenue."
The Natchez, Miss., "Courier" said that the States
of Louisiana, Mississippi, Alabama, and Arkansas imported 250,000 slaves in 1836. The "Baltimore American" published from a Mississippi paper a report
adopted by a citizens' meeting, held in Mobile, which
attributed "the money pressure of 1837 to the fact
that $10,000,000 had been paid out of the State an-
nually for slaves since 1833." The New Orleans
"Courier," of February 5, 1839, declared that "the
United States law against the African slave-trade put
millions of dollars into the pockets of the people
living between Roanoke and Mason and Dixon's
line. Yet we think it would require some casuistry
to show that the present slave-trade is a whit better
than the one from Africa."

Added to all this, in the interest of slavery, and
designed to afford an all-sufficient safeguard and
guarantee of its perpetual existence in America, was
the national statute of 1850, approved and signed by
President Fillmore. The full text of that law need
not be quoted. Its characteristics can be given in a
few sentences. It made each claimant of a fugitive
slave the master of all the Circuit, District, and Ter-
ritorial Courts, commissioners, marshals, and citizens

of the United States. The government of the nation became thereby a gigantic Briarean slave-catcher for the South. All American citizens were constituted kidnappers. Fines and imprisonment were the penalty of neglect to perform the work of blood-hounds, or for any hinderance to the slave-catcher, or any help to the fugitive. All fees and costs for legal services, for subsistence of runaway slaves, for hunting, catching, and holding them; for defense against rescue, and for transportation over the entire continent if necessary — that without any limitation of the expense—were provided for to be paid out of the Treasury of the United States.*

Such was the system of slavery in our nation when its enormity culminated. It had been growing for generations, all the while condemned by many good men, and hated of God. But good men were too few and feeble, and God was slow to anger and of great mercy, and his wrath delayed its manifestation.

Having anticipated somewhat in order to complete the monstrous portrait and fully set forth the system against which Wesleyan Methodism arrayed itself at the first, and afterward sought to extirpate, it is necessary to turn back to the point of divergence and resume the direct narration at the period when American Methodist history commenced.

* "The South had no right to claim that the policy of the Union should be established in sole reference to the condition of the blacks; in other words, that the whole country should become the slave of slaves!" — *Prentice's Life of Henry Clay*, 1819, p. 187. Yet, in 1850, he advocated and secured the adoption of this policy.

CHAPTER IV.

METHODISM VERSUS SLAVERY, 1766-1784.

WESLEYAN Methodism became an American institution by the emigration of its votaries to this country. Societies were formed in New York and Maryland about 1762 or 1766. The former is the date assigned by some to the organization of a Society in Maryland by Robert Strawbridge. The latter is the year of the organization of the Society in New York by Philip Embury, and is usually accepted as the beginning of Methodism in America. The first general movement which constituted Methodism a religious denomination was the meeting of the Conference at Philadelphia, in 1773, which was attended by Francis Asbury and nine other English preachers, acting under John Wesley's authority.

There was no action at this Conference on the subject of slavery. The subsequent utterances of the preachers only indicate their sentiments; and they were boldly expressed under the deepest convictions of duty.

Freeborn Garrettson, a native of Maryland, the companion of Asbury, thus writes of his personal experience the day after his conversion, in 1775: "It was the Lord's day. I continued reading the Bible till eight, and then called the family together for prayer. As I stood with a book in my hand, in the act of giving out a hymn, this thought powerfully struck my mind, 'It is not right for you to keep your fellow-creatures in bondage. You must let the oppressed go free.' Until then I had never suspected that the practice of slave-keeping was wrong. I had not read a book on the subject, nor been told so by any. I paused a minute, and then replied, 'Lord, the oppressed shall go free;' and I was as clear of them in my mind as if I had never owned one. I told them they did not belong to me, and that I did not desire their services without making them a compensation. I was now at liberty to proceed in worship. After singing, I kneeled to pray. Had I the tongue of an angel I could not fully describe what I felt. A divine sweetness ran through my whole frame. It was God, and not man, that taught me the impropriety of holding slaves, and I shall never be able to praise him enough for it. My very heart has bled since that for slave-holders, especially those who make a profession of religion, for I believe it to be a crying sin."—*Dr. N. Bangs' "Life of Garrettson."*

The following year he commenced a ministerial career which extended over more than half a century, and has left historical and ineffaceable traces on the Church from North Carolina to Nova Scotia. "He failed not to inculcate his opinions of slavery, and preached often to the slaves, weeping with them in their wrongs, rejoicing with them in their spiritual consolations. He was menaced by persecutors, threatened by armed men, and one of his friends was shot for entertaining him. 'But,' he says, 'the consolations afforded were ample compensation for all the difficulties I met with wandering up and down.'"— *Stevens' "History of Methodist Episcopal Church."*

Francis Asbury's Journals exhibit his methods and manner of antagonizing slavery, at the times indi-

cated by the dates affixed to each paragraph following. [1776.] "After preaching I met the class and
then the black people, some of whose unhappy masters forbid their coming for religious instruction.
How will the sons of oppression answer for their
conduct when the great Proprietor of all shall call
them to account? [1780.] Spoke to some select friends
about slave-keeping, but they could not bear it. This
I know: God will plead the cause of the oppressed,
though it gives offense to say so here. O Lord, banish the infernal spirit of slavery from thy dear Zion!
Lord, help thy people. The Lord will certainly hear
the cries of the oppressed, naked, starving creatures.
O my God, think on this land! [1783.] We all agreed
at the Virginia Conference in the spirit of African
liberty, and strong testimonies were borne in its favor
at our love-feast. I pity the poor slaves. O that God
would look down in mercy and take their cause in
hand! [1785.] At the Conference in Virginia I found
the minds of the people greatly agitated with our
rules against slavery, and a proposed petition to the
General Assembly for the emancipation of the blacks.
We waited on General Washington, who received us
very politely, and gave us his opinion against slavery.
[1788.] Other persuasions are less supine, and their ministers boldly preach against the freedom of the slaves.
Our Brother Everett, with no less zeal and boldness,
cries aloud for liberty and emancipation. [1798.] My
mind is much pained. I am brought to conclude that
slavery will exist in Virginia perhaps for ages. There
is not a sufficient sense of religion nor liberty to destroy it. On Saturday I had a close conversation with
some of our local ministry. We were happy to find
that seven out of ten were not in the spirit or prac-

tice of slavery. I assisted Philip Sands to draw up
an agreement for our officiary to sign against slavery.
Thus we may know the real sentiments of our local
preachers. We can never fully reform the people
until we reform the preachers. Hitherto, except
purging the traveling connection, we have been working at the wrong end. But if it be lawful for local
preachers to hold slaves, then it is lawful for traveling preachers also, and they may keep plantations and
overseers upon their quarters; but this reproach of
inconsistency must be rolled away. [1801.] In South
Carolina a Solomon Reeves let me know that he had
seen the address signed by me, and he was quite confident that there were no arguments to prove that
slavery was repugnant to the spirit of the Gospel.
What absurdities will not men defend! If the Gospel will tolerate slavery, what will it not authorize?
I am strangely mistaken if this said Mr. Reeves
has more grace than is necessary, or more of Solomon
than the name."

The names of Everett, O'Kelly, Rankin, and others who are incidentally named by Bishop Asbury,
are only specimens of the entire class of Methodist
preachers of the first generation who were a unit
against slavery, which they denounced publicly with
unsparing severity of language every-where. But
they were struggling with fearful odds against them.
Public sentiment generally upheld slavery. Private
interest, social standing, personal comfort, were all
sacrificed by the early converts to Methodism at the
South, who felt conscience-bound to emancipate their
slaves. And therefore their increase was very slow.
The temptation was strong to relax their vigorous on-
set upon slavery, for peace' sake, and the prosperity

promised thereby. How utterly this failed to affect
Mr. Asbury we have noted already. This is equally
true of others, and especially of his honored associate
in the episcopacy, of whom special mention must be
made.

Dr. Coke, who had been associated with Mr. Wesley in England seven years, was, in 1784, set apart
for the office of Superintendent over the Methodists
in America, and became the associate of Mr. Asbury
from 1785 onward. Before his arrival, for several
years successively, the Conferences in the United States
had considered and condemned slavery in plain, strong
words, and had adopted prohibitory laws against it.
With this legislation the doctor was in hearty sympathy. Besides, he added an open hostility to slavery,
in private intercourse and public denunciation, after
being in the country a few months. "While Dr.
Coke preserved a profound silence on the subject of
negro slavery all were pleased, and he was permitted
to go on his way in peace. But no sooner did he lift
up his voice against the injustice of the traffic than it
became the signal for the commencement of hostilities against him. In the province of Virginia, while
preaching in a barn, on Sunday, April 9, 1785, he
took occasion to introduce the subject of slavery, and
expatiated on its injustice in terms that were not calculated to flatter his auditors. Many were provoked
to hear those truths which, from their earliest infan-
cy, they had been taught to stifle, and which their
interest still instructed them to conceal. A small
party withdrew from the house, and combined to offer
him personal violence as soon as he came out. They
were stimulated by a lady who informed the enraged
mob that she would give them £50 sterling if they

would seize the doctor and give him a hundred lashes. This they would have done but for the vigorous action of a magistrate present, who arrested one of the leaders, and the threats of a colonel to repel force by force. The fruit of this sermon was, that the magistrate referred to emancipated fifteen slaves. Another master freed eight slaves, and another one slave. To this private and public action personally against slavery the doctor added his official influence as president of Annual Conferences. At the Conference of North Carolina, in which State emancipation was prohibited, he prepared a petition to the Assembly praying them to pass an act 'that in a land which boasted of its independence slave-holders should at least be allowed to emancipate their slaves.' This was signed by the Conference. Sanguine hopes were entertained of success for a time, as the governor had signified to Bishop Asbury his approbation. At the Virginia Conference, also, a petition was drawn up praying the Legislature to pass an act for the immediate or gradual emancipation of the slaves, a copy of which was given to each preacher to present to his circuit for signatures. This was a measure the doctor suggested, and it was approved by many prominent men in the State, who entertained sanguine hopes of its success."—Drew's "Life of Coke." The antislavery action thus inaugurated, which was directed against the system as it was sustained by the State, was not more vigorous and persistent than the antislavery measures adopted, designed to banish all slave-holding from the Methodist Episcopal Church, prior to 1800.

When the first Conference was held in 1773, and for a few years following, there was no rule forbidding slavery, any more than there was a Church law against theft, or adultery, or murder. It seems not to have entered into the thought of these English Wesleyan preachers. They denounced that and every other sin, as they did gambling and drunkenness, in their public ministrations. But to legislate against slave-holders in the Church, or for the regulation or removal of slavery, was never any part of Conference action until seven years afterward—in 1780. The reason of that reticence at first, and the subsequent outspoken action, may be found in the history of the times, to which we give brief attention.

"The year after the introduction of Methodism, by conference organization in this country, the friendly relations between Great Britain and the Colonies were disturbed, and finally destroyed by the war of 1776 for the space of seven years. In 1778 all the English preachers had returned except Mr. Asbury, and he was confined mostly to the small State of Delaware. The advice and control of the older preachers were almost entirely lost to the rising Societies. The extension of the cause and the founding of new Societies were committed to young and inexperienced men, most of whom had been as yet taught the way of the Lord but very imperfectly, and who had themselves been born and educated in slave-holding communities. For in this great revival of religion some preachers, almost immediately on their conversion, were sent, not only to preach, but to found Churches, receive members, and administer discipline. Most of these young preachers, with Freeborn Garrettson, were raised in the midst of slavery, and, with him, could say they had never read a book upon the subject, nor had been told that it was wrong by any body.

"The forty-eight preachers who were received into the itinerancy during the war belonged almost exclusively to this class. All the Conferences which were held from 1776 to 1787 were held within the limits of the recent slave-holding States. So entirely was Methodism confined to that section that from 1777 to 1783 there was not one appointment of a preacher north of some parts of New Jersey. [Of a membership of 8,504 reported in 1780, only about four hundred resided in what were called the free States.] And very many of their preachers, thus imperfectly taught, and always accustomed to slavery, had not, for years, the advice or supervision of Mr. Asbury.

"In 1779, mainly on account of desiring the administration of the ordinances, the more Southern preachers, amounting to more than one half of the entire body, seceded, holding a separate Conference in Fluvanna, Virginia, while Mr. Asbury held one, consisting of only seventeen preachers, in Kent County, Delaware. Each passed its own resolutions, stationed its own preachers, and exercised discipline over their respective Societies for that year. And even after the reconciliation, the administration of Mr. Asbury was received by the Virginia preachers with much caution. In view of all these transactions, there are very few historical facts so well attested as this: That slavery found its way into the American Societies during the confusion of the Revolution, when Mr. Wesley had no communication with this country; while Mr. Asbury was confined to the State of Delaware; when the reception of members and the government of the Church were in the hands of young, inexperienced men, and when more than one half of the Church was entirely under the control of those who had been born and raised in the midst of slavery, the sin of which they had not been taught.

"At the Conference of 1780, in Baltimore, some of the preachers so recently converted and sent out to preach were found to be possessed of slaves. There was at this time no written rule on the practice of slave-holding. Hence, the Minutes of that year: '*Question* 16. Ought not this Conference to require those traveling preachers who hold slaves to give promises to set them free? *Answer.* Yes. *Question* 17. Does this Conference acknowledge that slavery is contrary to the laws of God, man, and nature, and hurtful to society; contrary to the dictates of conscience and pure religion, and doing that which we would not others should do to us and ours? Do we pass our disapprobation on all our friends who keep slaves, and advise their freedom? *Answer.* Yes.'

"This was a noble testimony, worthy the men who made it, the Gospel they preached, and the Churches they were planting. It was put forth in the very seat of slavery, at the zenith of the slave-trade, in the midst of a revolution, when a timid or worldly policy would have suggested silence, and at a time when almost every man's hand was raised against them. There was a moral sublimity in their attitude. As embassadors from God they fearlessly proclaimed the doctrines of their commission. They did not wait until public opinion was ready to receive their principles. They were in advance of public opinion nearly a century. Circumstances were not to mold them; they set themselves to molding the world and its institutions to the doctrines of Christ. None were more willing to yield obedience to Cæsar in that which

was his; but then Cæsar must not invade the temple
of God, nor trammel them in carrying out their high
mission.   This record reared a moral monument in the
Monumental City that still towers splendidly above its
marble shafts, throwing a halo of glory around the memory of the men who raised it, and furnishing a with-
ering rebuke to the ministers who have since pleaded
for slavery or apólogized for it, while it grandly stands
as a beacon light to guide the antislavery followers of
the fathers in other generations.   This testimony at
the Baltimore Conference, after the union with the
Conference in Virginia was acquiesced in, was incorpo-
rated in the general Minutes, and became the opinion
of the entire Church of that day in reference to
slavery."—*Letter of Rev. D. De Vinne, "Zion's
Watchman,"* 1842.

Rev. Jesse Lee says: "If any rule was fixed at the
Baltimore Conference, the preachers in the South
were under the necessity of abiding by it."

The promise required of traveling preachers did
not remove their practice of slavery wholly.   Some
few cases must have continued, as the vigilant Superintendent secures the adoption of the following rules
in 1784 touching the preachers, traveling and local,
and laity as well.   "*Question* 12. What shall we do
with our friends that will buy and sell slaves?   *Answer*. If they buy with no other design than to hold
them as slaves, and have been previously warned, they
shall be expelled; and permitted to sell on no consideration.   *Question* 13. What shall we do with our
local preachers who will not emancipate their slaves
in the States where the laws admit it?   *Answer*.
Try those in Virginia another year, and suspend the
preachers in Maryland, Delaware, Pennsylvania, and

New Jersey. *Question* 22. What shall be done with our traveling preachers that now are, or hereafter shall be, possessed of slaves, and refuse to manumit where the laws permit it? *Answer.* Employ them no more."

This action was the last on that subject during the period that American Methodism was under the direct supervision of Mr. Wesley. The following session of the preachers at the Christmas Conference inaugurated a new era, and the year 1785 commenced the history of the Methodist Episcopal Church in the United States, with Thomas Coke, LL.D., and Francis Asbury, Bishops.

Twelve years only had elapsed since the first Conference in America. But so positive, uncompromising, and extensive had been the hostility of Methodism to slavery, that it was recognized in high places. It had conferred with the President of the Republic, with governors of States, and been listened to in legislative halls on behalf of the slave. And in the Convention where the Constitution of the United States was formed two years afterward, Methodism aided in holding back the oppressor's hand from blotting that document with the black words, "slave" and "slavery." For it is a fact of history that Mr. Marshall, of Virginia, afterward Chief-Justice, urged, in the discussion, with much emphasis and success, that if the Government thus countenanced slavery it would lose the support of the Methodists and Quakers. But these words never were allowed a place in the Constitution.

CHAPTER V.

THE METHODIST EPISCOPAL CHURCH VERSUS SLAVERY, 1784–1800.

THE Methodist Societies in America which had been organized by the preachers sent out by John Wesley, were, by his instructions, given through Dr. Coke, formed into an Episcopal Church in 1784. From that time forward the Methodist Episcopal Church takes its place in American history. At its organization the General Rules, prepared by Mr. Wesley in 1743 for the English Societies, were adopted, with the addition of a rule against slavery, as follows: "The buying or selling the bodies and souls of men, women, or children, with an intention to enslave them." This was forbidden. A more intensified form of expression could not be framed to indicate the abhorrence felt toward slavery as it then existed in America.

Besides forbidding the practice of slavery within the communion of the Church, the extirpation of the system of slavery was at once recognized as an object which demanded attention and action. The 42d question of the Minutes was: "What methods can we take to extirpate slavery?" And then followed, first of all, a sweeping indictment against slavery, which had never been so fully set forth in such few words, and which demonstrated its deserving to be instant death. The Church then said: "We view it as contrary to the golden law of God, on which hang all the law and the prophets, and the inalienable rights of mankind, as well as every principle of the Revolution, to hold in the deepest debasement, in a more abject slavery than is perhaps to be found in any part of the world except America, so many souls that are capable of the image of God." Then followed special rules designed " to extirpate this abomination from among us," as they were indeed well adapted to do : 1. Every slave-holding member, within twelve months, was required to execute a deed of manumission, gradually giving his slaves their freedom.   2. All infants were to have immediate freedom who were born after these rules went into force.   3. Members who chose not to comply were allowed to withdraw within twelve months.   4. The Sacrament of the Lord's Supper was denied to all such thenceforward.   5. And no slave-holders were to be admitted thereafter to the communion table or to membership in the Church.   6. And any member who bought, or sold, or gave slaves away, except on purpose to free them, was immediately to be expelled.

And these provisions were not a dead letter on the journal of the Conference. Mr. Samuel Davis, of New York city, who resided in the slave States from before the organization of the Church in 1785 until 1826, in a letter to Dr. Fisk, which was published in "Zion's Watchman," April 8, 1838, says : "I know it was required of all those who joined our Church, in our district, in those early days of Methodism, that they should execute an instrument of emancipation of all the slaves in their possession, which they had inherited, according to their respective ages and circumstances ; and if any members had bought, or

should buy, for their own use, any slave, a committee
was appointed to determine how long the slave should
serve; and this committee was regulated in its esti-
mates by the age, health, and cost of the slaves, after
which none of those thus emancipated were considered by us as slaves. So universally were these rules
attended to, that I never knew but one instance of
any member's neglecting them, and that was my next
neighbor, at whose house our presiding elder called
on business with a preacher who was then stationed
there in the year 1792. When the elder was about
to retire, the gentleman of the house invited him to
stay to dinner. The reply was, 'I never eat a meal
in a Methodist slave-holder's house,' and he immediately left him. I have heard Bishop Asbury and
many of the early preachers preach pointedly against
slavery. At our quarterly meetings, where hundreds
were present with their slaves, I have repeatedly
heard our preachers condemn the practice as a vile sin
against God, morally, socially, and politically wrong,
no one molesting nor interrupting the man of God.
And I have no doubt, had all our ministers done their
duty, there would not have been a slave left in this
country twenty years ago. For I know that about
that time, and a few years previous, there were hundreds of slaves set free by the members of the Methodist Episcopal Church."

In other sections of the country immediate opposition to these rules was very general. Bishop Asbury,
in his Journal, says: "At the Virginia Conference for
1785 several petitions were presented by some of the
principal members, urging the suspension of the rules
on slavery." But Dr. Coke and the Conference
brought affairs to this issue: that, unless the rules

were permitted to operate, preaching should be withdrawn from those circuits and places in which they
were too obnoxious to be suffered.   This decision,
mainly reached by the influence of Dr. Coke, settled
the affair for the time, and the preachers were appointed and the rules enforced.

The course pursued by Dr. Coke at the Virginia
Conference was not sustained by the action of the
body meeting at Baltimore subsequently, which exercised more authority.   There an informal action was
had which appears as a *nota bene*, with a recommendation preceding it, thus : " It is recommended to all
our brethren to suspend the execution of the minute
on slavery till the deliberations of a future Conference ; and that an equal space of time be allowed all
our members for consideration, when the minute shall
be put in force."   And then, before retiring their
battery from the boldly aggressive position now for
a few months occupied at the front, every gun was
loaded to the muzzle with an " N. B.," and a parting
shot fired point-blank at the system, the echo of
which has been reverberating now these many years
as a testimony and a prophecy both.   Here it is :
" We do hold in the deepest abhorrence the practice
of slavery, and shall not cease to seek its destruction
by all wise and prudent means."

The purpose of a future enforcement of the suspended rules was never accomplished.   Mr. Lee, in
his history of the Methodists, says : " These rules
were offensive to most of our Southern friends, and
were much opposed by many of our private members,
local preachers, and some of the traveling preachers ;
and they were never afterward carried into full
force."

Bishop Asbury relates, in his Journal of 1785, that great agitation against the rules existed. "Col. —— and Dr. Coke disputed on the subject, and the colonel used some threats. Next day, Brother O'Kelly let fly at them, and they were made angry enough. We, however, came off with whole bones." The standard-bearers of the Church kept her testimonies on their banners, in spite of opposition and danger.

The Discipline of 1786, however, indicates a yielding to outside pressure, inasmuch as nothing is retained relating to slavery, except the General Rule and the following: "What shall be done with those who buy or sell slaves, or give them away? *Answer.* They are immediately to be expelled, unless they buy them on purpose to free them." This did prevent Methodists from being slave-traders, but it did not forbid their continuing to be slave-holders. For six years no other change was made, but in 1792 the Discipline appears still further shorn of its antislavery power by the omission of this statute law against the domestic slave-trade, while the General Rule is retained, except the words, "the bodies and souls," and this was the only law of the Church until 1796.

This apparent inertia and actual repeal of legislation, was not, however, an index of the measure of antislavery action put forth by the Church. Antislavery preachers found sufficient warrant in the General Rule for the denunciation of slavery. And the embarrassments to proper discipline thrown in their way by the lack of Conference action, and by the rescinding of former statutes in favor of freedom, were soon removed by the return of the Church from its divergences to a renewal of testimony and prohibitory laws.

A new departure was inaugurated in 1796. The Discipline of that year, by the request of the General Conference, was published by the Bishops with notes prepared by them. To the General Rule on slavery they appended this note: "The buying and selling the souls and bodies of men—for what is the body without the soul but a dead carcass?—is a complicated crime. It was, indeed, in some measure overlooked in the Jews, by reason of the wonderful hardness of their hearts, as was the keeping of concubines and the divorcing of wives at pleasure; but it is totally opposite to the whole spirit of the Gospel. It has the immediate tendency to fill the mind with pride and tyranny, and is frequently productive of almost every act of lust and cruelty which can disgrace the human species. Even the moral philosopher will candidly confess that, if there be a God, every perfection he possesses must be opposed to a practice so contrary to every moral idea which can influence the human mind." This is supported by quotations from the prophets and apostles, including Nehemiah's sharp question: "Will ye even sell your brethren?" Isaiah's thundering edict: "Let the oppressed go free; break every yoke!" Ezekiel's denunciation against merchants who "traded the persons of men;" Paul's application of the law "for unholy and profane, for man-slayers and men-stealers;" and reached the climax of divine malediction with the curse of the Apocalypse on Babylon for making "merchandise of slaves and souls of men."

A new section, "Of Slavery," was put in the Discipline of 1796, opening with, "We declare that we are more than ever convinced of the great evil of African slavery," which renewed the direct assault upon the system of slavery after a suspension of hostilities for ten years, or since 1786. Again the extirpation movement is resumed, thus: "What regulations shall be made for the extirpation of the crying evil of African slavery?" The answer to this question then given was continued for eight years, with the addition in 1800 of two paragraphs, making six in all, which may thus be summed up: 1. All persons holding slaves, if admitted to official stations in the Church, must give security for their emancipation, such as the yearly Conferences might designate, which now had full power. 2. All slave-holders asking admission as members must be spoken to freely and faithfully by the preacher on the subject of slavery. 3. Slave-selling was to be followed by immediate expulsion; and slave-buying was allowed only on condition that the slave, and offspring thereof, should be held only for a term of years to be fixed by the Quarterly Conference. 4. The deep attention of the Church was asked for to the subject of negro slavery, and memorials thereon requested, to be imparted to the ensuing General Conference, in order to take further steps toward eradicating this enormous evil from ·the Church. 5. Any traveling preacher who became a slave-owner, by any means, forfeited his ministerial character, unless he executed, if practicable, a legal emancipation, conformably to the laws of the State in which he lived. 6. The Annual Conferences were directed to prepare antislavery memorials to the State Legislatures, have them circulated for signatures, and by every means in their power "further the blessed undertaking" for gradual emancipation of the slaves. "Let this be continued from year to year until the desired end be accomplished."

These regulations were far below the stringent rules of 1784, yet they were far beyond the position taken by any other Church, and quite in advance of the average public sentiment on slavery. Even as early as 1788 we have already noted Bishop Asbury's statement that other persuasions were active in the opposite direction, and that their ministers boldly preached against the freedom of the slaves. Methodism had been standing alone in the struggle for thirty years.

The provisions of the Discipline adopted in 1800, especially the last, inaugurated an aggressive movement. That political action meant work. Its originators believed in freedom. They had faith in the triumph of truth and right. Not satisfied with the enactment of this regulation, the General Conference authorized an "Address to all their brethren and friends in the United States," calling special attention to it. This was signed by Bishops Thomas Coke, Francis Asbury, and Richard Whatcoat; and by Ezekiel Cooper, William M'Kendree, and Jesse Lee. It was an earnest appeal against "the great national evil," which, they said, deprived "so many of our fellow-creatures of every trace of liberty," and which was, for the people of the United States, declared to be "an inconsistency which can scarcely be paralleled in the history of our race." "At this General Conference we wished, if possible, to give a blow at the root of this enormous evil." "We, therefore, determined at last to rouse up all our influence in order to hasten, to the utmost in our power, the universal extirpation of this crying sin." So said the Methodist Episcopal Church at the opening of the nineteenth century. Noble words and brave purposes were thereby put on record by the fathers!

CHAPTER VI.

SLAVERY TOLERATED BY THE CHURCH, 1800–1824.

THE antislavery platform on which the Church stood at this period was vigorously assailed by the extreme South. The Bishops were the leaders of the antislavery movement recommenced in the year 1800. Their action was not merely perfunctory. Besides bringing before the Annual Conferences this question for counsel and action, officially they published and circulated antislavery pamphlets all over the land on their personal responsibility.

A pamphlet attributed to Rev. Gabriel Capers, brother of Bishop Capers, referring to the action of the first Bishops of the Methodist Episcopal Church, says : "Many years ago the venerable Bishops Coke and Asbury published a pamphlet on slavery, which compelled the enlightened and benevolent Legislature of South Carolina to pass an act authorizing any person to repair to Methodist meetings and disperse the negroes, whether assembled with or without the consent of their owners. The act was justified by the first law of nature—self-defense—and was based upon the fact that Methodism at that period, whether at the North or South, was identified with the most deadly opposition to slavery. It continued in force — and with the utmost propriety, too—until the ministers of that denomination ceased to assail the institution of bondage and to expel the members of their Societies for buying and selling a slave under any circumstances." — *Letter of Rev. D. De Vinne, "Zion's Herald,"* 1844.

The antislavery doctrine and discipline of the Church evidently did prevail in South Carolina, as well as in New York, in those early days, but was soon displaced after persecution began to be suffered. The late Bishop Capers, then a member of the General Conference held at Cincinnati, in 1836, said that these persecutions ceased when Methodist people began to hold slaves. "At length people began to consider that many of them were slave-holders; why should they be insurrectionists? This went far to raise them above suspicion." And in the General Conference held at New York, in 1844, Dr. Capers further testified to the presence and influence of the Address of the Conference of 1800: "I never saw but one of those documents called Addresses to the Legislatures, and I regret that I did not preserve a copy of it. I can, however, assure you that Orange Scott never wrote or published a more violent, incendiary, and disloyal document. Some of the preachers would not circulate them because they believed they would do harm. Among these was George Dorr. He said he could not and he would not be the bearer of such a communication to the people of his charge. He preached in Charleston, and the paper found its way there and cost him much trouble. They came in some way to Brother Harper's store. He did not intend to circulate them, but one got out in some way and produced a great excitement. The people charged the bringing of the papers into town on poor Dorr, who had done all he could to oppose them. I saw the mob as I was going down town, and understood that they were going to duck the preacher. The feeling

became so deep and general, and the excitement rose
so high, that it became necessary to expurgate all that
related to slavery from the copies of the Discipline
that were sent to South Carolina." — "*Report of Debates*," *Matlack and Lee.*

The earnest and untiring zeal of the Bishops to
carry out the well-matured plans of the General Conference were not equal to the deep-rooted hostility of
the people of the South, who were diligently at work
upon the selfish fears of a rising Church, linked as
that hostility was with the supineness of a ministry
naturally ambitious of denominational success. Facts
similar to these now given could be recited, showing
the same state of feeling in other Southern States,
underlying a reactionary movement against the interests of freedom, and in conflict with the antislavery
plans and purposes of the Church, which became
dominant in a very few years. But without such detail, the retrograde action will be clearly understood
from what has come under notice already and by the
facts hereafter given.

Dr. Durbin said, in 1844, at the General Conference
held in New York city: "The history of the Church
shows this point indisputably, that the highest ground
that has ever been held upon the subject of slavery
was taken at the very organization of the Church,
and that concessions have been made by the Church
continually from that time to this in view of the
necessities of the South. Even the language of the
question about slavery was mitigated. It had been,
'What regulations shall be made for the extirpation
of the crying evil of African slavery?' In 1804 it
was changed to, 'What shall be done for the extirpation of the evil of slavery?' In 1808 all that relates

to slave-holding among private members was stricken out, and no rule on the subject has existed since."— *"Debates of* 1844," pp. 173, 174.

The Discipline of 1804, moreover, shows other changes than that made in the form of the question which heads the section on slavery. The section itself was materially altered. The "blessed undertaking" of the year 1800 to memorialize State Legislatures, which was "to give a blow at the root of the evil," and which the Church then purposed should "be continued from year to year until the desired end be accomplished," was entirely abandoned. Slave-selling was allowed, "at the request of the slave, in cases of mercy and humanity, agreeably to the judgment of a committee of the male members of the Society, appointed by the preacher who has charge of the circuit." The rules, as thus modified against traveling preachers holding slaves, on slave-holders being official members, on free and faithful talk with slave-holding probationers, on buying and selling slaves, and on gradual emancipation of all slaves, were all utterly canceled for four States in the South, embracing one fifth of the Church members, or about 123,000, by the provision: "Nevertheless, the members of our Societies in the States of North Carolina, South Carolina, Georgia, and Tennessee, shall be exempted from the above rules." Furthermore, the request made in 1800 of the whole Church to consider the question of negro slavery, and impart important thoughts to the General Conference, in order to take further steps toward eradicating this enormous evil, was withdrawn from the Discipline. And instead thereof a provision was adopted, as a present close and fitting inverted climax to this down

grade, in the interests of slave-holders every-where:
"5. Let our preachers from time to time, as occasion
serves, admonish and exhort all slaves to render due
respect and obedience to the commands and interests
of their respective masters."

And the Church entered upon the ensuing quadrennium with but little apparent zeal for "African
liberty," as Bishop Asbury termed it, and only "as
much as ever," instead of "more than ever," "convinced of the great evil of slavery," which had ceased
to be a "crying evil," and was not in the Discipline
now recognized as existing "in the United States."
The question was becoming a so-called delicate one,
and was not to be roughly handled as aforetime.
Smoother words, in moderate tones, began to be
spoken.

Four years were passed on this line. The Discipline of 1808 contained only the paragraphs about
official members being slave-holders, and on traveling
preachers who were slave-holders, with a new paragraph allowing the Annual Conferences to regulate
the traffic in slaves as they saw fit. The free and
faithful talk with slave-holding probationers, all the
restrictions against private members holding, buying,
or selling slaves heretofore contained in the section
on slavery, as well as the duty of exhorting slaves to
obey and respect their masters, are all omitted in and
after 1808. Four years later the paragraph relating
to Annual Conference powers was prefaced with the
words: "Whereas the laws of some of the States
do not admit of emancipating of slaves without a
special act of the Legislature." A clause was added
at the same time to the requisites for local eldership:
"Provided, nevertheless, that no slave-holder shall be

eligible to the office of an elder where the laws will admit of emancipation and permit the liberated slave to enjoy freedom."

In 1816 a verbal change only was made, and in 1820 the paragraph authorizing Annual Conferences to form regulations relative to buying and selling slaves was rescinded. But in 1824 the section on slavery was amended for the last time until 1860. What the position of the Church was on the question of slavery, and what plan the Methodist Episcopal Church then provided " for the extirpation of the evil of slavery," will be found quoted in full as given below :

The " General Rules " forbid " the buying and sell-ing of men, women, and children, with an intent to enslave them."

The " Section on Slavery " said :

" 1. We declare that we are as much as ever con-vinced of the great evil of slavery ; therefore, no slave-holder shall be eligible to any official station in our Church hereafter where the laws of the State in which he lives will admit of emancipation, and permit the liberated slave to enjoy freedom.

" 2. When any traveling preacher becomes an owner of a slave or slaves by any means, he shall for-feit his ministerial character in our Church, unless he execute, if it be practicable, a legal emancipation of such slaves, conformably to the laws of the State in which he lives.

" 3. All our preachers shall prudently enforce upon our members the necessity of teaching their slaves to read the word of God, and to allow them time to attend upon the public worship of God on our regu-lar days of divine service.

" 4. Our colored preachers and official members

shall have all the privileges which are usual to others in the District and Quarterly Conferences where the usages of the country do not forbid it. And the presiding elder may hold for them a separate District Conference where the number of colored preachers will justify it.

" 5. The Annual Conferences may employ colored preachers to travel and preach where their services are judged necessary; provided that no one shall be so employed without having been recommended according to the form of Discipline."

This summary of the antislavery sentiment and antislavery purposes of the Church, as set forth in the book of Discipline of 1824, and afterward for thirty-six years, gives us the following points: First, The system of slavery is declared to be a great evil. Second, The extirpation of slavery is the objective point of a stereotyped question. Third, Slave-trading is forbidden. Fourth, Traveling preachers might not hold slaves where emancipation was practicable. Fifth, Official members of the Church could hold slaves in every State where liberated slaves were not allowed to remain on the soil. Sixth, Private members could hold slaves anywhere, the only duty required or obligation imposed being put upon the preacher, " who shall prudently enforce" on the members the claims of their slaves to read the Bible and to worship God. Seventh, The usages of slaveholding communities made the measure of Church privileges for colored preachers and official members. Eighth, Colored preachers might be employed as itinerants. How far from the old testimonies were these modified regulations, and how powerless for the work of extirpating slavery!

With the latest years of Bishop Asbury's life came feebleness and lessened activity. From 1804 he had been without the companionship of Bishop Coke, who had returned to England, and, afterward, on the way to India, died in 1814. The inspiration of their joint zeal in the antislavery struggle was not at work in the Conferences as formerly. And Bishop Asbury, alone in the Episcopacy from 1806 to 1808, after Whatcoat died, had more than he could well accomplish as the chief executive in a Church of one hundred and fifty-one thousand nine hundred and ninety-five members, with a pastorate embracing five hundred and forty traveling preachers.

The recognition of the laws of slavery and the usages of slave-holding communities, by framing the Discipline of the Church thereby, and administering the same to please slave-holding Methodists, seems to have come very near extirpating the spirit of liberty, and did most certainly establish slavery with almost invulnerable ramparts.

So tenacious was this already "privileged class" of the sanctity of their institution, that any provision of the Discipline, or action of the General Conference, ever so remotely touching it, was condemned and must be removed out of the way. As early as 1796, "at the request of the Annual Conferences, colored preachers were occasionally ordained under a special arrangement. Bishop Asbury at this session [1800] desired that the arrangement should be formally adopted by the General Conference. Accordingly it was enacted that when the colored members had built a house of worship and had a person qualified, he might be ordained a deacon upon obtaining a rec-ommendation of two thirds of the male members of

the Society, and also one from the minister in charge
and his associates in the city or circuit. The rule,
however, was offensive to many of the Southern people, and, though acted upon locally, was never inserted
in the Discipline. — (Simpson's "Hundred Years of
Methodism," p. 84.)

The adjustment of the laws of the States to the
principles of truth and justice, as these were identified with freedom and equality of natural rights, was
not an impossible task for American citizens, members of the Methodist Church. And that would have
made so much better a history. How unfortunate
that such history was not made! In this country the
influence of ecclesiastical bodies upon the body of the
people is immediate and forcible, and the identity of
the people with the government is without parallel
in any part of the world. What might have been in
most of the Southern States, at an early day, is suggested by Dr. William A. Smith's remarks about Virginia: "I told Dr. Bond that Southern Methodists
concurred in making the laws—voluntarily did so, as
far as the system itself was concerned; and that in
Virginia, particularly, they could not avail themselves
of the benefit of his apology. Because, so strong is
the non-slaveholding interest, that at any time when
the membership of the Church shall unite their votes
with the non-slaveholders, in Western Virginia particularly, they are competent to overthrow the whole
system. But that we did not do so, because we considered it our solemn Christian duty to sanction and
sustain the system under its present unavoidable circumstances."—*Asbury's Letter*, "*Christian Advocate
and Journal*," *July* 31, 1844.

CHAPTER VII.

ABOLITIONISM—ENGLISH AND AMERICAN.

THE period now reached in the history of American Methodism marked the beginning of a movement against slavery in the West Indies, under the British Government, in which the English Wesleyans were zealous and effective co-workers. At the beginning of the antislavery movement there the number of Church members in the Methodist Societies in the West Indies, according to the British Minutes, in 1822, was 880 whites and 23,819 black or colored. About 80,000 adults and children were then under the instructions of the Wesleyan missionaries.

The British Antislavery Society, which was organized in 1823, included Jabez Bunting, Richard Watson, and many other Wesleyan ministers among its active and influential members. The advocates of slavery in Jamaica were offended thereby, and persecuted the missionaries, who were constrained to sign a declaration in favor of slavery and censuring the British antislavery men. To this the Wesleyan Missionary Committee responded by a public disavowal of the conduct of their missionaries, and an assertion of their positive antagonism to slavery, and their purpose to seek its overthrow. This was in 1825.

This manifesto, Lord Bathurst, principal Secretary for the Colonies, regarded so dangerous to the peace

of the West Indies that he communicated with Mr.
Watson, the missionary secretary, on the subject,
showing great uneasiness and excitement. The reply
of Mr. Watson reaffirmed prudently the Wesleyan
antislavery position and views, and then added : " We
could not shrink from the avowal of this opinion on
the general question of slavery when circumstances
obliged us either to make it or tacitly to profess the
contrary opinion. We cannot surrender our principles even to obtain that favor in the West Indies by
which we might increase our opportunities of doing
good. Wherever policy may be proper, we think it
out of its place in the proceedings of a religious society." Wise words, worthy of world-wide accepta-
tion.

At this period, and for seven years afterward, the
home government was almost a unit in favor of
continuing slavery in the West India Colonies, and
refused to hear with any patience any ope, except
indeed Mr. Brougham, in the House of Commons,
speak against the system. But the Wesleyan Conference was not silent, nor their West India missionaries inactive. Persecutions were suffered ; mobs
assailed their dwellings, assaulted their persons, and
destroyed their chapels. The Colonial authorities
imprisoned the missionaries in a loathsome dungeon,
enforcing intolerant laws. One died from broken-
down health induced by it. Others returned to England to recuperate slowly.

A bill reasserting religious tolerance for the missionaries in the West Indies having been brought
into Parliament by Mr. Buxton, in 1825, the Wesleyan Conference of that year adopted, unanimously,
a vote of thanks to him and to those who supported

it. And in 1830, when Mr. Brougham was the candidate for Parliament for the County of York, the
entire influence of Mr. Watson and the Wesleyans
was used in his favor. This was followed by the
adoption of six resolutions, with perfect cordiality, at
the Conference in Leeds, July 30, 1830. They declared slavery to be, 1. In direct opposition to all
the principles of natural right and to the spirit of the
religion of Christ.   2. That the system doomed a
great majority of slaves to labors inhumanly wasting
to human life, and to arbitrary, excessive, and degrading punishments.   3. That the system was necessarily
unfavorable to missions; inspired slave-holders with
contempt and fear of the negroes; nurtured violent
prejudices of caste which opposed formidable obstacles to the employment of colored teachers and
missionaries; discouraged marriage by violent separa-
tions, and encouraged grossness which corrupted the
young and polluted the most hallowed relations of
life; fostered irreligion, and rendered nugatory every
attempt at efficient religious instruction. 4. That the
right of a Christian brotherhood of 24,000 West India
slaves to freedom was, if possible, strengthened by
their being partakers with us of like precious faith.
5. That the Wesleyans throughout the kingdom are
earnestly recommended to petition Parliament for the
speedy and universal abolition of slavery. 6. The
members who enjoy the elective franchise are urged
to use that solemn trust, in the elections now on the
eve of taking place, in favor of those candidates who
pledge themselves to support measures for the entire
abolition of slavery."—*Condensed from "The Great
Secession,"* chaps. i, iv.

These aroused an antislavery agitation among the

Wesleyans, which was kept up with an unflagging zeal year by year at the Conferences, in all the chapels, under the lead of their principal ministers and laymen, until the desired end was accomplished and slavery ceased in all the British Colonies, Aug. 1, 1834. An apprenticeship system was continued until 1838. Then the day of jubilee came when liberty was proclaimed throughout all the land to all the bondmen thereof, numbering in all 800,000 souls.

"The Wesleyans kept watch-night in all their chapels on the night of July 31. One of the Wesleyan missionaries gave us an account of the watch-meeting at the chapel in St. John's. The spacious house was filled with the candidates for liberty. All was animation and eagerness. A mighty chorus of voices swelled the song of expectation and joy, and as they united in prayer the voice of the leader was drowned in the universal acclamations of thanksgiving and praise, and blessing, and honor, and glory, to God who had come down for their deliverance. In such exercises the evening was spent until the hour of twelve approached. The missionary then proposed that when the clock on the cathedral should begin to strike, the whole congregation should fall upon their knees and receive the boon of freedom in silence. Accordingly, as the loud bell tolled its first note, the crowded assembly prostrated themselves on their knees. All was silence save the quivering, half-stifled breath of the struggling spirit. The slow notes of the clock fell upon the multitude; peal on peal, peal on peal, rolled over the prostrate throng, in tones of angels' voices, thrilling among the desolate chords and weary heart-strings. Scarce had the clock sounded its last note, when the lightning flashed

vividly around, and·a loud peal of thunder roared
along the sky—God's pillar of fire and his trump of
jubilee! A moment of profoundest silence passed—
then came the burst: they broke forth into prayer;
they shouted; they sung 'Glory,' 'Alleluia;' they
clapped their hands, leaped up, fell down, clasped
each other in their free arms, cried, laughed, and
went to and fro, tossing upward their unfettered
hands; but high above the whole there was a mighty
sound which ever and anon swelled up—it was the
utterings, in broken negro dialect, of gratitude to
God. After this gush of excitement had spent itself,
and the congregation became calm, the religious exercises were resumed, and the remainder of the night
was occupied in singing and prayer, in reading the
Bible, and in addresses from the missionaries explain-
ing the nature of the freedom just received, and exhorting the freed people to be industrious, steady,
obedient to the laws, and to show themselves in all
things worthy of the high boon which God had conferred upon them."—*Thome and Kimball, "Journal
of West India Emancipation."*

Such was the outcome of English abolitionism,
and mainly through the agency of the English Wesleyans.

Jabez Bunting, President of the English Wesleyan
Conference in 1836, wisely said: "It must be admitted that there was a great difference between having to emancipate 800,000 slaves at a distance, separated by local situations, and those localities being
favorable for their emancipation, and emancipating
two or three millions of people [in America] living
among them, man to man, and house to house, and
so connected with their domestic life; and he was

not a candid abolitionist who did not admit that,
though slavery was the same all over the world, the
facilities for terminating it might be different."—
"*Great Secession,*" p. 151.

And so it proved. To grapple with it in a hand-
to-hand struggle at our doors, in our American homes,
was too much for our Methodist fathers of the first
generation. They grew old and feeble in a noble
but unsuccessful effort to destroy African slavery in
the United States.

Subsequent to 1824 the General Conferences and
the Church at large were occupied with questions of
polity, and had little time and a lessening inclination
to disturb slavery by any new measures for or against
its extirpation, for about ten years. But soon after
this the Annual and General Conferences, and the
Church, were greatly agitated by a movement designated " Modern Abolitionism." The origin of that
movement it is proper to put on record, as also its
character.

A " New England Antislavery Society" was organized in 1832, which recommended a national movement. The American Antislavery Society, consequently, was organized at Philadelphia, in 1833, by
a convention of sixty-three abolitionists, from eleven
States of the Union. Twelve of these were evangelical ministers. All professed to be Christians.
Beriah Green was president. Lewis Tappan and
the poet Whittier were the secretaries. Lucretia
Mott, Esther Moore, Lydia White, and other worthy
women, were members. The committee to prepare
a declaration of sentiments was : Dr. E. P. Atlee,
Elizur Wright, William Lloyd Garrison, S. S. Joselyn,
David Thurston, a Mr. Sterling, William Green, Jun.,

John Greenleaf Whittier, William Goodell, Samuel J. May. The declaration embodied an elaborate argument showing how trifling were the grievances of the Colonies in 1776 compared with the wrongs and sufferings of the slaves of 1833. These wrongs are recited in detail, and, " in view of the civil and religious privileges of this nation, the guilt of its oppression " is declared to be " unequaled by any other on the face of the earth."

It was furthermore declared as their belief, " that there is no difference in principle between the African slave-trade and American slavery ; . . . that every American citizen who retains a human being in involuntary bondage is a man-stealer; . . . that the slaves ought to be instantly set free ; . . . that all those laws which are now in force admitting the right of slavery are, before God, utterly null and void; . . . that all persons of color ought to be admitted forthwith to the enjoyment of the same privileges and prerogatives as others ; . . . that no compensation should be given to the planters emancipating their slaves;" and "that, if compensation is to be given at all, it should be given to the outraged and guiltless slaves."

It also recognized "the sovereignty of each State to legislate exclusively on the subject of slavery within its limits," but insisted that Congress had "a right to suppress the domestic slave-trade between the States, and to abolish slavery in the Territories;" and further, that the people of the free States were bound to do every thing "to remove slavery by moral and political action, as prescribed in the Constitution of the United States." And this was the argument in justification of the Society then organized.

During the year 1835 there was $30,000 expended by this society; one million publications were issued, and fourteen lecturing agents were employed, who organized more than five hundred auxiliary societies. A great excitement prevailed, which was more violent against these agitators, however, than against slavery. The Methodist Episcopal Church shared largely in this feeling.

The Ohio Annual Conference of 1835 said, "That, as the friends of peaceable gradual emancipation, we have no cause to regret the course which has been pursued by the Methodist Episcopal Church on the subject of slavery, as set forth in the Discipline, but retain undiminished confidence in the same; ... that we deeply regret the proceedings of the abolitionists and antislavery societies in the free States, and the consequent excitement thereby produced in the slave States."

The Baltimore Annual Conference of 1836 resolved, "1. That we are as much as ever convinced of the great evil of slavery. 2. That we are opposed, in every part and particular, to the proceedings of the Abolitionists, which look to the immediate, indiscriminate, and general emancipation of slaves."

The New York Conference of 1836 resolved, "That in the judgment of this Conference it is incompatible with the duty which its members owe to the Church, as its ministers, for them to be engaged in attending antislavery conventions, delivering abolition lectures, or forming antislavery societies, either in or out of the Church, or in any way agitating the subject so as to disturb the peace and harmony of the Church, and that they be, and hereby are, affectionately advised and admonished to refrain from all these things."

The Philadelphia Conference of 1838 "heard with surprise and much regret that the Rev. O. Scott, of the New England Conference, and the Rev. G. Storrs, a local preacher, have come within our bounds, and are engaged in delivering lectures on modern abolitionism, and promoting the formation of antislavery societies within the Church;" and resolved, "That this Conference strongly protest against the conduct of the said O. Scott and G. Storrs;" "and that we also earnestly recommend our brethren and friends to discourage the objects and plans of said Scott and Storrs on the subject of modern abolitionism, as they tend to disturb the peace and prosperity within our bounds."

The Pittsburgh Conference of 1838 resolved, "That while this Conference disclaims all intention of interfering with any man's private opinion; and while, as the Discipline says, 'we are as much as ever convinced of the great evil of slavery,' we judge it incompatible with the duties and obligations of Methodist preachers to spend their time in delivering abolition lectures, contributing to the getting up of abolition meetings, attending abolition conventions, or in circulating abolition papers."

Resolutions of similar import were adopted by the Michigan Conference of 1838. This will suffice as specimens of ecclesiastical action in that direction.

Several Southern States by their legislative enactments sought to induce the States of the North to suppress modern abolitionism. A few instances are quoted from Dr. Elliot's "Great Secession:" "*Resolved*, That the Legislature of South Carolina, having every confidence in the justice and friendship of the non-slaveholding States, announces her confident expectation, and she earnestly requests, that the governments of these States will promptly and effectually suppress all those associations within their respective limits purporting to be abolition societies." (Adopted December 16, 1835.) North Carolina, December 19, 1835 : " *Resolved*, That our sister States are respectfully requested to enact penal laws prohibiting the printing of all such publications as may have a tendency to make our slaves discontented." Virginia adopted a similar resolution February 16, 1836. The same year Georgia called on the people of the North to "crush the traitorous designs of Abolitionists." Alabama also insisted " on the Northern States enacting such penal laws as will finally put an end to the malignant designs of the Abolitionists." And circulars were sent by the governors of Southern States to the governors of the Northern States urging their concurrence in such action.

CHAPTER VIII.

ANTISLAVERY AGITATION, 1835, 1836.

THE organization of the American Antislavery Society, in 1833, was only one year in advance of the first Methodist society. That was formed at the house of Mr. N. Dunn, 73 Leonard-street, New York. La Roy Sunderland presided, and Bishop Hedding was chosen president of the society, but declined to serve as soon as he was informed of it. " The New England Methodist clergy very early identified themselves with this cause. June 4, 1835, the New England Conference, sitting in Lynn, organized an antislavery society on the basis of the immediate and unconditional abolition of slavery, and invited George Thompson to address them. He preached a very powerful sermon from Ezek. xxviii, 14, 16: " Thou art the anointed cherub that covereth; and I have set thee so: thou wast upon the holy mountain of God; thou hast walked up and down in the midst of the stones of fire. . . . By the multitude of thy merchandise they have filled the midst of thee with violence, and thou hast sinned: therefore I will cast thee as profane out of the mountain of God: and I will destroy thee, O covering cherub, from the midst of the stones of fire."

North Bennet-street Methodist Episcopal Church, in Boston, was opened to Mr. Thompson that year on Fast Day, for a sermon, and received warm words of commendation for their courage from the pen of

William Lloyd Garrison: "In these days of slavish servility and malignant prejudices we are presented occasionally with some beautiful specimens of Christian obedience and courage. One of these is seen in the opening of North Bennet-street Methodist Meeting-house, in Boston, to the advocates for the honor of God, the salvation of our country, and the freedom of enslaved millions in our midst. As the pen of the historian in after years shall trace the rise, progress, and glorious triumph of the abolition cause, he will delight to record, and posterity will delight to read, the fact that when all other pulpits were dumb, all other churches closed, on the subject of slavery in Boston, the boasted 'cradle of liberty,' there was one pulpit that would speak out, one Church that would throw open its doors in behalf of the down-trodden victims of American tyranny. The primitive spirit of Methodism is beginning to revive, with all its holy zeal and courage, and it will not falter until the Methodist Churches are purged from the pollution of slavery, and the last slave in the land stands forth a redeemed and regenerated being."—*Haven: Introduction to "National Sermons."*

The New Hampshire Conference formed an antislavery society the same year. Simultaneously, at the opening of the year 1835, a series of stirring articles appeared in "Zion's Herald," Boston, from Orange Scott; and an "Appeal," which was written by La Roy Sunderland, signed by Shipley W. Wilson, Abram D. Merrill, La Roy Sunderland, George Storrs, and Jared Perkins. The "Appeal" was addressed to the members of the New England and the New Hampshire Conferences, to which the appellants belonged. Besides, Orange Scott, during the same year, sent

"The Liberator," Mr. Garrison's paper, free, for six months, to all the ministers of his Conference.

The "Appeal" opened a discussion that continued for thirty years, occupying the pens of able writers, including bishops, editors, and doctors, as well as pastors and laymen. This initiative document set forth the views of the Abolitionists on the general question of slavery; its connection with the Methodist Episcopal Church; the duty and responsibility of the Church; all which was supported by the testimony of the Bible, the Methodist Discipline, John Wesley, and the English Wesleyans. It was well-matured and every way worthy of the grave matter now brought to the consideration of the Church and nation. After an exhaustive exposition of doctrines and duties, the appeal closed with urging all to become " well acquainted with the state of slavery in this country, especially as it is connected with the Christian Church; . . . to remember those in bonds as bound with them, at the family altar and at the monthly concert for prayer ; . . . to read and circulate the publications of the American Antislavery Society;" and to address the next General Conference as " congregations and Conferences on this momentous subject." The first battery, manned by Methodist Abolitionists, had opened its fire. The reply was not long delayed, nor was it a less vigorous fire when aroused.

A " Counter Appeal" of remarkable ability appeared in the same paper, in reply, which was written by Prof. D. D. Whedon, dated March 27, 1835, signed by Wilbur Fisk, John Lindsey, Bartholomew Otheman, Hezekiah S. Ramsdell, Edward T. Taylor, Abel Stevens, Jacob Sanborn, and H. H. White. It was published April 8, 1835, and addressed to the same two Confer-

ences.   The signers of the "Counter" understand the
"Appeal" as declaring "that no part of the system of
slavery is just or humane, that no Christian can consistently support any part of it, and that the whole
should be this moment abandoned ; . . . and that no
slave-holder is truly awakened, and that no slave-
holder can rightly be permitted a place in the Christian Church."   To the first of these positions it is
replied, on "the basis of the divine law of love and
the golden rule," that "the authority of the master
should terminate so soon as its cessation would not
produce more evils than would its longer continuance ; and the authority should be diminished in
amount and severity when such diminution would
not produce more evil than it would subtract."

To the second position objections are brought from
the Scriptures of the New Testament, which· it is
affirmed prove "that in the primitive Christian
Church at Colosse, under the apostolic eye, and with
the apostolic sanction, the relation of master and
slave was ·permitted to subsist ; . . . that there were
already such in the Church of Ephesus ; . . . that
the New Testament here (Ephes. vi, 5–9) and elsewhere enjoins obedience upon the slave as an obligation due to a present rightful authority ; . . . that
1 Tim. vi, 1, 2, presents an impregnable demonstration that slave-holding is not in all cases and inva-
riably sinful ; that we may not say that no slave-
holder is truly awakened ; and that it does not of
itself form ground of exclusion from the Christian
Church.   The "Counter" maintained, also, that the
Bible is opposed to slavery as a system, and disclaimed
all purpose of defending the system or proving its
perpetuity.   What it opposed is the dogma, "That

all slave-holding is sinful, and therefore should be universally and immediately abandoned."

Following this scriptural argument, the "Counter" vindicated the action of the General Conference prior to 1836, and defended the Discipline as it then was; and then expressed in earnest words the hope of the liberation of the slaves, without expatriation, in behalf of which an appeal is made "to our brethren of the South" that "they would now emulate the memorable stand of our brethren of England, and with the name of Wesley on their banners and his spirit in their hearts, would seize the timely honor of leading out the foremost van of the great Christian movement, which in some of our States is directing their onward march toward the ultimate achievement of universal emancipation." Bishop Hedding read the "Counter," and appended his signature, saying, in general, "I believe the arguments and statements are correct, particularly those which refer to the acts of the General Conference."

Thus commenced the early controversy, in which, besides the above-named ministers of distinction, many others of equal ability were engaged, *pro and con*, for more than twenty-five years ensuing. The immediate objects sought by the Abolitionists were, the expression of antislavery sentiments in the Annual and Quarterly Conferences, and, through memorials from the Church generally, the enactment of prohibitory rules against slavery by the General Conference; and, ultimately, the extirpation of slavery from the land. The necessary agitation of the Church, in order to secure all this, became a cause of solicitude to the Bishops and others, who sought to allay the excitement by discouraging and suppressing the discussion, which

they feared would embarrass and seriously injure the
peace and unity of the Church and nation. Bishops
Hedding and Emory therefore addressed a Pastoral
Letter, September 10, 1835, to the same two Conferences already twice appealed to. The Bishops say:
"We have now between us attended the Northern
and Eastern Conferences as far as the Troy, inclusive,
and have found no such excitement within any of
them, except yours." They regard the general agitation as "a deep political game," which they advise
the brethren not to be drawn into; and attest, from
personal knowledge, that "nothing has ever occurred
so seriously tending to obstruct and retard, if not absolutely to defeat, the cause of emancipation," as "the
modern agitation on this subject." After enumerating
the difficulties in the way of emancipation, the impropriety of insisting so vehemently on universal, unconditional, and immediate abolition, regardless of all
consequences, the Bishops refer to their own embar-
rassing duties as administrators of discipline in a very
emphatic manner, and appeal to the Church generally
to co-operate with them in discountenancing agitation.

They say: "And if any will persist in so doing,
whether from the pulpit or otherwise, we earnestly
recommend to our members and friends every-where,
by all lawful and Christian means, to discountenance
them in such a course. The presiding elders especially we earnestly exhort to discountenance such
practices, both by their counsel and example. And
if any, of whatever class, go beyond their own bounds,
or leave their proper appointments, whether under
the pretext of agencies or otherwise, to agitate other
societies or communities on this subject, we advise
the preachers, the trustees, the official and other mem-

bers, to manifest their disapprobation, and to refuse the use of their pulpits and houses for such purposes."

No further detailed statements are necessary to afford a correct view of the attitude of the parties engaged in this discussion, or to learn the position and purposes of the highest authorities in the Church as they were carried out in the Annual Conferences generally for seven years following. The two Annual Conferences addressed by the Pastoral Letter of the Bishops seem not to have been influenced thereby in their course of action. They had already elected Abolitionists the same year of the most decided character to the ensuing General Conference, with two exceptions. From New England: Orange Scott, Isaac Bonney, Phineas Crandall, Charles Virgin, Joseph A. Merrill, Daniel Fillmore, Daniel Webb. From New Hampshire: Charles D. Cahoon, John F. Adams, Samuel Kelley, Schuyler Chamberlain, Jared Perkins, Elihu J. Scott, E. Scott, George Storrs, Samuel Norris. With them were forwarded the first antislavery memorials that the General Conference had seen for a long time, a skirmish-line in advance of the solid columns of after years.

Joseph A. Merrill presented one memorial signed by two hundred Methodist preachers, asking for the restoration of the original rule on slavery. Another, asking the same thing, was presented, signed by two thousand two hundred and eighty-four members of the Church. Besides these, others were presented from within the bounds of the Maine, New England, New Hampshire, New York, Oneida, Genesee, and Troy Conferences, making the same request. They were referred to a committee of seven, two of whom were Abolitionists. The report was unfriendly.

The action of the General Conference of 1836 was associated with a discussion of much interest, at times very exciting, which was introductory to and prophetic of momentous consequences within the ensuing twenty-five years.

Dr. Nathan Bangs' report of an answer to the "Address" of the Wesleyans of England was presented May 4, which said: "Had the Wesleyan Conference fully understood how slavery was interwoven in many of our State constitutions, they would probably have censured us less or modified their language." The report also spoke of the "trouble abolitionism" had made. Tobias Spicer, of the Troy Conference, said: "I think slavery should be inserted, instead of abolitionism." O. Scott and others thought so too. But the motion of John Early, of Virginia, to lay the report on the table, prevailed. As finally adopted the next day the answer to the Wesleyan "Address" did not censure abolitionism nor condemn slavery. The entire session nearly was occupied with the discussion of the paragraph on slavery by those only who were not Abolitionists, during which the Abolitionists heard in silence some hard things. Abolitionism was called "an unhallowed flame that has burned to the destruction of both whites and blacks." John Early said: "Let the Methodists from Maine to Georgia come out and denounce Abolitionists, and it will place the Methodist Episcopal Church on an eminence that it never had before."

On the appointment of the committee to prepare the Pastoral Address, S. G. Roszel and S. Luckey moved to instruct them to incorporate a paragraph on "abolition;" when O. Scott moved to add, "and another on slavery." Their motions were withdrawn.

The next day, May 12, an opportunity was afforded for the amplest denunciation of Abolitionists and abolitionism, which was much enjoyed by their antagonists.

A regular weekly meeting of the Cincinnati Antislavery Society had been held on Tuesday evening, May 10. George Storrs and Samuel Norris were present, being on no committee, and having no appointment to preach. Each made a few remarks. This was the occasion of the resolutions already quoted in Chapter VIII of this volume. The discussion leading to their adoption is an essential feature of the history of those times. An abridged report of it is herewith presented. ("The Philanthropist," J. G. Binney, reporter.)

The preamble said: "*Whereas*, great excitement has pervaded this country on the subject of modern abolitionism, which is reported to have been greatly increased in this city recently by the unjustifiable conduct of two members of the General Conference in lecturing upon and in favor of that agitating topic; and, *whereas*, such a course, on the part of any of its members, is calculated to bring upon this body the suspicion and distrust of the community, and misrepresent its sentiments in regard to the point at issue; and, *whereas*, a due regard for its own character, as well as a just concern for the interests of the Church confided to its care, demand a full and unequivocal expression of the views of the General Conference in the premises, therefore," etc. (See Chap. IX.)

William A. Smith, of Virginia, insisted on inserting the names of the two guilty individuals. " Let them be brought forth in all the length and breadth of their damning iniquity," said he. But that proposition was lost, for their exposure to Lynch law was feared by some if they became known to the public.

Noah Levings censured the recklessness of those brethren who had lectured upon and agitated this miserable subject.

G. C. Light, of Missouri, thought the state of feeling too high for deliberate action. He was willing to condemn abolitionism, but could not subscribe to every expression of the resolutions. He wished to refer them.

H. G. Lehigh, of Virginia, opposed the reference. It would waste time.

L. Grant, of Genesee, favored it. He could not find it in his heart to grind the Abolitionists down. He was not an Abolitionist. But Abolitionists had been misrepresented as to their motives, designs, and ultimate objects.

S. G. Roszel, of Maryland, would not say that Abolitionists had bad motives. But he would take a strong and decided course with them. Nothing else would do for such people; for they had pledged themselves in the most sacred and solemn manner to prosecute their object, and they seemed by their earnestness to think they were doing God service. No language in the resolutions was any too strong for them.

Laban Clark, of New York, thought that the resolutions embraced more than the circumstances of the case called for. He also questioned the power of the Conference to censure its members.

Mr. Payne, of Alabama, said: " Can it be possible that such authority can be denied to the highest tribunal of the Church—to censure the conduct of its own members when that becomes offensive, crim-

inal ?" At this, P. P. Sandford, of New York,
called Mr. Payne to order, as such epithets should
not be used against our brethren. The speaker ·con-
tinued : " It would seem that nothing can cure them.
The Abolitionists stop at nothing. They persist, notwithstanding the impediments they are continually
encountering in popular hatred and persecutions."

Dr. Elliott, of Pittsburgh, wished to amend so as to
declare it to be highly imprudent for any of the
members to deliver lectures on abolition during its
session.

D. Young, of Ohio, was opposed to any amendment.

T. Crowder, of Virginia, would have the resolutions pass in their present form as the most beneficial
disposition of the matter.

Messrs. Storrs and Norris both said that had the
"two members" known the sentiments of the General Conference in relation to their attendance at the
meeting before they had promised to be present at it,
they would have taken a different course. Dr.
Elliott's amendment was lost. Some impatience was
manifested by several at the delay, and immediate
adoption urged. But the dimensions of the question
were extending far beyond the personal aspects first
presented, and the whole subject of slavery and emancipation were yet to be discussed. The number of
the Abolitionists were small. Their cause proved to
be too immense to be easily managed by their opponents, who outnumbered them ten to one.

Orange Scott, of the New England Conference, obtained the floor, and commenced a calm and dispassionate examination of the resolutions. An eye-wit-
ness * says: " He began by asking the patience of the

* James G. Birney, Editor " Philanthropist," Cincinnati.

members, as he would probably, by consent, do the
principal part of the speaking on behalf of the Abolitionists in the Conference.   It was a noble effort—
calm, dignified, generous, Christian.   He showed no
waspishness nor petulance toward those who differed
with him, and who had been so prodigal in their repro-
bation of Abolitionists.   He was several times inter-
rupted by his impatient adversaries, yet his calmness
and self-possession were in no measure disturbed even
for a moment.   The dignity of the experienced de-
bater, understanding his subject in all its aspects,
calmly taking up the admissions of his opponents and
routing them with the very weapons their own un-
acquaintance with the subject and their intemperate
passion had so abundantly supplied, directing them
all with consummate skill, yet with the kindness and
forbearance of the Christian—in all these essentials
of religious discussion Mr. Scott presented himself in
striking and honorable contrast with nearly all, if not
all, who supported the resolutions."

Mr. Scott's report of his own remarks may be briefly
stated thus:

"MR. PRESIDENT: Before condemning modern
abolitionism, this Conference would do well to hear
patiently the opinion of its friends as to what it is
and to what it stands related.   Plainly, then, it proposes to abolish slavery, an acknowledged evil in our
Church, which has always contemplated its extirpation as a legitimate work for Methodists to do.   The
principle of slavery, which justifies holding and treating the human species as property, is morally wrong;
its practice is a sin.   Aside from all circumstances,
the principle is evil, only evil, and that continually.
It is a reprobate, too bad to be converted, not subject

to the law of God, neither indeed could it be.   Circumstances might palliate or aggravate, but could not justify it.   The views of slavery held by modern Abolitionists were shown to be identical with those held by Wesley, by the fathers of Methodism, and our Wesleyan brethren of England from numerous quotations.   The peace of the Church, which is disturbed by agitating these views of slavery, ought to be broken.   It may not, perhaps, be always best that the Church be at peace.   There may be 'ease in Zion' connected with a wedge of gold and a Babylonish garment.   The Methodist Episcopal Church has an unholy alliance with slavery; she ought not, therefore, give herself any peace until she cleanses her skirts from blood-guiltiness.   Shall the dearest interests of undying millions be sacrificed upon the altar of the peace of the Church?

"An aged and venerable brother yesterday called the abolition excitement 'an unhallowed flame.'   This expression has been several times repeated on this floor.   Sir, this same unhallowed flame has burned off the chains of eight hundred thousand slaves who were goods and chattels in the West India Islands, and elevated them to the rank of human beings.   Abolitionism is one the world over.   We are not trying an experiment, but walking in a beaten track.   Our principles have been tested.   We have no fear as to the results.   The day of our own national jubilee may linger, but it will come at last, and it cannot tarry long.   The fires of abolitionism are burning deep and wide; the leaven of liberty is now working through the whole lump; the axe is laid at the root of the tree; the whole country is awake, and the day of our redemption is at hand!

"Sir, one of our brethren from Baltimore has told us that he came up here flush with the expectation that the brethren from the North would put their foot on abolitionism and crush it! Have our brethren yet to learn that free discussion is not to be put down in this way? When you can put your foot on one of the burning mountains and smother its fires; when you can roll back the thundering Falls of Niagara; when you can stop the sun in its course with a word, you may crush abolitionism! Sir, the die is cast. The days of the captivity of our bondmen are numbered. Their redemption is written in heaven!"

Mr. Scott was replied to by Mr. Crowder, of Virginia, and Mr. Winans, of Mississippi, who took high Southern ground in behalf of slavery. Dr. Capers narrated several circumstances showing the need of great prudence to prevent persecution, illustrative of the faithful labors of Southern preachers among the slaves. An amendment by Mr. Scott, to disapprove of slavery as well as abolitionism, was discussed, but rejected. After two days' discussion the resolutions were adopted. Only fifteen negative votes were given. The whole abolition strength of the body was represented by the delegates from the New England and New Hampshire Conferences and J. S. Barris, of Pittsburgh.

In the "Christian Guardian," of Canada, Rev. William Lord, who represented the English Wesleyans at the General Conference of 1836, said of this small band: "The Abolitionists were in a very small minority. Before another General Conference the case will be greatly altered. There I envied the position in which Brother Orange Scott stood, making a firm stand against the monstrous evil, opposed by an overwhelming and influential majority. But as in our country so in America—the storm will soon blow over and the question of emancipation become popular."

At the English Wesleyan Conference in 1836 President Bunting said : "Slavery is always wrong, essentially, eternally, and incurably wrong. Die it must; and happy should I have been had the General Conference of the Methodist Episcopal Church passed sentence of death upon it." So thought and felt many others of our trans-Atlantic brethren. But they knew very little about the magnitude of the struggle with slavery in America.

CHAPTER IX.

CONFERENCE ACTION ON SLAVERY, 1836-1840.

THE almost unbroken silence of the Church on slavery for many years, except its stereotyped official testimony, very mildly formulated, and that not generally enforced, was suddenly and violently disturbed by the irrepressible agitation of the Abolitionists. Their radical views were condemned by some of the largest Annual Conferences, and their methods and aims were repudiated with much greater zeal than slavery was by the same bodies. The New England Conferences, however, became identified with the Abolitionists prior to the General Conference of 1836, which was held in Cincinnati.

At that Conference the Southern members brought forward the name of Dr. Capers, a slave-holder, as their candidate for Bishop, but he was not elected. This they deemed and declared "a proscription"— "an insult;" and on the evening of the day of election they held a meeting, which prepared the way for a circular, in July following, which recommended such concert of action as would induce the Church to recede from that "proscriptive position" in 1840. For the time, however, the Northern friends of slave-holding Methodists were fixed in their purpose not to favor slavery to the extent of electing a slave-holder for Bishop. They, therefore, elected three non-slave-holders to the Episcopacy—Beverly Waugh, of the South, and Dr. Wilbur Fisk and Thomas Morris, of

CONFERENCE ACTION ON SLAVERY, 1836-40. 101

the North. Previous to the election of Bishops an expression had been given to the views held by the Conference on the subjects of slavery and abolition, which were accepted by the Southern men at the time as "indicative of a determination on the part of the Methodist ministry throughout the North not to interfere with the domestic institutions of the South." So said Rev. William A. Smith.

The Report on Slavery said: "The committee to whom was referred sundry memorials from the North, praying that certain rules on slavery, which formerly existed in our Book of Discipline, should be restored, and that the General Conference take such measures as they might deem proper to free the Church from the evil of slavery, beg leave to report, that they have had the subject under serious consideration, and are of the opinion that the prayer of the memorialists cannot be granted, believing that it would be highly improper for the General Conference to take any action that would alter or change our rules on the subject of slavery." "*Resolved*, That it is inexpedient to make any change in our Book of Discipline respecting slavery, and that we deem it improper to agitate the subject in the General Conference at present." This was adopted by a majority of nine tenths of the body.

Following this, an occasion was found for the adoption of the two following resolutions—the first by 122 yeas to 11 nays; the second by 120 yeas to 14 nays—the last part of it unanimously:

1. "*Resolved*, by the delegates of the Annual Conference in General Conference assembled, That they disapprove, in the most unqualified sense, the conduct of the two members of the General Conference who

are reported to have lectured in this city recently, upon and in favor of modern abolitionism."

2. "*Resolved*, That they are decidedly opposed to modern abolitionism, and wholly disclaim any right, wish, or intention to interfere in the civil and political relation between master and slave as it exists in the slave-holding States of this Union."

The fourteen prepared a protest, which was not allowed to be put on record.

The Pastoral Address—prepared by a committee— signed by all the Bishops, and published by order of the General Conference, after treating of the legal barriers in the way of antislavery action, and the supposed evil effects of agitation, adds: "These facts constrain us, as your pastors, to exhort you to abstain from all abolition movements and associations, and to refrain from patronizing any of their publications. . . . Those of you who may have honest scruples as to the lawfulness of slavery considered as an abstract principle of right and wrong, if you must speak your sentiments, would do much better to express yourselves in those terms of respect and affection which evince a sincere sympathy for those of your brethren who are necessarily, and in some instances reluctantly, associated with slavery in the States where it exists, than to indulge in harsh censures and denunciations. . . . From every view of the subject which we have been able to take, and from the most calm and dispassionate survey of the whole ground, we have come to the solemn conviction, that the only safe, scriptural, and prudent way for us, both as ministers and people, is wholly to refrain from this agitating subject, which is now convulsing the country, and consequently the Church, from end to end." This advice, however, was not accepted by all.

The Baltimore Conference of 1837 resolved : "That in all cases of administration under the General Rule, in reference to buying and selling men, women, and children, etc., it be, and hereby is, recommended to all committees, as the sense and opinion of this Con-ference, that the said rule be taken, construed and understood, so as not to make the guilt or innocence of the accused to depend upon the simple fact of purchase or sale of any such slave or slaves, but upon the attendant circumstances of cruelty, injustice, or inhumanity on the one hand, or those of kind pur-poses and good intentions on the other, under which the transactions shall have been perpetrated."

The Pittsburgh Conference of 1837 resolved: "That in the judgment of this Conference, all traffic in the souls and bodies of our fellow-men, under any circumstances which either originates or perpetuates slavery, is a direct violation, both of the spirit and letter, of our rule on this subject."

The Genesee Conference of 1837 resolved : "That in the judgment of this Conference, our Discipline, in declaring that slavery is a great evil, is to be un-derstood as pronouncing, not upon its civil or polit-ical, so much as upon its moral character." This Conference repeated the declaration of the Pittsburgh Conference also.

The Georgia Conference of 1837 said, by a unani-mous vote: "*Whereas*, There is a clause in the Dis-cipline of our Church which states that we are as much as ever convinced of the great evil of slavery; and, *whereas*, the said clause has been perverted by some, and used in such a manner as to produce the impression that the Methodist Episcopal Church believed slavery to be a moral evil; therefore, *Resolved*, 1. That it is the sense of the Georgia Annual Conference that slavery, as it exists in the United States, is not a moral evil; *Resolved*, 2. That we view slavery as a civil and domestic institution, and one with which, as ministers of Christ, we have nothing to do, further than to ameliorate the condition of the slave, by endeavoring to impart to him and his master the benign influence of Christ, and aiding both on their way to heaven."

The South Carolina Conference of 1838 said: "We hold that the subject of slavery in these United States is not one proper for the action of the Church, but is exclusively appropriate to the civil authorities; therefore, *Resolved*, That this Conference will not intermeddle with it further than to express our regret that it has ever been introduced, in any form, into any one of the judicatories of the Church." Dr. Capers, the mover, explained, that "if slavery were a moral evil, that is, sinful, the Church would be bound to take cognizance of it; but our affirmation is, that it is not a matter for her jurisdiction, and, of course, not sinful." Whereupon it was unanimously adopted.

The General Conference of 1840 was advised of this state of things in the Church generally by the Address of the Bishops, who also say, "We cannot withhold from you, at this eventful period, the solemn conviction of our minds that no new ecclesiastical legislation on the subject of slavery at this time will have a tendency to accomplish these most desirable objects," to wit: "Preserve the peace and unity of the whole body, promote the greatest happiness of the slave population, and advance generally in the slave-holding community of our country the humane and hallowing influence of our holy religion." Yet, in view of "the different constructions to which the general rule on slavery had been subjected, and the variety of opinions entertained upon it, together with the conflicting acts of some of the Annual Conferences of the North and South," the Bishops venture the opinion that it would "seem to require that a body having legitimate jurisdiction should express a clear and definite opinion, as a uniform guide to those to whom the administration of the Discipline is committed." But no such opinion was expressed.

Two subjects were brought before the Conference which led to action relating to the question of slavery. The first was the appeal of Silas Comfort from the decision of the Missouri Conference. Mr. Comfort had admitted negro testimony on the trial of a white man. This was declared by that Annual Conference to be maladministration, but considered in his case to be an error of judgment only, so that his character had been passed. He appealed from the decision that he had perpetrated any maladministration to the General Conference. The principal plea of the Annual Conference was, that colored testimony was received in no civil court in Missouri against a white person. A motion to reaffirm this decision was lost. But a resolution was adopted by a vote of 74 to 46, "That it is inexpedient and unjustifiable for any preacher among us to permit colored persons to give testimony against white persons in any State where they are denied that privilege in trials at law." A motion to reconsider was laid on the table by a vote of 76 to 42, and this became the law of the Church for four years.

The other subject was introduced by a petition from the official members of Westmoreland Circuit, Baltimore Conference, complaining that ordination was withheld from local preachers because they were slave-holders; and they prayed for a change or a construction of the rule which should allow of such ordination, or that their circuit be set off to the Virginia Conference. This petition was referred, May 8, to a committee, Rev. H. B. Bascom, chairman, who reported June 3, near midnight, the following resolution, which, with little examination, was adopted: " That under the provisional exception of the general rule of the Church on the subject of slavery, the simple holding of slaves, or mere ownership of slave property, in States and Territories where the laws do not admit of emancipation and permit the liberated slave to enjoy freedom, constitutes no legal barrier to the election or ordination of ministers to the various grades of office known to the ministry of the Methodist Episcopal Church, and cannot be considered as working any forfeiture of rights in view of such election or ordination."

The conclusions reached, or the position the Church occupied, in 1840, may be thus summarized: Slavery was acknowledged to be a great evil, the extirpation of which was inquired about, but not provided for in the Discipline of the Church. Whether it was a moral evil, or only a social and political evil, or merely a harmless, domestic institution, were questions upon which the Annual Conferences gave uncertain and conflicting testimony, while the General Conference declined to express any opinion, although advised to do so by the Bishops, and requested to do so by anti-slavery memorialists. The Conference, however, had in 1836 deliberately declared against "any change in the Book of Discipline respecting slavery," and against the "agitation of the subject in the General Conference;" it had condemned abolitionism, and passed its disapprobation on two of its members for "speaking in favor thereof;" it had exhorted all the Church "wholly to refrain from" the agitating subject of slavery; and now it had declared against receiving the testimony of the colored members of the Church against white persons where slavery forbade it; and, finally, had characterized slave-holding as no barrier to ordination where freedom was forbidden by State law.

Of that portion of these declarations made at the General Conference of Cincinnati, in 1836, an immediate and unfortunate use was made by a pronounced friend of slavery. Judge Lewis, of the State of Louisiana, wrote a pamphlet that was published the same year by the "Conservative Society of Louisiana." It was an argument to prove Jewish servitude and American slavery essentially the same, allowed by the divine law still in force under the Christian dispensation, and, therefore, not a sin. "In this," says the judge, "I am glad to find that I am sustained by the resolution of the General Conference of the Methodist Episcopal Church, passed in their late session at Cincinnati. In that body are many men of profound and extensive learning, who are deeply versed in Scripture, and whose piety is as deep and sincere as that of any others to be found in any denomination of Christians whatever. Such men are competent to judge correctly in this if any men on earth are. But they do not condemn slavery as a sin, taken as it exists here. On the contrary, they imitate their divine Master by wholly disclaiming

any right, wish, or intention to interfere in the relation between master and slave, which they consider
one of the established civil and political relations of
society in our country. I cannot but consider this as
an invaluable testimony in our favor. It is a testimony they could not have given if they had considered that slavery, as it exists among us, is a sin."

Three periods have now been compassed in the
history of our Church: the preliminary period, when
slavery was rooted and grounded in this country by
European cupidity and avarice, long before the coming of the Wesleyan pioneers, and anterior to their
organization in 1784 as an Episcopal Church; the
primary period, during which the fathers of the
Methodist Episcopal Church unsparingly denounced
and vigorously legislated against slavery for twenty
years; and the subsequent period of toleration, during
which their sons allowed and practiced slavery. This
last reached its culmination with the General Conference of 1840 in the action already noted, whose concessions in favor of slavery deeply mortified and subsequently awakened and aroused the Church to action.
For there was even then an immense antislavery
force in process of development, which was afterward
unfolded within and without the ecclesiastical lines.
The period of extirpation efforts had commenced
already.

CHAPTER X.

METHODISM VERSUS ABOLITIONISM, 1836–1840.

THE Methodist Episcopal Church, by the action of the General Conference of 1836, was arrayed against the views, objects, and measures of the modern Abolitionists. It had also decided against any change of regulations touching slavery among its own members, and condemned all further agitation of the subject. Subordinate Conferences and executive and administrative officers recognized generally their obligation to act in harmony with the General Conference in these matters. The exceptional Conferences and individuals, who chose not to accept the advice of the Pastoral Address, "wholly to refrain" from antislavery action, as practically the law of the Church, soon became aware of the odds against them in the struggle now commenced.

The New England Conference of 1836 appointed a committee on slavery and abolition, with instructions to report early. The report was offered three days before the Conference adjourned, but the Bishop refused to allow it to be read until every thing else was done. It was read the last night at eleven o'clock, but Bishop Hedding would not put a motion for its adoption unless it could be re-read and discussed in detail, as some things in it he thought he could not approve. The New Hampshire Conference was deterred by these facts from attempting any action.

The following year numerous memorials came up from different parts of the New England Conference asking an expression on the subject of slavery. A committee, under the sanction of Bishop Waugh, informed a committee of Abolitionists that "the Bishops had consulted together and agreed to prevent, as far as possible, all Conference action on the subject; that the Conference was not a legislative body, and the memorials could not be received; that it was not Conference business; that the proposed expression of antislavery views would unchristianize the South; that the General Conference had condemned abolitionism, with other considerations of equal weight. The Bishop himself informed a committee, consisting of Timothy Mérritt, O. Scott, Jotham Horton, La Roy Sunderland, and James Porter, that he should "decline to put to vote any question of reference on memorials which seek to keep up an excitement and produce agitation on topics which the wisdom and authority of the General Conference have sought to quiet and put to rest." On the 14th of June, 1837, the memorials from the people were presented asking the Conference "to bear its solemn testimony against the great sin of slavery, and to memorialize the General Conference on the subject." The Bishop refused to put a motion to refer to a committee, refused an appeal to the Conference from his decision, declined to give an opinion as to whether the memorials had been received and were in possession of the Conference, and refused to put a motion for the expression of an opinion by the Conference on that matter.

At the New Hampshire Conference for 1837 another of the Bishops stipulated six conditions for allowing the appointment of a committee on slavery,

which the Conference refused to accept, and hence
no antislavery action was taken. A motion which recited the action of the Baltimore Conference, (see
Chap. VIII,) dissenting therefrom and disapproving of
it, was also refused to be put by the same Bishop, because it would bring the two Conferences into collision.

To enforce more completely, and by argument show
the propriety of, the line of policy pursued by the
Church against abolitionism, Bishop Hedding prepared an address on the subject, in answer to the
questions, "What right have any of our members to
hold slaves? Or, what right has the Church to allow
them to hold slaves?" He said: "Owning or holding a slave does not include exercising all the rights
which the laws are supposed to give the master over
the servant, but only such rights as are necessary for
the good of the servant and the safety of the master,
all the circumstances taken into the account. Now
let us answer the question. The right to hold a slave
is founded on this rule: 'Therefore all things whatsoever ye would that men should do to you, do ye
even so to them; for this is the Law and the Prophets.' Matt. vii, 12. If no case can be found where a
man can own a slave, and in that act obey this rule,
then there is no case in which slave-owning can be
justified. But if one case can be found where a man
may hold a slave, and by the civil law own, and in
that act obey this rule, then there may be ten such
cases, or ten thousand. And that there are many
such cases among our brethren I firmly believe. . . .
And I am not authorized to be the instrument of
passing Conference resolutions which even imply that
they are all sinners."—*Address to Oneida Conference.*

The Conferences were not prevented from condemning abolitionism, as has already been noted, (Chap. VIII.) And, moreover, the Pittsburgh Conference and the Genesee Conference for 1837 both antagonized the Baltimore Conference construction of the General Rule. And the Genesee Conference had, also, construed the great evil of slavery to be a moral, and not a political or social, evil—which the Georgia Conference was allowed to contradict squarely two months afterward. When, in 1838, the New England Conference desired to reiterate the words of the Pittsburgh and Genesee Conferences of 1837, it was not allowed. So the conflict thickened.

A yet more vigorous action was adopted by several of the Annual Conferences to put down abolitionism, which action, however, was remarkable mainly for the increased agitation of the slavery question which it occasioned, adding fuel to the flaming excitement that ultimately swept, like a prairie fire, over the whole land. It was a fire, soon under too much headway, too deep and broad, for the heaviest footfalls to stamp out.

The New York Conference of 1836 promptly concurred in the advice of the General Conference just preceding, and also "*Resolved*, That although we would not condemn any man, or withhold our suffrages from him, on account of his opinions merely in reference to the subject of abolitionism, yet we are decidedly of the opinion that none ought to be elected to the office of a deacon or elder in our Church unless he give a pledge to the Conference that he will refrain from agitating the Church with discussions on this subject."

At the ensuing session, in 1837, Charles K. True

was elected to elder's orders. The vote was reconsidered, however, and his having read an address on slavery to his Church at Middletown, Conn., from the pen of the venerable Timothy Merritt, was urged by several leading ministers as a reason for denying him elders' orders. But, after consuming nearly all of one day in the discussion, he was re-elected by a large majority. The next year his character was arrested on the charge of "contumacy and insubordination." The specifications were: 1. Violation of his pledge on slavery at the last Conference; 2. Aiding in the publication of an antislavery tract; 3. Attending an antislavery convention at Utica. Luther Lee, of the Black River Conference, was his counsel, and defended him in a speech of great power. The trial lasted two days, and resulted in his suspension from all the functions of a gospel minister, by a vote of ninety-one to thirty-seven. He appealed to the next General Conference. The next day, however, he sent into the Conference a pledge to abide by its decisions on the subject of slavery while he continued a member of the body, and refrain from such action as it would forbid; whereupon the suspension was removed—not, however, until he had promised to withdraw from the American Antislavery Society.

At the same session of the New York Conference (1838) James Floy was tried on the same charge and similar specifications. He had acted publicly against slavery, and attended an antislavery convention. He was found guilty by a vote of 124 to 17, and suspended from the office of a deacon; 102 for, 31 against. The next day he also pledged to abide the decisions of the Conference on slavery, and the suspension was taken off by a vote of 127 to 1.

Paul R. Brown was arraigned and tried at the same time the above-named brethren were, on the same charge, for attending the Utica Convention. Before the committee he manfully asserted his purpose to do all he could to oppose slavery and promote abolition-ism. The committee reported "that he be required to refrain wholly from this agitating subject; that he be publicly reproved by the Bishop, and that he be not appointed preacher in charge, but in a subordi-nate station, with some one over him." This was adopted. He made a noble defense, sketching fully the pro-slavery action of various Conferences and leading men, as a good and sufficient reason for hold-ing antislavery conventions in the Church, and a justification of his attendance and co-operation with them. He concluded his defense in the following dignified and Christian manner: "I have taken my stand, and cannot go back. I am not ambitious. I feel it a solemn duty. I must stand if alone and all the world against me. I can bear to be censured; it may do me good. I am willing to be admonished by any one, anywhere. As to having charge of a cir-cuit or station, I do not wish it. I never felt worthy of it, and think wiser and better men should be placed there. But as for pledging not to discuss the subject, I never can do it. If you think you must censure or suspend or expel me, why, you must take your course, and I must bear it. But I feel it to be my duty to plead for the slave, and I must have the liberty."

He was publicly rebuked by the Bishop, and his appointment was in a distant field, where he suffered much inconvenience and many privations. Special contributions during the year were made by personal friends among the Abolitionists to meet his necessities.

The Pittsburgh Conference resolution of 1838 was practically reaffirmed the following year by refusing to rescind it, with this construction: that the delivery of a single lecture, or lending an abolition book or paper, was a violation of it, and that a brother so offending, after admonition, could have no more place among us as a traveling Methodist preacher. The case of Goodsill Buckingham was then taken up, a probationer of one year's standing, who had delivered two lectures against slavery. His presiding elder and colleague represented him to be " deeply pious, habitually serious, greatly devoted to his work, possessing far more than ordinary talent and education, and exceedingly anxious to continue and give himself wholly to God and his work." His address to the Conference, says the venerable Robert Boyd, was marked by great self-possession and a truly amiable manner. Such was the ability manifested on this occasion, that his warmest opposers admitted that he was no ordinary man. But he was firm to his purpose, and refused to pledge himself wholly to refrain from the agitating subject, and was dropped from the traveling ministry by a vote of 49 to 29. He took his place among the laymen of the Church, a monument of personal integrity, and a constant memorial of mistaken Church policy, seen and lamented when too late for correction in his case.

Edward Smith, also of the Pittsburgh Conference, a minister of twenty years' standing, was, in 1840, brought to trial under this resolution he had helped to frame and pass. The relation of persons and propositions were now beginning to change. More enemies of abolitionism became its friends than contrary-wise. The formulæ of charges, moreover, were more

guardedly expressed. Mr. Smith was charged with
"giving publicity to things respecting the Methodist
Episcopal Church and the ministry which are highly
slanderous in their character;" and "encouraging a
spirit of rebellion in others, and violating his own
ordination vows, by declaring that he would not take
an appointment in Virginia if the Bishop were to
send him there." The "things" given publicity to
were such facts as have been recited in the former
chapters of this history on the connection of the
Church and ministry with slavery. The declared
purpose not to take an appointment in Virginia was
admitted, and defended on the ground that he was a
member and officer of an antislavery society, and conscientiously bound to express his views of slavery
wherever appointed. This would subject him to the
penalty of the following law of Virginia, passed
March 23, 1836 : "That any member of an abolition
or antislavery society who shall come into this State,
and shall maintain, by speaking or writing, that the
owners of slaves have no property in the same, or advocate or advise the abolition of slavery, shall be deemed
guilty of a misdemeanor, and on conviction thereof
shall be fined in a sum of not less than fifty dollars
nor more than two hundred dollars, and suffer a term
of imprisonment of not less than six months nor more
than three years, at the discretion of the jury." Both
charges were sustained, and "Rev. E. Smith was suspended from all official relation to the Methodist
Episcopal Church until he shall give this Conference
satisfactory evidence of repentance and reformation."

The Erie Conference of 1838 had adopted a resolution forbidding abolition lectures, similar to that of
the Pittsburgh Conference, for violating which Ben-

jamin Preston was suspended for one year from his ministerial office. In his case it was proved also that he said hard things about the suspensions effected at the New York Conference as inquisitorial persecution with Satan at the bottom of it.

J. S. Barris, a presiding elder of the Erie Conference, was, in 1838, arraigned upon the charge of "Insubordination to the authorities of the Church," in 1. Disobeying the advice of the General Conference. 2. Contempt of the Erie Conference, by getting up and presiding in an abolition meeting, and delivering an abolition lecture in the Presbyterian Church on Sabbath evening, under pretense of preaching a gospel sermon. 3. Giving leave to a pastor on his district to attend the Abolition Convention at Utica, N. Y. The Conference adopted a vote of regret, and directed an admonition from the Bishop, further requesting him to desist from such conduct.

The Philadelphia Conference from 1837 for ten years put the question to candidates for admission: "Are you an Abolitionist?" and without each one answered in the negative he was not received. The author was thus questioned by that Conference, and was not received in 1837 and 1838. And the "Pastoral Address," by the Philadelphia Conference for 1847, affirmed it to be the rule then. Nor was that Conference singular. Others carried out the same rule. A detailed statement of such cases in many Conferences, duly authenticated, is within reach, but is perhaps unnecessary in this connection, which would show a loss to Methodism of a large number of really valuable young ministers, whose only fault was to have been Abolitionists too early in the day of the great struggle with slavery.

The attitude of the antiabolition Conferences, and their action against the Abolitionists, were generally assumed by the Quarterly Conferencés toward their members, and by pastors toward the leaders of the classes, within the bounds of all such Annual Conferences. The purpose was fixed ; the means of accomplishing it seemed for awhile equal to the task assumed; but suppressing the Methodist antislavery agitation by silencing the agitators was not the mission of the Methodist Episcopal Church.* Her work was "the extirpation of slavery!" To have turned aside from that purpose for a time, was her great mistake. To undertake another task and so signally fail, was her sad misfortune. To become again the old-time friend of "African liberty," was her destiny.

* NOTE.—*Letter of Cyrus Prindle, D.D.*

MY BROTHER:—No one who was not a participant in the ecclesiastical proceedings in the Methodist Episcopal Church from 1835 to 1840 can have an adequate idea of the embarrassments and sufferings of the Abolitionists in those years of terrorism. What I have seen and experienced in my connection with the antislavery cause is full enough for one life; and what I could not be tempted to endure again, especially needlessly, by all the gold in the treasuries of earth.

I will soon close my fourscore years of life, but the memory of events connected with this struggle, which with others I commenced fifty-five years ago, is clear and fresh with me now. The struggle and conflict in the Church that was the most trying and severe began about 1834. Thirty years of the vigorous part of my life I have battled with this Church sin, through "evil report and good report," until I have the unfeigned satisfaction of not only seeing this huge evil abolished in the nation, but of welcoming the fact that the Methodist Episcopal Church was never constitutionally pro-slavery.

When I became acquainted with the fact, over fifty years ago, that slavery had an existence of some sort in the Church, my surprise cannot be expressed. But I was assured that none held slaves, only those who held them by devisement and could not avoid this relation; and that no difference of sentiment existed in the Church in relation to the evil. When, at a later period, the facts were developed that members of all classes in the Church held slaves and traded in them, I was struck dumb and confounded, hardly believing it was possible for it to be true.

Beginning with the loss of antislavery principle, as indicated by a relaxation of disciplinary testimony and practice during a period of thirty years, followed up by a vigorous accumulation of slave-power, the way was prepared for an exercise of proscriptive power otherwise utterly impossible. The Pastoral Letter of 1835 is one example. At the New Hampshire Conference of that year, Bishop Emory refused to put to vote a report against slavery which had been prepared by a committee authorized by the Conference so to do; yet he had put to vote a series of antiabolition resolutions a few days before at the Maine Conference.

In the spring of 1839, in agreement with Bishop Hedding, I conveyed him from Western Vermont to the seat of the New Hampshire Conference, which was held in the extreme part of the State. As we rode together alone in my carriage, and were in each other's company for two weeks, and as the most cordial intimacy and friendship existed between us, the subjects of slavery, Conference rights, and episcopal prerogatives, were discussed and elaborated extensively. At the opening of the Conference a brother moved to have a committee on slavery. The Bishop paused and hesitated; but the request was pressed. He finally consented, but gave the Conference to understand that the report must be of a qualified character, or he should not consent to its adoption. I was invited to meet with the committee. Many things were said in relation to the assumption of the Bishop, and among others, John F. Adams, one of the most venerable and influential men of the Conference, said: "If the Bishop refuses to put our report to vote, I will rise in my seat and put it to vote myself."

I saw a storm was gathering, and said to the committee: "I will take the responsibility of pledging the Bishop to treat your report on slavery as he does others." I saw the Bishop during the day, and told him substantially what had occurred, and that I had pledged him to receive and treat that report as he did others; and he said he would honor my pledge, and so he did. The Bishop frankly acknowledged that I had rendered him much service during the session, and seemed thankful for it.

For no man during my entire life have I cherished a stronger regard than for Bishop Hedding. But that he was wrong in his views and official administration in relation to the slavery question, I never doubted for a moment. He told Merritt Bates in 1842, while pastor of

North Second-street Church, Troy, N. Y., that he was liable to be arrested, censured, located, or expelled, for no other crime than preaching that slave-holding was sinful under all circumstances.

In the New York, Erie, and Pittsburgh Conferences, measures were adopted and discipline enforced against ministers of these bodies for no other cause than their advocacy of such views and attendance upon antislavery conventions. An attempt was made to adopt similar measures in the Troy Conference in 1838, where I held my membership. But a few of us had the responsibility and the honor of confronting the measures brought forward, and we showed most triumphantly that the prohibition of antislavery action by Conference resolutions, which were attempted to be forced upon us, were in direct opposition to the whole history of Methodism. And I for one declared that I would trample them in the dust if they were adopted. I never had been so abused and honored up to this time in my life as on this occasion. I was told that Bishop Morris, who presided, said that the Abolitionists adhered closer to the Methodist Episcopal Discipline than their opponents. Whether he said so or not, it was true; and, thank God! we conquered. The early Abolitionists of the Church maintained from the first that the old Rule on Slavery was, by a fair construction, a prohibition of slave-holding, and that it placed the Church upon strictly antislavery ground.   C. PRINDLE.

CLEVELAND, OHIO, *February* 7, 1880.

To L. C. MATLACK.

CHAPTER XI.

THE CONTROVERSY REVIEWED.

BETWEEN the very equivocal position occupied by the Church at the opening of the modern antislavery movement and the position afterward maintained until the final triumph of liberty throughout all the land, there was a wide field of controversy to be traversed. The parties engaged in that strife employed words often which were harder than their arguments. The epithets need not be recalled. A faithful review of the course of reasoning pursued by the Abolitionists and their opponents respectively is essential to a correct history. The disputants, however, will be designated only as the Abolitionists and the Conservatives of the Church.

The official papers were not open to the Abolitionists for several years from 1835 onward. "Zion's Herald," of Boston, was their first medium of publication. Afterward "Zion's Watchman," of New York city, was published as a special organ of the Methodist antislavery men, from January 1, 1836. The "Wesleyan Journal," of Hallowell, Maine; the "American Wesleyan Observer," edited by O. Scott and J. Horton, of Lowell, Mass.; and the "New England Christian Advocate," of Lowell, Luther Lee, editor, were, at different periods, largely occupied with the early antislavery discussion. But the leading journal was the "Watchman," La Roy Sunderland, editor.

The prominent early abolition writers were: La Roy Sunderland, Orange Scott, George Storrs, Phineas Crandal, Joseph A. Merrill, Timothy Merritt, Frederick P. Tracy, Jotham Horton, Gershom F. Cox, James Porter, Luther Lee, Jonathan D. Bridge, Charles Adams, Cyrus Prindle, Daniel Wise, Robert Boyd.

Among the early conservative writers were: Dr. Fisk, Professor Whedon, Dr. N. Bangs, Dr. Durbin, Dr. S. Luckey, Rev. Amos Binney, Bishop Hedding, Bishop Emory, Dr. Bond. These had the advantage of position, were well intrenched inside the lines, and acted on the defensive mainly; while their more numerous antagonists were the assailants from the open field, and did not always move in concert nor dress up on the same line of battle. But the struggle was well sustained by them respectively during an almost "seven years' war" of words.

The propositions which were affirmed by the Abolitionists and denied by the Conservatives may be all briefly stated, thus: All slave-holding is sinful. No slave-holder should be retained in the communion of the Christian Church. The Methodist Episcopal Church is largely responsible for the continuance of slavery in the United States. The Discipline of the Church should be changed so as to exclude all slave-holders. Immediate and unconditional emancipation is the duty of every slave-holder and the right of every slave. All rights are for all men. Annual and Quarterly Conferences have the right to adopt antislavery testimonies. Methodist antislavery conventions and antislavery societies in the Church are necessary, lawful, and effective instrumentalities for the extirpation of slavery.

The Abolitionists emphasized the facts that slavery in the United States originated in man-stealing in Africa; chattelized manhood; perpetrated the crime of stealing human beings by enslaving every child born of slaves; and, therefore, insisted that slavery was the sin of oppression which is so unequivocally and universally denounced in the Bible.

The Conservatives replied that the Old Testament recognized the patriarchs as owning servants or slaves, who became such by purchase or by being born in their house; that laws regulating the purchase of servants or slaves were divinely authorized; and that the New Testament nowhere forbade either the owning or purchasing of slaves, but recognized both Christian masters and their Christian slaves as united in fellowship in the Grecian Churches.

The Abolitionists quoted the original Methodist testimonies against all slave-holding; their subsequent modifications, and the repeal of antislavery statutes; the abandonment of early systematic plans of agitation for emancipation; the opposition to modern abolitionism, and the toleration of the practice of slave-holding in the private membership from 1808 onward, as evidence of present responsibility for slavery.

The Conservatives answered that the original rules were abandoned after six months' trial had proved them to be impracticable and unwise; that the modifications made were the dictation of Christian prudence, and within the limits of actual necessity; that the abandonment of the plan of memorializing State Legislatures was only a change of methods; that modern abolitionism was an enemy to the peace and unity of both Church and State; and that Methodist slave-holders were allowed to be such only so far as the good of the slave and the safety of the master required that the relation be continued for a time, without violating the law of love or the golden rule.

The Abolitionists argued that the perpetual rule against "buying and selling men, women, and children," and the ever-recurring inquiry, "What shall be done for the extirpation of slavery?" were unmeaning formulas without providing also for the actual prohibition of all slave-holding, and the exclusion of all Methodist slave-holders from the Church.

The Conservatives challenged anew the doctrine that slave-holding was in itself a sin under all circumstances, and urged the injustice of applying a new test of membership to those who had already been recognized as worthy Christian communicants for many years.

The Abolitionists insisted on instant repentance and full restitution as God's law for sinners, slave-holders included; while the Conservatives favored gradual emancipation as necessary both to the safety of the master and the good of the slave, with the proviso that compensation was due the former for loss of property value in the slave if emancipated.

The Abolitionists demanded that all men should be equals before the law, without discrimination on account of color or previous condition, in respect to natural rights and political privileges. The Conservatives, on the contrary, favored preparing the slave for freedom by a system of tutelage, and then not to make the right of suffrage universal.

The Abolitionists claimed that the primitive usages of the Annual and Quarterly Conferences had established a precedent equivalent to an ecclesiastical right to testify against slavery. The Conservatives disclaimed all inherent rights for the Conferences, and regarded them as strictly confined to the business assigned them by the General Conference. This view was sustained by the highest executive authorities.

The Abolitionists, therefore, fell back upon their individual right and duty as Christians to organize local societies and hold voluntary conventions for the discussion of the question of slavery, and for adopting antislavery measures in the Methodist Episcopal Church. But the Conservatives earnestly opposed such societies and conventions in the Church as irregular and unauthorized, besides being necessarily revolutionary and schismatic in their influence and tendency.

Not that each individual of the respective parties held every view here introduced to notice; but all these views were entertained and canvassed by one or another of the disputants. The discussion, which first consisted of articles in the newspapers already enumerated, afterward was embodied in the form of circulars, pamphlets, and small volumes. Meanwhile it was transferred to Methodist antislavery conventions, and thence scattered through the Church in the addresses and reports issuing therefrom.

The first Methodist Antislavery Convention was held in the Methodist Episcopal Church at Cazenovia, New York, August 3, 1837, of which Rev. Schuyler Hoes, Rev. Joseph Cross, and other prominent ministers and laymen, were members and participated in the discussions. Another convention of antislavery laymen was held at New York Mills, which was largely attended, August 16, 1837. It was severely denunciatory of the authorities of the Church, and adopted resolutions too radical for the convention at Cazenovia. And yet another convention was held at Lynn, Mass., October 25, which discussed the subject of "Conference rights."

The second large convention was held at Utica, N. Y., May 2 and 3, 1838, and was attended by delegates chosen by Conference and local societies from within many of the non-slaveholding States. The venerable Timothy Merritt, who was editor of the "Christian Advocate," with Dr. Durbin, from 1832 to 1836, called the convention to order. The permanent officers were Jared Perkins, of New Hampshire, president; Seth Sprague, of Massachusetts, vice-president. La Roy Sunderland, Wilbur Hoag, of New York, and James Porter were secretaries. Rev. James Floy and Rev. Charles K. True were prominent members. Rev. Orange Scott preached a sermon at the opening of the convention from Isaiah's words, "Cry aloud, spare not; lift up thy voice like a trumpet." Isa. lviii, 1.

An address was prepared to be presented to the English Wesleyan Conference. Orange Scott and Luther Lee were chosen delegates to represent the Methodist Abolitionists of America before that body and the Canada Wesleyan Conference. Luther Lee visited the latter Conference the ensuing summer. The venerable president, in a private interview, said to him: "We are with the Abolitionists in principles, and they may rest assured of our sympathies and prayers; but it would be improper to receive you, in a Conference capacity, as an antislavery delegate, lest it should disturb the friendly relations between the two bodies." From considerations growing out of these circumstances, Orange Scott was deterred from prosecuting his mission to England. But the influence of the convention, directly, and the antagonism it developed, indirectly, in several Annual Conferences, united to propel the antislavery agitation wider and deeper throughout the Church.

A third general convention was held November 21, 22, 1838, in Lowell, Mass., pursuant to a call first issued by Rev. James Porter, and afterward signed by nearly fifteen hundred names. Of this body Rev. Joseph A. Merrill was president; Timothy Merritt was first vice-president; La Roy Sunderland, Elihu Scott, and L. C. Matlack, secretaries. The unfriendly criticisms of the official Methodist papers, from the hands of conservative writers, upon these conventions, did not prevent their being powerful agencies for extending the antislavery sentiment very rapidly. And to the immediate actors and witnesses they were occasions of deep and thrilling interest. Convictions of duty to God and the slave, which were not allowed expression in the Conferences, there found utterance and opportunity for action. Individual ministers, who in some instances stood almost alone in strong antiabolition bodies, there found congenial associates and warm sympathy, which inspired them with needed courage when they returned home and were arraigned and treated as offenders for having been present at these conventions. And no seasons of worship were more solemn and intensely emotional and spiritual than the prayer-meetings held daily, when for the slave and the master and the Church good men poured forth strong cries and tears. The recollection of them by the writer stands out among the most vivid and pleasant memories of the past. Furthermore, the crowded audiences, the rapt attention, the logic of truth, and the eloquence of freedom that characterized these occasions, evidenced the strength of feeling and conviction that was increasing constantly, with certain prospect of ultimately overcoming all opposition.

It was indeed a great discussion, not free from extravagances of expression, nor faultless on either side, but fruitful of good in disturbing the stagnant waters of public lethargy, and in clearing the way for a final controversy that settled all disputed points on slavery in the Methodist Episcopal Church.

CHAPTER XII.

PROSECUTIONS—PROGRESS—PASTORAL LETTER OF 1840.

THE increase of antislavery feeling, and sentiment in harmony with the Abolitionists, was manifested at the sessions of the Annual Conferences coming after the conventions of 1838, and prior to the General Conference of 1840 at Baltimore. Numerous smaller conventions were held in 1838–1839, which aided to develop these results. Apposite to the matter before mentioned is the action of the New Hampshire Conference for 1838, at Danville, which "*Resolved*, That it is the sense of this Conference that an attendance on the part of any of its members on abolition conventions, delivering abolition lectures, or circulating abolition periodicals, does not involve immorality, or militate against his ministerial character." Bishop Morris allowed an appeal from his decision that the resolution was not in order, and then put it to vote, afterward recording his exceptions thereto. Hereby was marked a turn in the tide of affairs—a relaxation in the exercise of Episcopal prerogative.

Unfortunate prosecutions of prominent Abolitionists were instituted before their Conferences, by chief ministers in the Church, for words spoken or written in debate, which in the main, however, promoted the spread of abolitionism, and will be briefly noted.

At the New England Conference for 1837, held in Nantucket, Bishop Hedding addressed the Conference in relation to certain letters which had been published in the "Watchman," by Rev. O. Scott, implicating his official conduct. His remarks were read from manuscript, and took him four hours to deliver. It was a document of great weight, ingeniously planned and well written, arguing the law-points of the Episcopal administration, and showing wherein he personally had been misrepresented. He was followed by two members of the Conference presenting charges against Rev. O. Scott, which were tabled.

The reply of Mr. Scott went into an examination of these points, and of the alleged misrepresentations, some of which last were confessed and corrected publicly afterward. He said: "I am convinced that my letters contain a number of statements which are erroneous and injurious to the reputation of Bishop Hedding." After specifying and retracting, he says: "I will only add, that I have now, and always have had, unlimited confidence in Bishop Hedding's moral integrity, purity of motive, and general character for fair and impartial administration—though we differ, and agree to differ, on the question of Conference rights and the powers of Bishops." The charges above named were not taken from the table.

The next year the Bishop again presented to the Conference formal charges, founded upon subsequent utterances by Mr. Scott, which were not sustained. The case was appealed to the General Conference ensuing, there referred to a committee, but afterward withdrawn by the Bishop in the interests of peace.

At the New England Conference for 1836 charges were preferred against La Roy Sunderland for "repeated instances of slanderous misrepresentation." Dr. N. Bangs was prosecutor. The evidence con-

sisted mainly of matters relating to the question of
slavery.   One specification was sustained, but the
charge was negatived by a two-thirds vote.   At the
session for 1837 the same prosecutor presented the
charges of slander and falsehood against Mr. Sunderland, with the same result—not sustained.   Mr.
Sunderland was also tried again in 1838, and acquitted,
at the time Rev. O. Scott was, when both cases were
appealed.   Again, in 1839, charges were preferred
against him, on behalf of the New York Annual
Conference, represented by Dr. Bangs and Rev. T.
Hodgson, of which he was acquitted.   Finally, a
committee in New York City proceeded, against his
protest, in his absence, convicted him, and declared
him suspended from the ministry until the ensuing
session of the New England Conference for 1840,
when the proceedings were set aside.   A new bill
of accusations was then and there presented by Rev.
C. A. Davis, of the New York Conference.   One
item charged Mr. Sunderland with having slandered
Bishop Soule.   The Bishop was reported, in 1839, to
have said, at Washington, Pa., "I have never yet
advised the liberation of a slave, and think I never
shall."   He also had said that he had advised a slave-
holder, who consulted him, not to free his slaves.
This was the occasion of a severe criticism, in verse,
by a lady correspondent, which Mr. Sunderland published in the "Watchman" with the remark, that
"every word of it was justified."   The offensive character of the words will be judged by a quotation:

> "Receive this truth—deep, dark thy stain;
>   Thy very soul is tinged with blood;
> Go, do thy first works o'er again—
>   Go, cleanse thee in the Saviour's blood."

Unfortunately for Mr. Sunderland, Bishop Soule presided during this trial.* The charge of slander was sustained by a small majority, but the only penalty was, that he publish the finding in "Zion's Watchman" without note or comment. He did so, inserting the words in display type, with deep mourning border around them. He withdrew from the traveling ministry at this Conference by location.

At the same period, during the years 1836–1840, the movements of the American Antislavery Society were provoking antagonisms in the National Legislature, whose mistaken efforts at suppression were scattering the living coals of truth upon the nation's naked heart. Memorials in favor of the abolition of slavery in the District of Columbia, and for the suppression of the slave-trade between the States, were forwarded to Congress in large number. Beginning with 1836, and for successive years, a resolution was passed refusing to receive or heed the memorials sent, until, in 1840, it was made a standing rule of the House, that "no petition, memorial, resolution, or other paper

* The defense was ably conducted by Mr. Sunderland, whose voice was husky and on the lowest key. Of the prosecutor, whose voice was full and even boisterous, he said, apologetically and sarcastically, "My voice is weak, and will not be equal to the task after the overwhelming appeals you have heard against me. I envy the vocal power of my enemy. But, sir, that is all I do envy about that man!"

The rulings of the Bishop in his own behalf, during Mr. Sunderland's plea, were such as to provoke sharp words from him. The Bishop had occasion, therefore, to maintain his dignity by a very stern rebuke. "In all my experience, and in all my intercourse with my fellow-men, I have this to say, that La Roy Sunderland is the first man that ever dared to speak to me in that manner." Nothing daunted, but rather provoked, Mr. Sunderland almost screamed in reply, "I thank God, sir, that you have lived long enough to find one man who will tell you to your face what many others say of you behind your back."

praying the abolition of slavery in the District, or
any State or Territory of the United States, in which
it now exists, shall be received or entertained in any
way whatever." The rule of 1837 was passed by a
majority of fifty-eight. The "gag law" of 1840 had
only a majority of six. In 1836 the memorialists
numbered thirty-seven thousand. Afterward they
numbered hundreds of thousands. Then followed
the action of Northern State Legislatures in favor of
the Abolitionists, Massachusetts leading the way in
1838 by declaring the "gag law" to be "a usurpation
of power, a violation of the Constitution, subversive
of the fundamental principles of the government,
and at war with the prerogatives of the people."
Every thing worked together to unsettle the foundations of slavery both in Church and State. The
elements of public sentiment were in a state of revolution and decomposition, ready to take on new forms,
freed from temporary chaotic confusion, and crystal-
lized in purer molds of thought.

The Annual Conferences just prior to 1840 were
called upon to pass judgment on the proposed change
in the general rule on slavery, which originated with
the New England Conference, so that it should forbid "the buying, or selling, or holding men, women,
or children as slaves, or giving them away, except on
purpose to free them." In the Genesee Conference
thirty voted for it, and sixty against it. The Pittsburgh Conference gave five votes for it. All the
other Conferences outside of New England gave less
votes than these two, and in most cases none at all.
The Michigan Conference gave one vote for it, and
the Erie Conference three. The North Carolina,
Philadelphia, Missouri, Indiana, New Jersey, Troy,

Black River, Illinois, Kentucky, Georgia, Baltimore, Virginia, and others, were unanimous for non-concurrence, or reported no votes in favor of it.

Memorials were adopted by four Annual Conferences asking antislavery action — the Maine, New Hampshire, New England, and Genesee. Abolition delegates were elected by the three first named, and four of the six from Genesee were Abolitionists. The antislavery memorials forwarded to the General Conference of 1840 contained the names of over ten thousand private members, and represented at least five hundred traveling preachers. These were from within the bounds of the three New England Conferences and the New York, Genesee, Ohio, Black River, Oneida, Michigan, Pittsburgh, Indiana, Erie, and Troy Conferences.

The aggregate of results reached, considered numerically, was far below the hopes of sanguine Abolitionists. Four only out of twenty-eight Annual Conferences asked for antislavery action, or one in seven. The Abolition delegates were about the same proportion of the General Conference, while the whole number of traveling preachers represented by memorial was a much smaller proportion than the one seventh, and the lay memorialists were not in number equal to one in seventy of the whole membership of the Methodist Episcopal Church. But there were probably tenfold more of the body of the Church who were identified with the Abolitionists, both in sentiment and action.

The session of the General Conference in Baltimore was more than usually agitated on the slavery question. Small as was the number of memorialists, they were more numerous than the Antiabolitionists

expected. A memorial from New York City of
nearly twelve hundred surprised the delegates from
that region. Its validity was challenged, but vindicated. An intense excitement prevailed for two days
over it on the wild assumption of fraud on the part
of Orange Scott. He coolly withstood the assault,
although in committee a Southern delegate from
Georgia moved that O. Scott be expelled as an unworthy member. Dr. Elliott said : " In this whole
affair the case seems to be this—There seemed to be
more Abolitionists in New York City than their opponents supposed, wished, or knew of. The Conference was pushed into a temporary excitement by
the warmth and haste of the New York brethren,
cherished by a pretty warm flame from the South.
But on calm reflection the whole temporary commotion subsided."—"*Great Secession.*"

In the Committee, of twenty-eight, on Slavery, as
the writer was informed by a member of it, the
Northern members who were not Abolitionists were
unwilling to express an opinion of slavery in the
report. This was displeasing to the Southern members, who wanted them to say that slavery was a
moral evil, if they thought so. Several very ultra
pro-slavery measures were proposed by William A.
Smith, which were so amended as to neutralize their
force. Mr. Smith then appealed to the committee to
know if they held slavery to be a moral evil, or not.
"If," said he, "you hold slavery to be a moral evil,
hands off that brother, [pointing to Orange Scott;]
you ought not to condemn, but cover him. If, indeed, slavery be a moral evil, I will defend him as
long as there is a plank on the deck. If slavery be a
moral evil, he reasons like a philosopher. The South

will never be satisfied by your passing resolutions against O. Scott and Co. while you hold the same doctrines he contends for. If slavery be a moral evil, the conclusion is irresistible that it ought to be immediately abandoned."—*Matlack's* "*Life of Orange Scott.*"

This will explain the brief and indefinite report on slavery, which did not condemn nor approve either abolitionism or slavery, and only set forth the expediency of General Conference inaction, and advised "the Annual Conferences, in their action upon this subject in future, to adhere closely to the language of the Discipline." A minority report, by a vote of 59 to 52, was not allowed to be presented. But the representative of New England Abolitionism, Orange Scott, obtained the floor and spoke for two hours in opposition to the report of the committee. The usual limitation of fifteen minutes was suspended. Dr. Elliott says: "Mr. Scott made a strong and temperate speech which took a wide range, comprising important matter." The New York "Christian Advocate and Journal" said: "The speaker's manner throughout was dispassionate and conciliatory, and his whole address free from offensive or inflammatory epithets. He was heard with the greatest respect and attention by the body and by a very large audience, which had convened to listen to the debate."

A spirited discussion ensued, but no action was had by which the resolutions of the report became the language of the General Conference. In connection with the stir about the New York memorial, a severe condemnation of all abolition movements was reported, but never acted upon. Thus no direct issue was made on the subject of slavery. Indirectly, the colored-testimony resolution, and the resolution on the ordination of slave-holders, were in the interests of slavery. But the Pastoral Address of the General Conference was entirely free from any reflection upon the course of the Abolitionists, and contained no word of admonition against the agitation of the subject of slavery. On the other hand, it was conciliatory, and even apologetic, in its reference to those who had asked for antislavery action. The entire paragraph is quoted below:

Since the commencement of the present session of the General Conference, memorials have been presented, principally from the Northern and Eastern divisions of the work, some praying for the action of the Conference on the subject of slavery, and others asking for radical changes in the economy of the Church. The results of the deliberations of the committees to whom these memorials had a respectful reference, and the final action of the Conference upon them, may be seen among the doings of this body as reported and published. The issue in several instances is probably different from what the memorialists may have thought they had reason to expect. But it is to be hoped they will not suppose the General Conference has either denied them any legitimate right, or been wanting in a proper respect for their opinions. Such is the diversity of habits of thought, manners, customs, and domestic relations among the people of this vast republic, and such the diversity of the institutions of the sovereign States of the confederacy, that it is not to be supposed an easy task to suit all the incidental circumstances of our economy to the views and feelings of the vast mass of minds interested. We pray, therefore, that brethren whose views may have been crossed by the acts of this Conference will at least give us the credit of having acted in good faith, and of not having regarded private ends or party interests, but the best good of the whole family of American Methodists.

CHAPTER XIII.

ANTISLAVERY SECESSION, 1842-1843.

THE abolition controversy in the Methodist Episcopal Church commenced with an effort to induce the Conferences, both Annual and General, to renew their old-time testimonies against slavery. The refusal of the latter to condemn all slave-holding, and the prohibition of the antislavery action in the former by the presiding officers, who claimed to be, and subsequently were constituted, both judges of law and order in the Annual Conferences, without allowing an appeal thereto from their decisions, precipitated an unfortunate collision between the Abolitionists and the authorities of the Church. There arose a personal struggle between them. Abolition writers assailed individual Bishops, by name, with severe and ill-advised criticism. These, in self-defense, preferred charges against their assailants, who were usually acquitted by their Annual Conferences. Thus a strife was engendered which produced alienation and disaffection with some leading Abolitionists, who, therefore, became objects of suspicion, and were charged with designing to divide the Church, or purposing to withdraw from its communion.

All such designs were promptly repudiated, and earnestly and honestly disclaimed, at first. But, being constantly reiterated, and the subjects of these suspicions being very largely regarded and treated as enemies of the Church, and stigmatized as such, they afterward reluctantly recognized the possibility of a division of the Church, or the necessity of withdrawal from it.

During the quadrennium preceding 1840 a large amount of disaffected material had been accumulated in and around the Church by the unwise and unjust proceedings against Abolitionists. Many young men on trial had been discontinued from the traveling ministry, and more had been denied admission thereto by the Annual Conferences, solely because they were Abolitionists. Many local preachers had been deprived of license to preach, and many others were refused license to preach, by Quarterly Conferences, for the same reason. And not a few leaders had been deprived of their class books by pastors who were anxious to carry out the constructive law of 1836, which was that Methodists must wholly refrain from agitating the subject of slavery.

Perhaps it was the inevitable consequence of such proceedings that secessions from the Methodist Episcopal Church are noted as commencing in 1839. In Ohio, New York, and Michigan, small societies were organized in that or the ensuing years which, in some instances, were independent congregations. But a small connection was formed May 13, 1841, in Michigan, called "Wesleyan Methodists," which in two years reported seventeen stationed preachers, nine circuits, and one thousand one hundred and sixteen members. Numerous individual secessions occurred in many different sections of the country, which had been absorbed with other Churches, while a still larger number of persons left the Methodist Episcopal Church, who stood waiting in expectation of a secession of the main body of the Abolitionists.

During the winter of 1840–41 Rev. Orange Scott was living retired at Newbury, Vermont, because of poor health, but he occasionally wrote for the press. In some of his articles he deprecated his own past mode of conducting the antislavery controversy; questioned the present advantage of Church anti-slavery societies; doubted the possibility of reforming the Church on the subject of slavery until the State should move in the matter; and declared, that "I have no hope that any improvement will take place in regard to Church government, and that there is no alternative but to submit to things pretty much as they are, or secede. I have never yet felt prepared for the latter, but my opinion is that those who cannot conscientiously submit to Methodist economy and usages had better peaceably leave."

As his biographer, seven years afterward, the writer had access to a large correspondence, a portion of which was from a few men of prominence in the Church then and since, who urged him to secede, to prepare a plan of Church government, and to call a convention, assuring him of their hearty co-operation. The above quotations, from his correspondence with the press, are the reply he made to these importunities at the time.

The following year, 1842, Mr. Scott announced a change of opinion and purpose in this matter, and with the other ministers, Jotham Horton and La Roy Sunderland, published a withdrawal, coetaneous with the issue of the "True Wesleyan," a weekly paper, which advocated the duty of secession, and announced a convention of all agreeing with them to prepare for a new. Church organization, non-episcopal in government, and free from slavery. Of those who united in this movement, whose names were familiar as Abolitionists, are found Luther Lee, Cyrus Prindle, Edward Smith, W. H. Brewster, S. Salsbury, P. A. Ogden, Marcus Swift, L. C. Matlack, and others. At the convention for organization, held at Utica, N. Y., May 31, 1843, when "The Wesleyan Methodist Connection of America" was formed, the whole number giving in their adhesion was nearly six thousand. Among these were twenty-two from the traveling ministry of the old Church, who, with as many more from the "Protestant" and "Reformed Methodists" who were present, joined to twice as many more who reported by letter, were divided into six Annual Conferences, which reported at the first General Conference, eighteen months afterward, a total membership of fifteen thousand.

The antislavery secession did not inflict so serious a loss numerically upon the Methodist Episcopal Church as was anticipated. Yet its influence was felt very deeply over the connection from the character of the men composing it, and by the energy with which the new body renewed the agitation of the slavery question. The men who constituted the mainspring of the movement gave unmistakable evidence of unselfish devotion to principle by leaving behind them, voluntarily, positions of comfort and ample support, and going out with the deliberate expectation of forming part of a small organization of feeble means and giving no hope of personal aggrandizement. Mr. Scott had written to Mr. Prindle, months before his withdrawal, that "within one year we may have a new Church, with more than one score of ministers, and more than one or two thousand members."

The considerations moving these men to action

were stated by themselves, thus: "I confess that the conviction deepens daily upon my mind that the Bible, the slave, and every thing in the sacred rights of man and religion, is calling upon us to take a stand in opposition to that oppression which our Church is protecting." Another said: "I can live either in or out of the Church; but the cause, the precious cause of human rights! Shall I keep silence, and go to my grave in peace? My inclination is in favor of retirement and silence, but conscience is not exactly quiet. I would not do any thing to hedge up the way of my brethren in the Church from pleading the cause of the slave, though I have but little faith they will ever loosen his chains till the country is free." A third wrote: "I have been waiting the openings of Providence. Hitherto God has gone before and opened my way. I am trying to live near God. I hope the Lord will direct in all our designs and movements."

It was believed and charged at the time, that an extensive secret correspondence had prepared the way for an iniquitous complicity, in order to a violent disruption of the Church for the gratification of personal ends. Such was the relation of the writer to these men and their movements, that much of their correspondence has been in his hand for examination. And, however liable they may be to the charge of ultraism, or fanatical zeal on the subject of abolitionism; whatever grounds any may have had for questioning the wisdom of their course or the fitness of their measures, no one could detect in their freest intercourse, even in confidential letters, any sinister motives or selfish designs. They had the seeming of men who were "prayerfully considering a question of

duty to the slave, looking meanwhile at their responsibility to God, to their families, and to the world,"
as they claimed.

The organization effected by them was doctrinally,
and in its worship, as well as general policy, on the
model of the Methodist Episcopal Church.   No
Bishops were provided for; * and chairmen of districts were appointed instead of presiding elders.
They, however, retained the connectional principle
through the Quarterly, Annual, and General Conferences.   On the main question of doing all in their
power for the extirpation of slavery, their position
was unequivocal.   The general rules forbid "buying
or selling of men, women, or children, with an intention to enslave them; or holding them as slaves; or
claiming that it is right so to do."   The Article of
Religion, VIII, held that: "We are required to acknowledge God as our only supreme ruler, and all
men are created by him equal in all natural rights.
Wherefore, all men are bound so to order all their
individual and social and political acts as to render
to God entire and absolute obedience, and to secure
to all men the enjoyment of every natural right, as
well as to promote the greatest happiness of each in
the possession and exercise of such rights."   And the
restrictive rules forbid making "any distinctions in
the rights and privileges of our ministers and. members on account of ancestry or color."

The antislavery secession was based upon distinctive Methodist ground.   The friction between Wesleyan and Episcopal Methodists resulted in a more

* Orange Scott said to the writer, that he was in favor of a moderate episcopacy, which should have a limitation of time and of jurisdiction, with eligibility to re-election quadrennially.

rapid development of antislavery power, which has-
tened, perhaps, the ultimate triumph of freedom.

That this statement is not a partial judgment by
one who was identified with the movement, but is an
important historic truth, will be accepted on the testimony of two distinguished and disinterested witnesses.

Bishop Thomson and the writer, in 1866, were
canvassing this question at the residence of Thomas
W. Price, Philadelphia. He said : " We have always
had a very high opinion of the Wesleyan brethren,
because their separation from our Church was not
caused by personal jealousies, or personal offenses,
real or imaginary, nor opposition to Church polity,
but entirely upon moral grounds ; and these were
your hatred to slavery and your zeal for its overthrow. And I came very near being one of their
number. For I, too, was almost discouraged at the
dark prospect for efficient antislavery action in the
old Church. But I hoped on and prayed for it, and
at last the old ship righted up, and moved off gal-
lantly in line of battle." To these remarks it was
answered : " Withdrawing as the Wesleyans did,
when they did, for the reasons they assigned, and organizing just outside the lines of the Methodist Episcopal
Church on an antislavery platform, they constrained
a development of antislavery activity within the ' old
Church,' which they could not have accomplished by
remaining members of it." " I have no doubt of
that," the Bishop replied ; " that was the work of the
Wesleyan Church, and it was well done."

Dr. Whedon, editor of the " Quarterly," in the
October number for 1865, said : " Especially would
we rejoice in the return of that Church, the WES-

LEYAN, who seceded from us rather than make our concessions to the Southern slave power. We honor and love those men. Their secession, as we believe, saved our Church in 1844 from accepting a slaveholding Bishop. They, honorably to themselves, left the Church for the Church's good; and for that same Church's good we trust that they will return with a full, triumphant welcome. Never, in such a crisis, may the Church want those who will desert her ranks and frighten her soul from bowing her knee to Baal." *

* NOTE.—*Letter of Moses Hill to Cyrus Prindle.*

In the summer of 1847 the Erie Conference held its session at Meadville, Pa. Dr. Bond, with other visitors, was in attendance. I was residing there, and finished my second year's labor. Dr. Bond took tea with us. We had a long conversation. He talked of his controversy with the old radicals, his part in the great antislavery rupture of 1844, and of his controversy with the antislavery men in the Methodist Episcopal Church, with Scott, Lee, Prindle, and Horton. He told me of his tour through New England before the secession of those brethren; how he found the influence of these brethren in New England, and the prejudice he found there against himself; how he looked over the whole ground, and became convinced that the only way to save the Church in New England was to get these men out of the Church, bring on the crisis as soon as possible, and change the issue of the controversy so as to divide the antislavery men of New England, and at least weaken the influence of Scott and others; how he calculated that when these men should leave the Church and set up for themselves, many who were in hearty sympathy with them while in the Church would become their opponents when outside. "With these convictions settled in my mind," said he, "I returned to New York with the determination to write them out of the Church." This led to a series of articles in the "Christian Advocate," under the caption, "Radico-Abolitionism" and "Politico-Abolitionism."

Whether the doctor was right in his calculation as to the best course to pursue, I am not prepared to say. Some men who were in deep sympathy with these men soon took quite strong ground on the issue of leaving the Church. But it is evident that if the General Conference of 1844 had not dealt as they did with Bishop Andrew, the Wesleyans would have become a power in the land.   MOSES HILL.

CHAPTER XIV.

ANTISLAVERY AWAKENING, 1840-1843.

DURING the autumn of 1840 an effort was made to rally the Abolitionists of the Church generally by holding a convention in New York city, which brought together a large number of them, but so divided in sentiment that the measures proposed by the more radical were strongly opposed or defeated. An American Wesleyan Antislavery Society was organized, with much opposition, but died at its first anniversary. A proposed Methodist Antislavery Missionary Society was so unpopular as to have scarcely a show of favor, except with a few.

The condition of the Church generally on the subject of slavery, in 1841, and the feeling of the Abolitionists, were noted by Dr. Tefft, then a resident of New England, who said: "In regard to abolition associations and organizations, I believe they are all now in the wrong. Time was when they were a source of good. But the scale is turned." Dr. Elliott remarks: "Nevertheless, the Methodist antislavery societies were not given up, though they had a sickly existence. The brethren in New England could not, with any face, give up the form, although the thing itself was languishing. The American Wesleyan Antislavery Society held its first and last anniversary at Albany, New York, October 6, 1841. The energy of the Abolitionists was not now combined. Various influences united to scatter their power. The Providence Conference formed a society, met, passed resolutions, and finished their business without a shred of radicalism. The New England Conference Society had a meeting, passed resolutions, with but little done any way except to keep up appearances. The New Hampshire Conference Society went through the rounds with all patience and earnestness, and all passed off very pleasantly." — "*Great Secession*," *col.* 233. And Dr. Stevens, then editor of "Zion's Herald," testified in 1842 that it was "a time of profound peace."

And so it was. The "Watchman" had become the organ of mesmerism. Many who had written extensively against slavery had withdrawn from the public journals. "Zion's Herald" was occupied but little with the subject of slavery. Nothing was published, for months together, of correspondence nor editorially. All was quiet along the shore of New England. Bishop Hedding said to Rev. M. Bates, in the fall of 1842: "The antislavery excitement in the Church is at an end." And the official journal at New York. pronounced abolitionism to be dead! "These appear to be gloomy and dark times to the Methodist Abolitionists," said a Boston pastor. Another writes to Mr. Prindle: "I confess I feel somewhat as you express it — like waiting in sullen silence for others to produce some change, or submit to things as they are. I fear this feeling is prevalent, but I doubt whether it is right."

The American Antislavery Society had become divided and paralyzed, on the one hand by the prejudices of the clergymen against women speaking in public, and on the other hand by the non-resistant sentiments of William Lloyd Garrison and his friends,

who insisted on the sinfulness of voting under the
Constitution of the United States, and who persisted
in the public advocacy of antisabbath, antichurch,
antiministry, and no-government views. And so indifferent were the mass of the Abolitionists to the
claims of the cause, that not one of all the antislavery
journals were self-supporting. All were published at
a loss to their proprietors. A temporary pause ensued. Many said abolitionism was dead. It was
sleeping.

At the General Conference of 1840 a memorial was
prepared by forty official members of Sharp-street
and Asbury Churches, in Baltimore, protesting against
the colored-testimony resolution. It was put in the
hands of Rev. Thomas B. Sargent, and by him given
to one of the Bishops. Through the efforts of Dr.
Bond and others the memorialists were pacified,
without the Conference knowing any thing of the
document. Dr. Elliott says: "The colored members
of the Church were greatly afflicted. This matter had
like to have done great mischief."—"*Great Secession,*" col. 223. This document was afterward published. Among other things, equally pungent, the
memorialists said: "We have learned with profound
regret and unutterable emotion" of the resolution
adopted May 18, which "has inflicted, we fear, an
irreparable injury upon eighty thousand souls for
whom Christ died — souls which, by this act of your
venerable body, have been stript of the dignity of
Christians, degraded in the scale of humanity, and
treated as criminals, for no other reason than the color
of their skin. . . . The adoption of this soul-sickening
resolution has destroyed the peace and alienated the
affections of twenty-five hundred members of the

Church in this city, who now feel that they are but spiritual orphans or scattered sheep. . . . The deed you have done could not have originated in that love which works no ill to its neighbor, but in a disposition to propitiate that spirit, which is not to be appeased, except through concessions derogatory to the dignity of our holy religion." And, therefore, they protest against it, and conjure them "to wipe from the Journal the odious resolution."

Although this was not done, nor their wishes made known to that body, an opportunity was soon after afforded for Dr. Bond and the Baltimore Methodists to give a substantial proof of their identity with and sympathy for free persons of African descent. "A pro-slavery movement in the winter of 1841 and 1842 was the occasion of manifesting the antislavery spirit of the Methodists of Maryland. A small fraction of the slave-holding interest, assuming to act for the whole, held a convention, and recommended to the Legislature a course of action, the effect of which would be to drive from the State, or reduce to bondage, those who, by the laws of the State, were free, a great many of whom were Methodists and claimed the sympathy and protection of Methodists. The pro-slavery men had taken advantage already of the fears induced by abolition agitation, and passed laws that made the friends of humanity to blush. Although a majority of the people were opposed thereto, the enforced silence on slavery prevented outspoken opposition. But this last was too much for the good people of Maryland, especially when, to their astonishment, a bill was passed by the House in conformity with the resolutions of the convention." — "*Great Secession*," col. 237, 964.

A meeting of the male members of the Baltimore Methodist Churches was held February 28, 1842, from which a memorial went up to the Senate, signed by Thomas E. Bond, Sen., G. C. M. Roberts, and Robert Emory, Committee, remonstrating against the bill of the House. They declare that the provisions of the proposed "act for the better security of negro slaves, and for promoting industry and honesty among the free people of color," do not correspond with its title; that they tend "to perpetuate slavery in the State, a calamity hitherto deprecated alike by Christians and patriots;" that they must inevitably banish from the State many free persons, and subject to hopeless slavery many others." And they boldly declare that "the making slaves of freemen has been denounced by Christendom as piracy, but by this bill every citizen is tempted to engage in the unhallowed work. . . . Many of the people who are to be the subjects of these enactments are united with us in Church fellowship, and we implore your honorable body to save them from a persecution more horrible than the African slave-trade."

The following week Dr. Bond, in the "Christian Advocate," overflowed with indignation at "this mad movement of the slave-holders' convention," "beyond the ordinary folly and wickedness of men. To our brethren we say, and to all who fear God we say, You are released. The slave-holders' convention have taken off your strait-jackets. The questions which we were told it was dangerous to discuss are now forced upon us by those who conjured us to be silent for the sake of mercy and humanity; and, with the blessing of God, we will discuss them to the hearts' content of the slave-holders' convention." Such was the effect of the movement thus heralded, that the rejection of the offensive bill was promptly secured in the Senate.

And hereby was demonstrated what Methodism could do if she had a mind to work in this direction; and this recalls Thomas Whitson's quaint remark on Methodism. He was a Quaker, and the first signer of the Declaration of Sentiments adopted by the American Antislavery Society in 1833. "I have been at one of the camp-meetings of thy people, and heard them shout and pray with much inward comfort. And I tell thee, Lucius, what I think, moreover, that if the Methodist people would try it, they might shout and pray down slavery in a short season. They have much power in that direction!"

Immediately following the antislavery secession in 1843, and to some extent manifestly a consequent movement, a great awakening occurred among the Abolitionists and in the Church generally, renewing the antislavery agitation. It became necessary to remove all cause of dissatisfaction with the position of the Church to prevent secession. It was desirable to develop antislavery activity to take away the reproach that the seceders were not backward to indulge in liberally. Besides, a quickened conscientious sentiment was aroused which never slept again.

Prior to 1843 no Annual Conference was allowed to say that all slave-holding was sin. Subsequently no form of expression was objected to by the presiding officer of any Annual Conference. Immediately following the withdrawal of Orange Scott and others, and before their organization in May, 1843, arrangements were made in the Methodist Episcopal Church for holding three large conventions—in Boston, January 18; in Hallowell, Maine, February 22; and in

Claremont, New Hampshire, March 22. The Methodists of New England moved *en masse*, as it were, in their support. The utterances at these conventions were full, strong, and clear. Nothing equaling their ultraism had before been adopted. The Boston Convention affirmed that "slave-holding is sin; that every slave-holder is a sinner, and ought not to be admitted to the pulpit or the communion; that the Methodist Episcopal Church is responsible for slavery in its pale; and that nothing short of a speedy and entire separation of slavery from the Church could satisfy the consciences of honest Abolitionists, and therefore reformation or division is the only alternative." The Hallowell Convention declared, "that, from a careful collection of documentary evidence, with other well-attested facts, there are within the Methodist Episcopal Church two hundred traveling ministers holding sixteen hundred slaves; about one thousand local preachers holding ten thousand; about twenty-five thousand members holding two hundred and seven thousand nine hundred more." And the Claremont Convention represented, as the conclusion of the whole matter, "that the only way to prevent an entire dissolution among us as a Church, is an entire separation from the South." And a plan was agreed upon for memorializing the General Conference to divide the Church, North and South, or to set off the New England Conferences by themselves. Subsequently, in discussing the "Plan of Separation," so-called, Dr. James Porter, in his "Compendium," referring to 1844, says: "Our choice was between having a slave-holding Bishop, the transfer of our churches to Wesleyanism, so-called, or a general New England secession."

The columns of the " Christian Advocate " at this time were opened editorially to the discussion of slavery; first in denouncing the Slave-holders' Convention, and then by the discussion of the two questions —" Ought the General Conference to enact a rule of discipline by which all slave-holders, whatever be the peculiar circumstances of the case, shall be expelled from the communion of the Church ? " or, " If it be admitted that there are circumstances which will justify a Methodist in holding slaves, then, whether it is possible to make a rule which, while it will·reach all others, shall spare those exempt cases ? "   The editor maintained the negative of both questions. Afterward Rev. Robert Boyd was allowed to publish two articles on the other side, to which Dr. Bond replied, expressing modified antislavery views, which provoked criticism in the " Southern Advocate," and called forth the condemnation of sundry Quarterly Conferences in Georgia and Alabama.

With characteristic independence Dr. Bond charged that, upon the Southern side of the question, there was ultraism not less dangerous to the common welfare than that of the Abolitionists.   And he summed up the case thus pointedly : " The Southern ultraism would leave us without hope of a better state of things; for slavery must not only be endured, but purposely propagated.   Our Discipline admits that slavery is a great evil, and of course a moral evil, as it would be unbecoming the Church to make so grave a declaration about a physical evil."   He concludes by declaring, that whenever the Church shall require him to advocate or defend the opinion contained in the resolutions from Georgia and Alabama, he will resign as editor.   And should the Church ever cease

to testify against slavery as a moral evil, as he had
defined that term, he should seek a more pure community. ("Christian Advocate," vol. xviii, page 10.)
The controversy thus introduced was participated in
by Southern correspondents. And Dr. Wightman,
editor of the "Southern Advocate," reviewed the
whole subject involved. He regarded the position
of the "Christian Advocate," at New York, "as the
embodiment of the feeling and opinion of that portion of the Church which will hold the balance of
power at the approaching General Conference, and
will then decide the destiny of the Church for good
or evil. He notes two things worthy of remark:
First, That this position was an advance upon what
the Book of Discipline affirms, and the doctrines heretofore maintained by the Journals of the General
Conference. Secondly, There is an implied admission
that the antislavery feeling—that which denounces
slave-holding in existing circumstances as a sin—is
gaining ground and winning converts, else why such
earnest discussion upon it?"

And so it was. The time of awakening had come.
The Church was aroused. These many earnest words
betokened action. What would be done by the General Conference of 1844 no man knew. That slavery
had nothing to hope for, its best friends feared.

CHAPTER XV.

THE GREAT CRISIS, 1844.

A T the General Conference of 1844, in New York city, the Abolitionists and Conservatives of the Church were a unit in action, because of the issues made by the Southern delegates on behalf of slavery. The South asked that a slave-holding traveling preacher, who had been suspended by the Baltimore Annual Conference, should be restored, and that a slave-holding Bishop should be allowed to remain undisturbed in his office. But to allow a Bishop to be a slave-holder would conflict with the usage of the Church from its organization; would yield a point contended for by the South, in vain, at the three preceding General Conferences; and would compel a violent disruption of the Church throughout the North, East, and West. While, on the other hand, to unfrock a Bishop, or suspend or censure him, when no canon, or statute law of the Church had been violated, was to tread on new ground, having no precedent, and possibly in conflict with the principles of ecclesiastical law. Besides, the demand for a slave-holding Bishop, long-continued, with ever-growing importunity, and now gratified in the case of James O. Andrew, would guarantee a united South in favor of dividing or disrupting the Church, if he was disturbed in his bishopric. Continued unity seemed impossible. Where should the lines of division be drawn? Across the continent from east to west?

or indefinitely through the length and breadth of the land? The crisis was at hand.

Preliminary and prophetic was the vote on the appeal of Rev. F. A. Harding from the action of the Baltimore Conference, which had suspended him from the ministry for refusing to manumit his slaves, which action was sustained by 117 yeas to 56 nays— more than a majority of two thirds for manumission.

The action in Bishop Andrew's case was, first, a report from the Committee on Episcopacy, giving his written statement of the facts in relation to his slaves. Then followed a resolution which "affectionately requested" him to resign. This was substituted by another, which declared, "That it is the sense of this General Conference, that he desist from the exercise of his office so long as this impediment remains." The discussion continued through ten days.

Alfred Griffith argued that a Bishop is only an officer of the General Conference, created for a specific purpose, and for no other than the purposes specified. The Annual Conferences had fixed this office on the General Conference, which they had instituted, and provided in one of the restrictive rules that the General Conference should not do away with that office. At the same time they reserved in their own hands the power to do away with the office altogether when it should so please them. Consequently they never intended to constitute the Bishop an officer for life under all circumstances. And the question is now, Has the General Conference power to regulate her own officers, to provide for any exigency which may operate as a barrier in the way of the accomplishment of the objects and purposes for which the officers were chosen?

Peter P. Sandford deemed it expedient that Bishop Andrew should not any longer exercise his office as a Bishop, in order to prevent convulsions in the Church and the loss of very large numbers of members, but he would not do any thing to affect the ministerial character and standing of the Bishop. He proposed only to place him where they found him when they put him into the superintendency.

William Winans did not deny the right to request Bishop Andrew to retire from the episcopacy, but the expediency of such action by the General Conference he did deny, as that would create an uncontrollable necessity that there should be a disconnection of a large portion of the Church from that body. Such a vote would cut off thirteen hundred preachers and four hundred and fifty thousand members.

Elias Bowen reiterated the views of Mr. Griffith and Mr. Sandford, and moreover expressed his preference for a secession by a portion than to have schism run through the whole Church from center to circumference. "If any portion of the Church should deem themselves called upon to secede, however we must deprecate such an event, it is unavoidable."

Lovick Pierce indorsed all that Mr. Winans had said, and declared that if by a two thirds vote Bishop Andrew was requested to resign he could not do it, and would not do it, knowing as he did the effects that would grow out of the movement. "Shall that be done which is inexpedient for us, because it is expedient for you? Show that Bishop Andrew has violated any one of the established rules and regulations of the Church, and that he refuses to conform himself thereto, and you put yourselves in the right and us in the wrong."

Thomas Crowder pressed the point that, placing the argument on the ground of expediency, and insisting that Bishop Andrew's ministerial and Christian character was not to be impeached, was a concession of two facts: first, That he had violated no precept of Christianity; and, second, That he had violated no rule of Discipline in becoming connected with slavery.

John Spencer replied to the question, What specific rule has Bishop Andrew violated? that the mere silence of the Discipline in regard to a particular case is no evidence that action in that case would be contrary to our rules. But we have a rule. A Bishop may be expelled for improper conduct. "Improper conduct," says one of our Bishops, "is a small offense, less than an immorality." The General Conference must determine what improper conduct is.

Seymour Coleman had expected a peaceful Conference, supposing, as he did, that the fire-brands had left the ranks last year. But give our Southern brethren a slave-holding Bishop, and they would make the whole North a magazine of gunpowder and the Bishop a fire-brand in the midst.

Nathan Bangs said: "I think there are many things that would disqualify a man for holding the office of Bishop that do not amount to immorality. Should Bishop Hedding declare that it was a sin to hold slaves under any circumstances, it would identify him with the ultra party, and I would vote for his retiring, because that would disqualify him for his work as superintendent over the whole Church."

Stephen Olin was unwilling to request Bishop Andrew to resign. He favored the substitute, which expressed the judgment that he ought to "desist from the exercise of his office so long as the impediment remains. Because the concurrent testimony of the accredited, venerable, and discreet men from the Northern Conferences was, that if things remain as they are the difficulty is unmanageable and overwhelming, pregnant with danger, and threatening manifold disasters and disaffections throughout the Church, it is for this General Conference to grapple with the difficulties and dispose of them in some way. Our powers are so great as to allow us to make some provision against them. We cannot do away with the episcopacy, nor infringe upon its character as a general superintendency. Within these limits we have plenary powers for carrying out, through the episcopacy, the general purposes of the Conference and the Church. I trust some measure may be adopted that will greatly palliate and diminish, if not wholly avert, the dangers that threaten us. The substitute now proposed I regard as such a measure."

Benjamin M. Drake proposed to meet the difficulty, and obviate the objections to a slave-holding Bishop presiding in Northern Conferences, by recommending the episcopacy to assign to each superintendent his sphere of labor for the next four years.

Henry Slicer, as a Conservative and friend of the slave, favored the substitute. Bishop Andrew might become disincumbered of slavery, and that very moment the full powers of the general superintendency would inure to him. The Bishop had not infracted the Discipline, but he had offended against the great law of expediency.

Phineas Crandal would have voted for the request to resign, but he was in doubt about expressing merely a judgment that the Bishop should desist. He was apprehensive that if the brother refused submission, and four years more passed over, it might be very difficult to control the matter.

William D. Cass regarded it morally wrong to be a slave-holder, and that Bishop Andrew had done wrong in becoming a slave-holder, and thereby disturbing the peace of the Church. "Four Annual Conferences and thousands of our members in New England have solemnly protested against having a slave-holding Bishop; and if he holds his office there will be large secessions, or whole Conferences will leave. If this Conference does any thing less than declare slavery a moral evil we stand on a volcano at the North."

George F. Pierce urged that the question involved more than was affirmed of the disqualification of Bishop Andrew and the expediency of suspending the exercise of his functions. The proposed measure was part and parcel of a system, slowly developed, yet obvious in its designs and unwearied in its operations, to deprive Southern ministers of their rights, and to disfranchise the whole Southern Church. "I do not feel a great deal of solicitude about the issue, because I regard the great question of unity as settled by the previous action of the Conference in the Harding case." He doubted if the argument of expediency had half the force assigned to it. He said: "I do not believe the people of New York would decline to receive Bishop Andrew, or that he would be objected to in New Jersey, Pennsylvania, Maryland, or in any of the Conferences of the Western States. The difficulties are with the New Englanders. I will allow that there may be secession, societies broken up, Conferences split, within the New England Conferences. I prefer that all New England should

secede, or be set off, with her share of the Church
property, than that this General Conference should
make this ruthless invasion upon the connectional
unity and the integrity of the Church. Let New
England go with all my heart. If the New England
Conferences were to secede the rest of us would have
peace. But set off the South and you multiply divisions. There will be secessions in the Northern
Conferences if Bishop Andrew resigns or is deposed.
Prominent men will abandon your Church. I venture to predict that when the day of division comes, ten
years from that day, and perhaps less, there will not
be a shred of the distinctive peculiarities left. The
venerable man who now presides over the Northern
Conferences may live out his time as a Bishop, but he
will never have a successor. Episcopacy will be
given up, presiding eldership will be given up, the
itinerancy will come to an end, and congregational-
ism will be the order of the day."

A. B. Longstreet cited the successive steps of authority assumed by the Romish Church which resulted in its present monstrous pretensions to supremacy, as illustrative of the possibilities of Methodist
history, as seen already in the exactions made of the
South, and in test rules on slavery and other subjects.
He would never consent to any test rules other than
those which obtained when Methodism first took root
in our land. "Every Conference for ten years has
been oppressed with petition after petition on the
subject of slavery. The petitioners are informed by
our committees that they were applying to a jurisdiction which is incompetent to give relief. At length
one who occupies one of the first places among us
finds himself connected with slavery. He finds the

Conference in commotion. He convened the dele-gates from the slave-holding Conferences, and, for the sake of peace, proposed to resign; but we, to a man, declared to him that if he sought the peace of the Church by that course he would be disappointed of his object; that his resignation to appease the clamor of the Abolitionists would spread general dis-content through the whole South. 'We cannot lie down and see you deposed. If it comes to this, that being connected with slavery disqualifies you, we are disqualified.'"

Jesse T. Peck replied to Mr. Pierce, and denied that the question of unity was decided, or that the disfranchisement of the whole Southern Church and ministry was an ultimate design. He also insisted that no constitutional rights were to be invaded, for no man had a constitutional right to be a Bishop. And as to whether a man will do for a Bishop, the General Conference is the sole judge, either as to his election or retention. "We might as well talk of a constitutional right to be an editor, or a Book Agent, or any other General Conference officer."

"But," continued Mr. Peck, "our brethren of the South utterly mistake the truth in this matter. This has never been a question of principle, but measures, between us and New England. We have always been agreed in fundamental antislavery sentiment. The united West and North and East form an insuperable barrier to the advance of slavery. We are happy that New England is with us to a man in this fearful con-flict. But my friend from Georgia says, 'Let New England go!' That exclamation vibrates in my soul in tones of grating discord. What is New England, that we should part with her with so little reluctance?

New England! the land of the pilgrims—the land of many of our venerated fathers in Israel—the land of Broadhead, of Merritt, of Pickering, and a host of worthies whom we have delighted to honor as the bulwarks of Methodism in its early days of primitive purity and peril. 'Let New England go?' No, sir, never! And our Southern brethren can't induce us to use such language. They can't provoke us to say, 'Let the South go!' No, sir; we cannot part with our brethren whom we love so well. We will not let them go unless they tear themselves from our arms bedewed with the tears of affection."

A. L. P. Green took issue with the position several had maintained—that a Bishop was nothing more than an officer of the General Conference, and argued that he was the officer of the Conference simply in the character of a chairman, but that as Bishop he was an officer of the Methodist Episcopal Church in the United States of America. And he declared that if any one who should vote to depose Bishop Andrew "was to be elected in his place, and should go South to attend our Conferences, and we were to sustain him, and thereby also the action of the Conference in deposing him, I do not know, sir, but the people would rise *en masse* and escort us out of town in a genteel dress of tar and feathers." He thought the South would stand the rescinding of the colored-testimony resolution, the decision in Harding's case, and the election of a non-slaveholding Bishop; but as to saying, "Here, take Bishop Andrew and crucify him, for I find no fault in him," as the passage of that resolution would say, he must pray, "God save us from such a course."

Leonidas L. Hamline said, "There are two questions

involved: Has the General Conference constitutional authority to pass this resolution? Is it proper or fitting that we should do it?" He argued this authority from the genius of our polity on points which most resemble this, such as the removal of class-leaders, exhorters, preachers, pastors, and presiding elders, whose amenability related not only to the vices, but to the improprieties, of behavior. His second argument for authority to depose a Bishop summarily for improprieties, morally innocent, which embarrass the exercise of his functions, was from the relations of the General Conference to the Church and to the Episcopacy. This Conference is supreme while acting within its constitutional limits, and its decisions are final and all-controlling. It can make rules of every sort for the government of the Church. It has legislative, judicial, and executive supremacy.

The General Conference is the fountain of all executive authority. Everything conveyed to Bishops, presiding elders, pastors, etc., by statutory provision was in the General Conference. All it can confer it can withhold, and also resume at will if no constitutional restriction forbids. And the constitutional grant of power to the General Conference is in mass, and no more excludes the executive than it does either the legislative or judicial. And that our powers are administrative do not we declare by inspecting and passing judgment upon the Minutes of every Annual Conference, and by putting the administration of our Bishops under severe inquisition for approval or disapproval. And the " power to expel" a bishop "for improper conduct," he said, "is recognized as existing in the General Conference, in the Discipline, answer to Question 4, page 28." "Improper" means simply not suitable, or unfitting. Whatever is unfitting a Bishop's office, and would impair his usefulness in the exercise of its functions, is embraced in the phrase "improper conduct." Finally the words "if they see it necessary," accord to the Conference discretionary power, and invite them to proceed on the ground of expediency, of which some so loudly complain. These summary removals are from office, and not from orders. And all ranks of officers are included up to the point where the officer has no superior; which, Mr. Hamline showed, included the Bishops, as they were subordinate to the General Conference. Finally, the expediency of the action proposed was to be determined by the extent of the evil to be prevented; and if the calamities were likely to be heavy, long continued, and scarcely ever ended, the call for summary proceedings is loud and imperative. If in such circumstances this Conference declines to act, it will betray its trust and dishonor God. When the Church is about to suffer a detriment, which we by constitutional power can avert, it is as much treason not to exercise the power we have as to usurp in other circumstances that which we have not.

Silas Comfort called attention to the third restrictive rule, which guarded the itinerant general superintendency. The law enacted under that article of the constitution is found on page 29 of the Discipline, answer to Question 6, which requires that if a Bishop cease from traveling at large among the people he should not exercise the Episcopal office without the consent of the General Conference. Bishop Andrew could not, under his present embarrassment, travel at large throughout the connection : and, therefore, with-

out the consent of this Conference, he must suspend
the exercise of his office till his embarrassment be removed. According to Bishop Hedding, in his "Notes
on the Discipline," he was "the servant of the elders."
If so, it is within the province of the great body of the
eldership now present by representation in this Conference to suspend the jurisdiction of Bishop Andrew.

William A. Smith criticised Mr. Hamline's analogy
respecting the summary removal of officers as not to
the point, and denied that Bishop Andrew had acted
improperly, and affirmed that in no offensive sense
was he a slave-holder. He said a friend died some
short time after his appointment as Bishop, in 1832,
and left him a girl to raise, and at a given age to send
her to Liberia, if she would consent to go. He faithfully fulfilled his trust. She refused to go to Liberia,
and remains his property, as free as the laws will permit her to be. In the second instance, he inherited a
boy by the death of his wife, who is also as free as
the laws of the State will permit him to be. In the
third instance, he married a lady who was the owner
of slaves, which he did not wish to become the owner
of, and relinquished to her at once the legal title
which fell to him by marriage. Two attributes must
attach to the act of holding this property to make it
offensive in the sense of the Discipline: it must be
received and held with an intention to enslave; and
the holder must of purpose omit to manumit when
by doing so freedom could be secured. No such intention or omitted duty is charged in this case.

Mr. Smith then classified the parties in the General Conference as on one side thirteen Southern Annual Conferences, on the other the four New England

Conferences and a few Northern Conferences, leaving
between the two parties all the Conferences, including
New York and those south and west of it, as the
umpires in this controversy, to whom he appealed as
having the entire responsibility of this decision. He
further argued that the rule of the Discipline on the
eligibility of slave-holders to office was a compromise
act, a basis of union, a common platform on which
the opposite parties have stood since soon after the
organization of the Church ; and therefore, no petitions nor memorials on slavery should be received or
considered. And as the Bishop's connection with
slavery is provided for in the compromise rule, the
" unacceptability " complained of is not his fault, but
theirs who make the complaint, and they, not he,
should suffer the consequences. Should you append
a request that he free himself from his present relation to slavery if it be practicable, we could not absolutely object to it ; at least, the consequences would
not be so serious. But the adoption of either the
substitute or the original resolution will be in the
highest degree proscriptive, will put in jeopardy all
our missions among slaves, and a division of our
ecclesiastical confederation would become a high and
solemn duty.

John A. Collins took issue with the claim that a
compromise act on slavery could be found in the constitution of the Church. He thought that, as the
Bishop knew when he was elected that a slave-holder
could not have been elected, he did commit an improper act in afterward becoming connected with slavery.
The Bishop had offended a portion of the brethren in
the ministry and membership, and the Discipline required that a Bishop should be blameless. He, how-

ever, knew a ground on which he could meet the South, and hoped it might be acceptable. It consisted of three resolutions: one, an expression of regret; another, a request to free himself from his connection with slavery within the ensuing four years; a third, erasing all action in the case of Silas Comfort in 1840.

James B. Finley, the mover of the substitute, reviewed the position of its opponents, reiterated uncompromising opposition to slavery and to its connection with the episcopacy. He was not an Abolitionist. They called him pro-slavery. Southern men called him an Abolitionist. He was Southern born, of slave-holding parents; but they had early seen the evil, freed themselves from the curse, and removed six thousand dollars' worth of slaves, and set them up for themselves in a free State.

Edmund W. Sehon had been in favor of a voluntary resignation by Bishop Andrew, but was opposed to both propositions before them, as involving a forced resignation, which would be equivalent to punishment by suspension from office.

William Winans denied that the General Conference had any original administrative power. He deemed it a creature having delegated attributes and none others. These were few, and found in the Book of Discipline, and not in abstract reasoning. The administrative power was found only in the rules and regulations of the Discipline, and did not include plenary power to be used at will.

Peter Cartwright was in favor of the substitute, was no friend of slavery, nor yet an Abolitionist. But when any body told him it was none of his business, and he had no right to meddle with slavery, he begged to enter his protest. Somebody of the South had said that Bishop M'Kendree intended to have purchased a slave, but he had heard Bishop M'Kendree say five hundred times that if he owned a thousand slaves, he would not die a slave-holder, he would set them free.

Jonathan Stamper sustained Mr. Smith's view of there being a compromise in the Discipline on slavery which would be broken by the proposed action in Bishop Andrew's case; besides it would throw impediments in the way of intercourse with the benighted colored brethren of the South. He thought the principles of ultra abolitionism would result in the destruction of the whole colored race.

Samuel Dunwody discussed the character of slavery, arguing, from the Old Testament and from the New, that it was not a moral evil. The excitement produced at the South, Mr. Dunwody was informed by correspondents, by this discussion and proposed action, was such that he did not know but if the Conference broke up, another would be called in the South to take measures to secede from the Church altogether.

Bishop Soule spoke in favor of further deliberation. He referred to the action of former General Conferences against agitating the question of slavery, questioned the power of the General Conference by a mere majority vote to depose a Bishop, and earnestly entreated them not to pass the resolution relating to Bishop Andrew. He favored sending the matter out to the Church at large to consider for the next quadrennium, and then act upon a complete knowledge of the mind of the whole Church.

John P. Durbin challenged Mr. Longstreet's assumed analogy between Romanism and Methodism, vindicated the action which confirmed the suspension of Harding, and affirmed the entire unity of the Northern Conferences on one point—that the episcopacy of the Methodist Episcopal Church ought not to be trammeled with slavery. He showed that the highest ground ever held on slavery was taken at the very organization of the Church, and that concessions had been made continually from that time to this in view of the necessities of the South.

The power of the episcopacy was shown to be derived from the suffrages of the General Conference, by which it could be removed if judged necessary. The Minutes of 1785 declare that "the episcopal office was made elective, and the elected superintendent or Bishop amenable to the body of ministers and preachers." The "Notes on the Discipline" assert that "the Bishops are perfectly subject to the General Conference; their power, their usefulness, themselves, are entirely at the mercy" of that body. Further, Rev. John Dickins, in a pamphlet published in 1792, says: "Now, who ever said the superiority of the Bishops was by virtue of a separate organization? If this gave them their superiority, how came they to be removable by the Conference? . . . We all know Mr. Asbury derived his official power from the Conference, and therefore his office is at their disposal. . . . Mr. Asbury was thus chosen by the Conference, both before and after he was ordained a Bishop; and he is still considered the person of their choice by being responsible to the Conference, who have power to remove him and fill his place with another if they see it necessary. And as he is liable every year to be removed, he may be considered as their annual choice." And Bishop Emory declared that "this may be considered as expressing the views of Bishop Asbury in relation to the true and original character of Methodist episcopacy;" and he gives it the sanction of his own authority by quoting and using it in the twelfth section of the "Defense of our Fathers."

Mr. Durbin closed his speech by suggesting a resolution referring the case to the judgment of the Church as that should be expressed by the General Conference for 1848.

William Capers answered the plea, that a slaveholding Bishop would involve the North, by insisting that the North was already involved by the unity of the Church and the unity of the ministry, the Southern portion of which contained slave-holders; and that there was no way of escape from being thus inextricably involved, except by breaking up the Church.

The Bishops, Joshua Soule, Elijah Hedding, Beverly Waugh, and Thomas A. Morris, subsequently presented a unanimous recommendation to postpone action for four years, from which document Bishop Hedding the day afterward withdrew his name. It was laid on the table by a vote of 95 to 83. The vote was then taken on the following resolution:

Whereas, The Discipline of our Church forbids the doing any thing calculated to destroy our itinerant general superintendency; and *whereas*, Bishop Andrew has become connected with slavery, by marriage and otherwise, and this act having drawn after it circumstances which, in the estimation of the General Conference, will greatly embarrass the exercise of his office as an itinerant general superintendent, if not in some places prevent it; therefore

Resolved, That it is the sense of this General Conference that he desist from the exercise of his office so long as this impediment remains.

The resolution was adopted. Yeas, 111; nays, 69.

A different conclusion was quite probable, and came much nearer being accepted than appears from any direct action taken. Mr. Collins proposed to substitute a request for the Bishop to free himself from connection with slavery within the ensuing four years. Dr. Durbin had proposed to defer action for four years; and the Bishops had united in a recommendation to the same effect.

"Abolitionists regarded this as a most alarming measure. Accordingly, the delegates of the New England Conferences were immediately called together, and, after due deliberation, unanimously adopted a paper declaring, in substance, that it was their solemn conviction that if Bishop Andrew should be left by the Conference in the exercise of episcopal functions it would break up the most of our Churches in New England; and that the only way they could be holden together would be to secede in a body, and invite Bishop Hedding to preside over them. The proposition was also concurred in by some of our most distinguished laymen who were present, and a committee of two were appointed to communicate this action to Bishop Hedding. On the morning of June 1 the Bishop was fully informed of the aforesaid action. He then publicly withdrew his name from the paper he and the other Bishops had signed, because 'facts had come to his knowledge which led him to believe that it would not make peace, but only increase the difficulty.' Thereupon the recommendation was laid upon the table by a vote of 95 yeas to 84 nays, showing very clearly that it would have carried had not Bishop Hedding withdrawn his name."—*Rev. James Porter, "Quarterly Review," April*, 1871.

CHAPTER XVI.

THE SOUTHERN SECESSION, 1844, 1845.

THE primitive antislavery sentiment of Methodism, too long dormant, now quickened by earnest discussion, had concentrated at a single point. The General Conference of 1844, under the control of this sentiment, had said to the slave-holding Methodists, who were constantly advancing their claims to toleration and indorsement, Thus far ye shall go, and no farther. It did not antagonize all slave-holding, nor explicitly condemn slavery generally, but it did say, There shall be no extension of the sphere of slavery; into the territory of the episcopacy slavery shall not go; having invaded that territory without our knowledge or consent, we insist that it shall leave at once. That is "the sense of this Conference," was the emphatic declaration.

"If that expression is adopted," said the representatives of the South in open session, "then thirteen thousand preachers and four hundred and fifty thousand members are cut off from the jurisdiction of this General Conference." And yet that opinion was deliberately uttered by the vote of nearly two thirds of the body. It was an important decision; it assumed a great responsibility, and it was grandly significant of a new departure in behalf of human freedom.

To mass so immense a force in position, facing the foe, is a work second only in power to the forward movement which afterward sweeps the field triumphantly. And the force now massed against this extension of slavery, headed by one hundred and eleven delegates, included also more than three thousand traveling preachers, three thousand local preachers, and six hundred thousand members, who were all organically arrayed against the extension of slavery, if not personally committed in favor of its extirpation. Such was the relative strength and the positive antagonism of the two sections of Methodism June 1, 1844.

A Declaration was presented to the General Conference three days afterward from the delegates of the Southern and South-western Conferences, signed by fifty-two of them, which referred to the "agitation of the subject of slavery in a portion of the Church; the frequent action on that subject by the General Conference; and, especially, the extra-judicial proceedings against Bishop Andrew," and stated that "a continuance of the jurisdiction of the General Conference over these Conferences is inconsistent with the success of the ministry in the slave-holding States." This impeachment of jurisdiction was followed with a protest the next day, which was more direct and indignant in tone, and stigmatized the action of the Conference as "an attempt to degrade and punish, a lawless prosecution, an illegal arrest, an anomalous quasi-suspension, imperative and mandatory in form," and closed by saying, "The South cannot submit, and the absolute necessity of division is already dated."

The General Conference answered the cavils of the protest by resolutions providing "that Bishop Andrew's name stand in the Minutes, Hymn Book, and Discipline as formerly; that the rule in relation to the support of a Bishop and his family applies to

Bishop Andrew; that whether in any, and if any, in what, work Bishop Andrew be employed, is to be determined by his own decision and action, in relation to the previous action of this Conference in his case." And, besides this, a special committee reported a statement, which was adopted, declaring that "the action of the General Conference was neither judicial nor punitive. It neither achieves a deposition nor so much as a legal suspension. Bishop Andrew is still a Bishop, and should he, against the expressed wish of the General Conference, proceed in the discharge of his functions, his official acts would be valid."

Notwithstanding these unqualified disclaimers, the Southern delegates moved on directly toward the disruption of jurisdiction as suggested, and the "antedated division" named in their declaration and protest. Dr. Capers offered a proposition providing for jurisdiction in partnership, which, after brief consideration, was withdrawn. Rev. J. B. M'Ferrin offered a resolution of instruction to the Committee of Nine, to which had been referred the Southern declaration, that they "devise a constitutional plan for division, mutual and friendly."

This committee, through Dr. Paine, chairman, presented a report which very considerately said, "We esteem it the duty of this General Conference to meet the emergency with Christian kindness and the strictest equity." And a plan was presented by them, to be adhered to "in the event of a separation, a contingency to which the declaration asks attention as not improbable." This plan indicated a boundary line; provided for border Conferences, stations, and societies choosing their position; recommended to the

Annual Conferences a change of the sixth restrictive
rule; provided contingently for the division of the
stock and assets of the Book Concern, and resolved
"that all the property of the Methodist Episcopal
Church in meeting-houses, parsonages, colleges,
schools, Conference funds, cemeteries, and of every
kind, within the limits of the Southern organization, shall be forever free from any claim set up
on the part of the Methodist Episcopal Church, so
far as this resolution can be of force in the premises."

All these provisions were conditioned upon the
occurrence of a state of things indicated thus: "Should
the Annual Conferences in the slave-holding States
find it necessary to unite in a distinct ecclesiastical
organization." Dr. Paine, speaking for the South,
said: "If found necessary to keep down faction and
prosecute their ministry at home they should feel
bound to separate, to carry out the provisions of this enactment, but not unless driven to it." "They should
be one people until it was formally announced by
a convention of the Southern Churches that they had
resolved to ask an organization according to the provisions of this report."

Such was the attitude and relation of the parties to
this great question when, at midnight, June 10,
1844, the General Conference adjourned *sine die.*
So spake the Conference of its willingness to meet
the contingency equitably and kindly. And so said
they of the South respecting their contingent purpose
and method of proceeding. No such scene had ever
been witnessed as had been exhibited in that highest
tribunal of the Church. And no such record of
magnanimity, gentleness, and generous dealing finds
a place in ecclesiastical history as that of the majority

of this General Conference of the Methodist Episcopal Church.

The morning after the adjournment, however,
found the Southern delegates in session as a convention in New York city. They proceeded to assume
the initiative of separation, which prerogative had
been specifically assigned, by their own consent and
request, to the Annual Conferences. A delegated
convention was called to meet at Louisville, Ky.,
May 1, 1845; the ratio of representation was fixed,
and an Address was issued to the ministers and members of the Southern States and Territories, which
declared "that the legislative, judicial, and administrative action of the General Conference, as now organized, will always be extremely hurtful, if not
ruinous, to the Southern portion of the Church; . . . and
that unless the South will submit to the dictation and
interference of the North there is no hope of any
thing like union and harmony." And thus the contingent plan proposed by the General Conference,
and accepted by the Southern delegates, was virtually
set aside by them within three days after its adoption, and a secession inaugurated.

The Annual Conferences of the Southern States
below Delaware and Maryland accepted the programme of the New York Convention, and thereby
ignored the plan adopted at the General Conference.
The Louisville Convention, May 17, 1845, by a vote
of 94 to 3, separated from the Church, and constituted a new body known as "The Methodist Episcopal Church, South."

Meanwhile, the proposed change in the sixth restrictive rule was being submitted to all the Annual
Conferences, and was not adopted. There lacked

269 votes of the three-fourths majority required, and therefore the division and transfer of the capital and produce of the Book Concern was disallowed. The negative vote was 1,070. The opposition, numbering one thousand traveling preachers, was largely increased before the ensuing General Conference, as was manifest by the election of delegates thereto. Only forty-one, out of one hundred and eleven who were members in 1844, were elected to the Conference of 1848, and eleven of these had voted against the plan. Various influences combined to affect this result. Opposition upon conscientious and constitutional grounds was alleged by many. The unauthorized precipitate action of the New York Convention of Southern delegates, and the disregard of the contingent boundary line, and the consequent strife and invasions of Northern territory following, was regarded as a repudiation of the plan by those who had favored it at the North.

Anticipating the history of the ensuing General Conference in part, it is noted that immediate and earnest attention was given to questions connected with the disruption of the Church. They were referred to a committee of forty-six, two from each of twenty-three Conferences, the first day, whose report was adopted May 26. In a vote of 143, sometimes one dissented, and never more than sixteen, on any one of four declarations. The first stated a principle : "That there exists no power in the General Conference to effectuate, authorize, or sanction a division of the Church." The second declaration affirmed the inviolability of the right of Church membership, "unless guilty of a violation of its rules." The third declaration set forth the universal right of trial

and appeal, declaring also that separation from the
Church otherwise contravenes constitutional right.
The fourth declaration stated the character, contingency, and conditions of the provisional plan, with
sundry contraventions thereof and the consequences.
These points were embraced in eight items reconstructed from the one lengthy paragraph of the
original report, amended by Dr. Matthew Simpson
of Indiana, and Dr. Daniel Curry of New York, and
accepted as a substitute in substance as follows:
1. The report of the committee of nine adopted in
1844 was intended to meet a necessity which it was
alleged might arise.   2. A part of its regulations were
made dependent upon the concurrence of three
fourths of the members of the several Annual Conferences.   3. It was made dependent also upon the observance of certain provisions respecting a boundary
by the ecclesiastical connection separating from us,
should such connection be formed.   4. Without waiting for the anticipated necessity, action was taken in
the premises by the Southern delegates.   5. The Annual Conferences have refused to concur with that
part of the plan submitted to them.   6. The provisions respecting a boundary have been violated by
the highest authorities of said connection which separated from us, and the peace and harmony of many
of our Societies have been destroyed.   7. No obligation exists on the part of this Conference to observe
the provisions of said plan, in view of the facts and
principles in these declarations.   8. Therefore the
plan is hereby declared null and void.

The committee designate the action of the separa-
tists as "revolutionary," in contravention of the
" plan," " reducing it to a nullity by the violation of

its first great and fundamental condition ; . . . and as an abandonment of the plan proposed by the General Conference. . . . And hence, that for the reason above alleged the plan has been of no real force since the date of the Call and Address issued by the New York Convention, June 11, 1844." So thought the General Conference of 1848 by unanimously adopting the report.

The opinion of the Supreme Court of the United States was otherwise, however. In support of its decision awarding to the Methodist Episcopal Church, South, the portion claimed for it of the common fund in the Book Concern at New York and Cincinnati, the Court said :

"We do not agree that this division was made without the proper authority. On the contrary, we entertain no doubt but that the General Conference of 1844 was competent to make it. . . . The same authority which founded that Church in 1784 has divided it and established two separate and independent organizations, occupying the place of the old one."
—"*Formal Fraternity,*" *p.* 39.

The Church South on its own behalf, through its College of Bishops, as recently as May 11, 1869, officially reiterated its uniform declaration as to the cause of separation. In reply to a communication from the Board of Bishops of the Methodist Episcopal Church, through Bishops Janes and Simpson, it is said by Bishops Paine and M'Tyeire: "You say that the great cause which led to the separation from us of both the Wesleyan Methodists of this country and of the Methodist Episcopal Church, South, has passed away. . . . If we understand your reference we so far differ from you in opinion that it may help any negotiations hereafter taking place, to restate our position. Slavery was not, in any proper sense, the cause, but the occasion only, of that separation, the necessity of which we regretted as much as you. But certain principles were developed in relation to the political aspects of that question, involving the right of ecclesiastical bodies to handle and determine matters outside of their proper jurisdiction, which we could not accept; and, in a case arising, certain constructions of the constitutional powers and prerogatives of the General Conference were assumed and acted on which we considered oppressive and destructive of the rights of the numerical minority represented in that highest judicatory of the Church. That which you are pleased to call, no doubt sincerely thinking it so, 'the great cause' of separation, existed in the Church from its organization, and yet for sixty years there was no separation. But when those theories incidentally evolved in connection with it began to be put in practice, then the separation came." —*"Formal Fraternity,"* p. 11.

CHAPTER XVII.

THE BORDER CONFERENCES, 1845–1847.

ON the Northern border of the thirteen Annual Conferences which were identified with the Church South, are four Annual Conferences of the Methodist Episcopal Church—the Baltimore, Philadelphia, Pittsburgh, and Ohio—which had within their limits the States of Maryland, Delaware, and part of Virginia. This border-land became a field of strife between the two Churches, as the contingent plan of 1844 had provided for border Conferences, circuits, and Societies making choice between remaining with the old Church or adhering to the new organization.

The considerations of identity with the South in local interests and institutions, the antislavery tendencies of the North, with the possible exclusion hereafter of all slave-holders from the communion of the Methodist Episcopal Church, were freely urged by the friends of the Church South in their own behalf; and it became the natural and necessary work of the friends of the old Church to offset these considerations, and save the border from disturbance as far as possible. And to accomplish this all the energies of the Church for a time were concentrated upon it as an object of supreme importance. The influence of the course pursued in this emergency was seen quickly in the temporary suspension of antislavery activity at the North and East, and the earnest vindication of the "Discipline as it is," became the rallying cry of the Methodist Episcopal Church very generally.

The Church South had left the rule and the section on slavery unchanged. They did not expunge the rule against slavery until their General Conference of 1858. The same words were used against slavery in both Disciplines. They could not, then, be reproached with having disturbed the modified testimony of the fathers on that subject, while the Methodist Episcopal Church was charged by them with designing to add thereto. "It is only a question of time," said they, with much plausibility, in view of the antislavery memorials sent up to the General Conferences for the twelve years previous to the separation. And when, at the first General Conference of the Church South, the subject of change was canvassed by them, Bishop Andrew said, "It would be extremely hazardous to attempt any change. If the tenth section be removed the border might suffer." Mr. Sullens said, "That they were in trouble in East Tennessee, and that he hoped they would not increase the trouble of that region by the change in the Discipline on the subject of slavery." Dr. Winans said, "It is not important to repeal it, and such repeal might bring on them the charge of being a pro-slavery Church." And in order to urge the lay members of Kentucky and Missouri into the new Church, Messrs. Parsons and Boyle, leading men, had pledged that the Discipline should not be changed. ("Great Secession," col. 559.) And it was not for several years.

The official papers of the Methodist Episcopal Church were very full and explicit in their assurances, also, that there would be no change in its

Discipline on that question. And the Annual Conferences on the border reiterated the statement, and repudiated all sympathy for, or identity with, the modern abolition sentiment of the North and East. The Baltimore Conference of 1846 said, "That this Conference disclaims having any fellowship with abolitionism. On the contrary, while it is determined to maintain its well-known and long-established position of keeping the traveling preachers composing its own body free from slavery, it is also determined not to hold connection with any ecclesiastical body that shall make non-slaveholding a condition of membership in the Church, but to stand by and maintain the Discipline as it is." The Philadelphia Conference of 1846 said, "That we will abide by the Discipline of the Church as it is, and will resist every attempt to alter it in reference to slavery so as to change the terms of membership."

Besides these Conferences others at the North took similar positions. The Oneida Conference of 1845 said: "We ask for no change in discipline or fundamental policy. And, finally, the sympathies of this Conference are most cordially tendered to those brethren who, beyond the proposed line of separation between the North and South, are still disposed to adhere to the Methodist Episcopal Church; and we hereby pledge them any aid which circumstances may allow us to render them." The Providence Conference of 1845 also said, "That we are satisfied with the Discipline of the Church as it is on the subject of slavery; and as we have never proposed any alteration in it, so neither do we now; and that, in connection with our brethren of the other Conferences, we will ever abide by it." And again, in 1847, they "pledge themselves to maintain the same conservative and true antislavery ground by which the Providence Conference has already become distinguished."

There seemed to be a correct summary of the facts at this period in the remarks of Dr. Bond, then editor of the "Christian Advocate:" "We learned, during our visit to Providence, New England, and Maine Conferences, (1845,) that the membership, as well as the more efficient and useful of the ministers, longed for repose. They were weary of the long strife of abolition controversy, and had resolved, if possible, to prevent the agitation of the subject in the Churches. Upon the whole we may confidently assure our brethren elsewhere that no furious ultraism, no rash, impracticable measures are to be expected hereafter from our New England brethren. We believe that excesses and extravagances are as likely to be rebuked by the present sound opinions, good temper, and pious feeling of the New England ministry and membership as in any other part of the Union." And so also judged Dr. Stevens, then editor of "Zion's Herald," who copied and indorsed this statement. There was a temporary suspension of antislavery activity, caused by sympathy with the general solicitude for the peace and harmony of the border.

A paper in "Zion's Herald," however, appeared, signed by Rev. James Porter and other leading Abolitionists of New England, headed, "Things as They Are," which took issue with the editors of the "Advocate and Journal," and of "Zion's Herald," giving all parties to understand that abolitionism was in full force. The editor of the "Western Advocate" fell upon the writer with great violence, but refused to allow him to reply in his paper to the extent of one word — an injustice afterward confessed privately. The South made good use of "Things as They Are," believing it to be a correct statement, as indeed it was.—*Porter, " History of Methodism," p.* 459.

The strife, however, was severe and prolonged. The friends of the Church South gave prominence to the outcry against abolitionism. That was the strong argument, or prejudice, made use of, and the excitement was pushed to the climax of mob violence, sometimes through the denunciation of Northern preachers by the friends of the Church South, who called them "abolitionists, incendiaries, revolutionists, and traitors." Even the Southern Methodist press stigmatized the Methodist Episcopal Church as an " Abolition Church," and declared its jurisdiction anywhere in the slave-holding States to be "an enormity that enlightened public sentiment cannot, and will not, tolerate." The natural results followed.

On Sunday, July 12, 1846, Rev. Valentine Gray, preacher in charge of Northampton Circuit, Philadelphia Conference, when about to commence services in the Salem Church, was assailed by a mob, seized, and forcibly taken out of the pulpit and church—and the next day he was driven from Eastville, the seat of justice for the county, by a mob, without redress or protection, and his life threatened if he did not leave the county. The alleged cause was, that he was a Northern preacher, but the essential fact, antedating it, was a lecture by a friend of the Church South, in which Northern preachers were stigmatized as all Abolitionists " who would sow dangerous opinions among the slaves."

A public meeting was held in Accomac County

presided over by Judge Scarborough, to discuss the
necessity of Virginia Methodists all withdrawing from
the Philadelphia Conference, and uniting with the
Virginia Conference of the Church South.   A labored
argument, in pamphlet form, was published and circulated extensively by the judge.

Rev. J. Hargis, of the Philadelphia Conference,
was mobbed at Guilford, Accomac County, while
preaching on the Sabbath day, November 26, 1846.
And a few months later the "Christian Advocate and
Journal" was formally presented by the grand jury
of that county as an incendiary sheet inciting slaves
to rebellion, and forbidding its circulation through
the post-offices; notice whereof was sent to all the
postmasters.   An attempt to drive out the preacher
on Accomac Circuit was defeated by the superior
number and firmness of the Church members.   But
a few months subsequently one of the preachers
was advised by the brethren to leave the circuit, as
the persecution was made to burn more fiercely by
an inflammatory speech of an influential Southern
preacher, in July, 1847.

Similar influences were at work in that part of
Virginia which was embraced in the Ohio Conference.   A mob was provoked at Parkersburgh, and
for a time succeeded in keeping away the preacher,
Mr. Dillon.   The grand jury for the Superior Court
of Wood County also made presentment of the
"Western Christian Advocate," as "an incendiary
publication, printed with the intent to make insurrection within the Commonwealth of Virginia."
This was procured through the agency of Prosecut-
ing-Attorney Jackson's zealous hostility, and after a
charge to the jury by Judge M'Comas, which was an

attempt at a scriptural argument in favor of the
divine right of slavery. Thereupon to read the "Advocate," or even receive it by public or private con-
veyance, was deemed an act of felony, and the person
"convicted thereof shall be punished by imprisonment in the penitentiary of this Commonwealth, for
a term not less than two years, nor more than five
years." The indictment was noticed by the Richmond and Nashville "Advocates" as a thing to be
regretted, and yet to be expected, and really deserved.
It was condemned in decided terms by the Northern
press. Large lists of new subscribers were forwarded
from the North, giving substantial proof of approbation, and repairing all damage suffered by diminished
circulation. (See Dr. Elliott's "Great Secession.")

These will suffice as specimen cases of violent persecution in the interests of the Church South, although not by its agency directly. It seemed an immediate advantage to them probably, but made many
life-long conservatives on the slavery question see
cause for becoming very decided Abolitionists soon
afterward. This strife annoyed the friends of the
Methodist Episcopal Church not a little for a time,
but it did deadly work for slavery in the long run.
That which could not be reasoned with was deemed
madness, and that which could not brook the sight of
an opponent demonstrated itself to be tyranny. The
mad tyrant, slavery, thereby procured its own verdict, and was doomed to death, although sentence
against that evil thing was not executed speedily.

CHAPTER XVIII.

THE GENERAL CONFERENCE OF 1848.

THE exciting affairs along the border, and the protracted discussion thereon, joined with the action of the Annual Conferences on the question of providing for a division of the capital and assets of the Book Concern, had diverted the attention of the Church from the antislavery discussion. And at the General Conference of 1848 there was no committee on slavery appointed, and only one memorial reported on that subject, which Rev. James Floy presented from Middletown, Conn. That went to the Committee on the State of the Church.

In that committee, or growing out of its action, the only discussion of slavery during the session occurred. It was brief and inconclusive, however. The committee reported in part, May 5, as follows:
' " That they have had under consideration the letter from the Rev. Dr. Pierce, and that they recommend to the General Conference the adoption of the following preamble and resolutions: *Whereas*, a letter from Rev. L. Pierce, D.D., delegate of the Methodist Episcopal Church, South, proposing fraternal relations between the Methodist Episcopal Church and the Methodist Episcopal Church, South, has been presented to this Conference; and, *whereas*, there are serious questions and difficulties existing between the two bodies, therefore: *Resolved*, That while we tender to the Rev. Dr. Pierce all personal courtesies,

and invite him to attend our sessions, this General Conference does not consider it proper at present to enter into fraternal relations with the Methodist Episcopal Church, South."

This report was amended, on motion of Dr. Tomlinson, thus: "*Provided*, however, that nothing in this resolution shall be so constrained as to operate as a bar to any propositions from Dr. Pierce, or any other representative of the Methodist Episcopal Church, South, toward the settlement of existing difficulties between that body and this." In support of this amendment Dr. Tomlinson said: "The sympathies of this General Conference are entirely on the side of liberty. But he would now say, although it was a little premature and was a painful fact, that the prevailing sympathies of the Church South were on the side of slavery. And he would now express the opinion, as a conscientious man, that he could not fraternize with that Church as a genuine branch of the Wesleyan Methodist family. He would say, on the other hand, that if they wished to break up the Methodist Episcopal Church they would do so by fraternizing with the Church South." Others, from different considerations, favored the amendment. It prevailed—147 yeas; nays, none.

When reporting this action for the columns of "Zion's Herald," the editor, Rev. Abel Stevens, wrote:

This morning the report of the Committee on the State of the Church brought the subject before the full Conference. It was a momentous hour, for this question is important not only for the peace of the Church, but vastly so in its relations to the enormous evil of slavery. The discussion on it in the Conference was solemn and impressive, and you have the result—a unanimous affirmative vote for the report of the committee.   It may not be an unworthy ground of congratulation that the preamble and resolution by which this great body has thus remarkably expressed itself, on this the gravest question before it, is of New England origin.   And the interest of this fact is enhanced greatly to all New England Methodists by the consideration that the West—the noble West—sustained the preamble and resolution manfully in the committee; they were seconded by Dr. Elliott.   All amendments proposed in the committee and in the Conference failed, except the explanatory proviso of Dr. Tomlinson.   They were numerous, but the language of the report was at last agreed to as the best we could harmonize on.   It is certainly sufficiently courteous and definite.

This important act is not only a declinature of fraternal relations, but its whole import is a verdict against slavery and ecclesiastical alliance with slavery.   It was the design of the framer of the preamble and resolution that the phrase "serious question and difficulties" should include not only the ecclesiastical "difficulties" between the bodies, but the "question" of slavery; it was so explained in the committee, and indeed who does not know that the relation of the Church South to slavery is *the* great point of obstruction to such relations as it proposes.   The action of the Conference on the subject is, therefore, a most solemn and emphatic protest against slavery.   The unanimity of the act stamps it with peculiar significance.   Let it go forth, then, that the Methodist Episcopal Church rejects all alliance with pro-slavery ecclesiastical bodies.   It has taken its stand, and will never, we trust, depart.

On the 24th of May the order of the day was suspended by the motion of Rev. J. B. Finley, "to correct certain misrepresentations which have been made concerning the sentiments of the Conference."   The above extract was read by the secretary, and Mr. Stevens took the floor.

He explained the history of the matter.   The delegations from the East had come here virtually instructed to protest against the pro-slavery character of the Methodist Episcopal Church, South, by rejecting all overtures of fraternization with it. The division of the vested funds was an important question with the people of the East; the abolition of the oppressive boundary act was of still higher importance to them; but paramount, supremely paramount, to these was the question of fraternization with the South; and I avow here distinctly, and let your reporter send forth the avowal to the people of the East, and to the people of all this land—I avow that the hostility of our people, and of all of us their delegations here, to the recognition of the Church South, is based on the consideration for which the Wesleyans of England, the Churches of Protestant Christendom, the civilized world protest to-day against — slavery. We question not unqualifiedly the individual piety of the Church South, but in its organic position it stands as a mighty rampart about that enormous evil; in its collective character we denounce it. But let me not be misunderstood here. The Methodists of the East must not be confounded with any class of ultraists. Troubles they have had, indeed, growing out of the question of slavery. Those who were not of them, and therefore have gone out from them, spread desolation among their altars; but those altars have been repaired and flame up with the divine fire. Methodism in the East stands erect—erect on the integrity of old-fashioned antislavery Methodism, as the antislavery writings of Wesley, and the antislavery protests scattered all through the history of our Discipline, characterize primitive Methodism. I stand here, sir, a member of no other antislavery society than the Methodist Episcopal Church. As such I have acted here against the South; and I believe a large majority of this Conference voted on the question referred to in the character of antislavery Methodists.

I repeat that, standing on this Methodistic antislavery position, the Methodists of the East have looked to their delegates to reject the overtures of the South, chiefly because of its pro-slavery character, and especially because it has allowed slavery to intrude into and desecrate the highest function of the ministry, contrary to the usages transmitted by our fathers; and they have expected us to do so frankly and manfully, and without disguise. The delegates from the East, on their way hither, consulted respecting their duty in the premises; they will bear me testimony here, that it was their determination to demand not only resolutions against fraternization, but a full report—an exposition—a candid, conclusive, demonstrative exposition of the character of American slavery, the relations of the Church South to it, and our consequent refusal of its fellowship. But on our route we met our brethren of the border: we learned their critical difficulties; we sympathized with them; and I affirm here, that no part of our work sympathizes more profoundly with those afflicted brethren than New England. Her delegates showed their sympathy in the present instances. Believing that the proposed report might be misconstrued to their harm, we abandoned the design. We went further, and made every possible concession to them in the Committee on the State of the Church. Brethren of all parties will witness that in that committee I stood up incessantly imploring that in all verbal matters, in all points but essential principles, we should concede to the brethren of the border. The purpose of an elaborate report being abandoned, it was insisted by some that our resolutions should at least be specific, and specify slavery among the reasons of our declinature. Even this was abandoned, and a more general phraseology admitted, namely: "questions and difficulties." I had the honor, sir, to frame the preamble and resolution which you adopted; and in using the phrase mentioned, I designed and explained before the committee that while the word "difficulties" comprehended the misconstructions and infractions of the plan of separation, the word "questions" comprised the subjects of slavery, and the relations of the Church South thereto. The committee, I believe, voted with this distinct understanding. They can witness.

Having thus, in consideration of the delicate circumstances of our border brethren, abandoned the high ground which we should have otherwise felt called upon to assume, it was necessary that our people at home should be guarded against a misapprehension of our position. It has heretofore been alleged by our enemies that Northern men have in the General Conference, like Northern men in Congress, cowered before the brass front of slavery. We knew the expectations of our people, and we knew that if the general language of the resolution were not explained, it would again be said we had succumbed—that the resolution had been forced upon us—foisted upon us. What shall we do, then? Why, we tell them that we ourselves originated the resolution. I hope brethren have no quarrel with this; it would be child's play to complain here; for the facts relating to the history of this affair are known to the committee. We tell them, also, the sense of the resolution, as we understood and asserted it in committee. It was necessary for our honor and security that we should do so. The explanation may have been too early— it might have been safer for others, if not for ourselves, to have delayed it; but it was quite natural for us not to have thought so. The explanation was written at yonder table, immediately after the solemn moment in which the important measure was adopted. It was written under the conviction that the hour of a great achievement in our history had just passed.

I little supposed that such an act, declining the recognition of a great religious body, was formally or chiefly on ecclesiastical squabbles; that, while the world is ringing with remonstrances against slavery, we were acting on a matter so intimately connected with it, and yet did not consider it the highest, gravest reason of our action. Sir, if I was mistaken, the mistake ought certainly to be considered excusable.

But I was not mistaken. I introduced this article yesterday to the committee where the resolution was prepared, and if unusual demonstrations there have any meaning, they sustained my sense of the resolution. I have not denied other reasons than slavery for our course; the article expressly refers to the phrase "difficulties" as comprehending others, but it affirms that the "question" of slavery was the great reason; and I here declare, without qualification, that I understood a large majority of the committee to mean this; that I understood the vote of the Conference to mean this; and I wish it to be understood, here and elsewhere, that thus I voted, and would have never voted otherwise.

What, sir! will brethren say that slavery was not an essential consideration in this extraordinary measure? Would we

presume before the world to have cast away the brotherly
overtures of the South merely or chiefly because of misconstructions or infractions of a boundary arrangement? Would
not the world call upon us indignantly, as honest and honorable men, to accept of fraternization and appoint committees
to adjust these comparatively small troubles, and live on in
brotherhood, if these were our only or principal reasons? I
say here boldly, that if brethren insist upon this construction
of the resolution, we are bound in honor to reconsider and
rescind it, and recognize the fellowship of the South. We
did not mean slavery! Did we then mean that if the other
obstacles or difficulties were out of the way, the proslavery
position of the Church South would not be an obstruction to
fraternization? Is it then to be understood that, after resist-
ing slavery in the episcopacy to the very dissolution of the
union of the Church, we would, nevertheless, receive to our
communion the slave-holding Church with its slave-holding
episcopacy which our resistance had cast away from us?
Sir, this is not the sentiment of the Methodists of these free
States; this was not the sentiment of the vote of this Conference. If I am herein mistaken, let me know it. I will make
reparation. I will send forth an acknowledgment of my misapprehension; but hear me: while God gives me strength to
stand up, I will labor to bring about a different and a better
sentiment. I am astonished, sir—I am astonished at this
interference with the rights of the press, in a matter so obvious—so palpable.

Two members of the Baltimore Conference followed. Rev. John Davis said: "It was stated in the
Committee on the State of the Church, distinctly,
that it could not reject Dr. Pierce on the abstract
ground of slavery—that the Discipline of the Methodist Episcopal Church, South, on that subject, is
identical with ours; the witness against the great evil
of slavery stands out in as bold relief as in our own
book. Besides, slavery is not now a difficulty existing, to be settled between us and the Church South,

and it could not, therefore, be consistently and properly referred to as a ground of refusal to receive Dr. Pierce. There were other reasons, no doubt, in the minds of some of the members of the committee for the course adopted, such, for instance, as the connection of slavery with the episcopacy in the Church South. It was so stated in the subcommittee, and with this and one or two other exceptions, the question of slavery was never mentioned in either committee. Certainly this Conference never intended to give utterance to the sentiments contained in that article. It would be our ruin."

Rev. John A. Collins would refer the communication of A. Stevens to a committee of five, but the motion to suspend the rules was laid on the table; and no correction of the misrepresentations was made by the Conference.

Subsequently, the Southern Methodist papers quoted Mr. Stevens' construction of the language of the General Conference, and these facts, as an argument against the Methodist Episcopal Church along the border. But Dr. George Peck, chairman of the committee that reported the language, then editor of the "Christian Advocate and Journal," New York city, denied most unequivocally that it had any such application, or could be properly construed to mean any thing about slavery.

Whatever uncertainty may attach itself to the exact intent and meaning which a majority of that committee associated with the words "serious questions and difficulties," or however equivocal the position of any member of that committee on the question of slavery, there is no uncertainty nor equivocation in the action of June 1, on motion of J. J. Steadman of the Erie

Conference, which rescinded the resolution of 1840, that had declared slave-owners eligible tō the various offices of the ministry. The resolution on colored testimony having been rescinded four years previous- ly, the Church was now redeemed from the reproach of all that most objectionable legislation in the inter- est of slavery which was enacted at the Baltimore General Conference.

The absence of antislavery petitions at the General Conference in Pittsburgh was accepted by some as evidencing the close of the agitation in the Church on that subject. But subsequent facts so completely refute this assumption that another more satisfactory explanation is needed. Perhaps it may be given by the fact, that it was very generally believed for a long time, by the mass of the membership of the Church, that the separation of the South had wholly removed slavery from the Methodist Episcopal Church, or would do so by drawing all Methodist slave-holders within the communion of the Church South.

CHAPTER XIX.

CORRELATED ANTISLAVERY ACTION.

THE citizen is nowhere else so identified with the government, and so directly responsible for its action, as in the United States of America. And every Christian is bound, by " the two great commandments which require him to love God supremely, and his neighbor as himself, so to order all his individual and social and political acts as to render to God entire and absolute obedience, and to secure to all men the enjoyment of every natural right, as well as to promote the greatest happiness of each in the possession and exercise of such rights."—"*American Wesleyan Discipline*," *Articles of Religion, VII.* Slavery denied God's right to the supreme regard of every slave. It would destroy the slave man's right to himself. It assumed to veto the law of love. It made merchandise of his most sacred instincts, virtue being a salable quality; and reputation for piety being held at a premium, the price of a human soul was graded according to the measure of the Spirit of God dwelling therein. The horrible indictment needs no further extension to demonstrate that slavery embodied every element of hatred to humanity and of opposition to God. Toward such a system Christian duty and the responsibility of the citizen were exactly equal.

Christian duty, therefore, was recognized by many citizens as including such a use of political power as would eventually repeal all legislation in support of slavery by national authority. By the authority of the whole people the return of fugitive slaves had been guaranteed in 1793; slavery had been extended over free territory; the African slave-trade was connived at from 1808 onward; the slave-trade between the States was allowed; slavery and the slave-trade were practiced at the capital; and last, and not least, of all, the so-called "Omnibus Bill," in 1850, practically enacted the unlimited expansion of black slavery over the entire republic, and made slaves, virtually, of white citizens, so far as the compulsory service of catching and holding slaves might enslave freemen. The responsibility for all this was equally shared by all the citizens of all the States, both Northern and Southern. And furthermore, the slave laws of the respective slave States, and the black laws of many of the free States, added to the responsibility and burden of this great national crime.

The first efforts to perform duty in this direction were by discussion, conventions, and petition. Rev. George Bourne, a Presbyterian of Virginia, in 1809 freely canvassed this question, and published a book ten years afterward, in New York, which stirred up other agencies in later years. Elias Hicks, the dissenting Friend, published, in 1814, a work on African slavery, denying the right of property in slaves, and affirming Wesley's old doctrine as to the equal guilt of men-stealers and slave-holders. Benjamin Lundy, a member of Friends' meeting, formed in 1815 an antislavery organization—"The Union Humane Society"—which within a few months had nearly five hundred members, residents of several counties adjacent to Wheeling, Virginia. Numerous addresses on slavery were delivered by him in North Carolina, and twelve societies organized within three years, numbering three thousand members, comprising many persons of position and eminence.*

"The American Convention for the Abolition of Slavery" was held in Baltimore in the year 1826. Eighty-one societies were represented, seventy-three being located in slave-holding States. There were then one hundred and forty societies in existence, of which one hundred and six were in the Southern States. Mr. Lundy's influence brought that convention together. A County Convention, held in Ohio the next year, passed a resolution that its members would support no persons for office who were not opposed to slavery. Mr. Lundy then said of this action: "If the friends of genuine republicanism would act upon that principle a change for the better would soon be witnessed. The people of the free States guarantee the oppression of the colored man. Slavery is no States-rights matter. All the citizens of the republic are interested in its extinction, and if we ever abolish it the influence and government of the United States must effect it. The question of abolishing slavery, when it shall be acted on, must be settled by ballot."

William Lloyd Garrison, then a Calvinist Baptist and a strict sabbatarian, became identified with Mr. Lundy, a Quaker, in 1828, and entered upon his public antislavery career. He says: "Now if I have in any way, however humble, done any thing toward calling attention to slavery, or bringing about the glorious prospect of a complete jubilee in our country at

* This and several pages following are compiled mainly from Henry Wilson's "Slave Power," vol. i.

no distant day, I feel that I owe every thing in this matter, instrumentally and under God, to Benjamin Lundy." As early as 1834 Mr. Garrison advocated the organization of a Christian party in politics. Professor Follen suggested, two years later, a new progressive democratic party, of which the abolition of slavery should be a fundamental principle.

For several years, however, political action was limited to petitioning Congress in favor of antislavery enactments. The result, reached after much earnest effort and great expense, was the annual adoption, by the national House of Representatives, of a resolution which, in 1840, became a standing rule, that refused to receive or entertain any "petition, memorial, resolution, or any paper" on the subject of antislavery legislation. Then followed the plan of questioning candidates for public office and voting for the most friendly, whether Whig or Democrat. In 1838 William H. Seward, then candidate for Governor of New York, was largely supported by the Abolitionists on this ground. Millard Fillmore, then candidate for Congress in New York, and Caleb Cushing, a candidate for Congress in Massachusetts, were also supported for the same cause by antislavery men. But the action of Fillmore and Cushing did not correspond with their antislavery words when party interests were at stake.

The necessity for a more positive course of action was manifest to many Abolitionists. But now Mr. Garrison, Wendell Phillips, and their immediate followers deprecated the use of political action, and denounced those who favored the formation of a political antislavery party. The Convention held at Albany, in May, 1839, issued an address favoring

political action in general terms. A county convention was held at Rochester, New York, at which
Myron Holley led the way in securing the adoption
of a series of resolutions and an address enjoining
the duty of a distinct political organization. This
was followed by the action of the New York State
Antislavery Society, January, 1840, which issued a
call for a National Convention at Albany on the first
day of April ensuing, to discuss "the question of an
independent nomination of Abolition candidates for
President and Vice-president of the United States,
and, if thought expedient, to make such nominations
for the friends of freedom to support at the next
election." Much opposition existed. The State Societies for Massachusetts, Rhode Island, and Connecticut
unanimously condemned this movement as unauthorized, unnecessary, and premature. But the Convention assembled. Only six States were represented.
One hundred and twenty-one delegates were present.
Seventeen only came from outside of New York
State.*

Such names as Myron Holley, Alvan Stewart, Ger-
rit Smith, Henry B. Stanton, Luther Lee, Orange
Scott, Lewis Tappan, William Goodel, and Benjamin Shaw, to those who knew them, gave ample
guarantee of large will, strong purpose, and tireless
energy, well adapted to this beginning of a new
national departure from the old political landmarks.
Of these men the first-named was recognized as the
father of the LIBERTY PARTY. The second presided over
the Convention. One only, the fifth, is living, (1880.)
Three of them were ministers of the Methodist Episcopal Church, one of whom, Rev. Luther Lee, made

* Thus far Wilson's History is quoted.

the conclusive argument that decided the action of the Convention. The nominations were made. James Gillespie Birney, of Kentucky, and Thomas Earle, of Pennsylvania, were the candidates. The first was a Whig in politics, and while residing in Huntsville, Alabama, was Solicitor-General of the State and an elector on the Whig ticket in 1832. Then he was a slave-holder, and an elder in the Presbyterian Church. But he had returned to Kentucky in 1833, freed all his slaves, and become identified with the Abolitionists in 1834. For this the Supreme Court of Alabama expunged his name from the roll of its attorneys; the University of Alabama, of which he was a trustee, and several literary societies of that State, expelled him from their fellowship. In 1839 his father deceased, leaving him and an only sister a large property in land, money, and twenty slaves. The last-named were, by his request, set off to him. These he emancipated and provided with a comfortable settlement in a free State. (May's "Recollections of the Conflict.")

Mr. Earle, with whom the writer was personally intimate for years, was a member of Friends' meeting, an able lawyer, and had always acted with the Democratic party. But in the State convention for constitutional reform, of which he was the recognized author and originator, he stood almost alone in opposing "white suffrage" as the basis of representation. He thereby sacrificed all hopes of political preferment, but maintained firmly and constantly the doctrine of human rights, without distinction of color or race. Such were the men selected by the Liberty party when Abolitionists first entered the arena of politics.

Notwithstanding all these peculiar recommendations to the Christian citizens of the Union, and to the suffrage of antislavery men especially, and although in natural and acquired abilities both superior to the candidates of the other parties, they were not supported by thousands of voters whose cause they represented. Of two million and a half of votes cast at that election, Birney and Earle received less than seven thousand. The privilege of being one of that "seven thousand" who repudiated the Baal worship of America is among the pleasant memories of the writer. And the members of the Methodist Episcopal Church were perhaps more numerous than any other class in that band of political pioneers. Next in number were the Friends; thus fulfilling in part the prophecy of Judge Marshall, fifty years before, that the government would lose the support of the Quakers and Methodists if it supported slavery.

The feeble exhibition of Liberty party votes was largely ridiculed as a conclusive demonstration of the folly of "throwing away your votes" until after the next presidential election. Then Mr. Birney and Thomas Morris, of Ohio, received sixty-two thousand three hundred votes — an increase of nearly tenfold. The first balloting was a sowing of seed; not votes thrown away, but producing fruit in measures not to be scorned even by ambitious politicians; for the majority of the popular vote in 1844 was less than forty thousand for the Democratic candidate, and the Liberty party had that much strength and twenty thousand votes to spare, thus holding the balance of power in New York and Michigan and also in the nation. Especially was this true in the State of New York, whose electoral vote decided the election of

James K. Polk, by a majority much less than the Liberty party vote in that State.

During this period the Liberty party was able to elect a few members of the State Legislatures. These sometimes held the balance of power therein, and determined the choice of United States Senators. John P. Hale, of New Hampshire, in 1846, and Charles Sumner, of Massachusetts, in 1851, with Salmon P. Chase, of Ohio, in 1848, were thus chosen. The first was elected by a coalition with the Whig members, and the two latter by a union with the Democratic members of their Legislatures, respectively. These disturbances of political equilibriums were felt sensibly at preliminary meetings for nomination, so that in a brief period a new class of men were brought forward by the old parties, and both were represented in part, in Congress and elsewhere, by men who were outspoken and true to the cause of freedom.

In 1848 a large number of influential Democrats of New York repudiated the nomination of General Cass by their party, and called a convention at Buffalo. At the same time the Liberty party held a convention there. The two conventions united in adopting a platform of antislavery principles, and took the name Free Soil party. The candidates chosen were Martin Van Buren and Charles Francis Adams, for whom hundreds of thousands of votes were given. In New York alone they received over one hundred and twenty-one thousand votes, which was seven thousand more than General Cass received in that State. General Taylor received nearly twice as many votes as were given to Cass, in New York, and was elected President. The defection in the Democratic party was, however, speedily remedied by the reconciliation of the leaders, but many of the Democratic voters never returned to their old association. And the Free Soil party candidates in 1852, John P. Hale and George W. Julian, received nearly three times as many votes as Mr. Birney did in 1844. And in 1856 John C. Fremont and Julius F. Le Moyne received over half a million votes.

The adoption of the principles of the Free Soil party by the Whigs generally, shortly afterward, and the organization of the National Republican party from the material of both, secured a triumph over a divided Democracy in 1860, and made Abraham Lincoln — the great emancipator — President of the United States.

The attention and activity of the antislavery men in the Church was thus, for the years immediately following 1840, directed more and more to new and palpable issues made on the slavery question. Whether it was "always a sin," or "not a sin always," were questions less absorbing now that each white man faced the intensely interesting personal questions, "Am I a slave?" or " Am I not a slave?" To be, or not to be, a freeman—that was the question of the times. Whether all the Methodist slave-holders along the border had left the Methodist Episcopal Church voluntarily, or ought to be expelled therefrom, although grave and important matters for consideration, were less pressing than the question, Shall all the Methodists of the Southern borders, and through all the valleys of the West to the Pacific Ocean, and along the Atlantic coast to the Northern Lakes, be compelled to become slave - hunters and slave-holders both?

The small number of memorials at the General

Conferences of 1848 and 1852, therefore, or the infrequency of Annual Conference resolutions during the interval, were not so much evidences of indifference to slavery as evidence of a new direction given to antislavery zeal. An illustration is given by the action of the preachers of the Methodist Episcopal Churches in New York, Brooklyn, and Williamsburgh, at a meeting held November 9, 1850. A very able paper was prepared by Rev. Davis W. Clark, and adopted with enthusiastic unanimity. In this meeting the Fugitive Slave bill was declared at variance with the writ of habeas corpus and the right of trial by jury, and that it encouraged perjury by allowing the unquestioned assertion of the claimant of a slave ; and, also, further declared it to be inconsistent with the Declaration of Independence, the Constitution, and the objects of the Federal Union, besides being, worse than all, iniquitous and unrighteous in its provisions, and in flagrant violation of the divine fugitive law which was proclaimed three thousand three hundred years before. That ancient law reads thus : " Thou shalt not deliver unto his master the servant which is escaped from his master unto thee : he shall dwell with thee, even among you, in that place which he shall choose in one of thy gates, where it liketh him best : thou shalt not oppress him." Deut. xxiii, 15, 16.

Similar sentiments were proclaimed in hundreds of Methodist pulpits, including the " Wesleyan " and the " Protestant " as well as " Episcopal." But a unanimous voice in opposition to these declarations was heard from the Methodist Episcopal Church, South. And the law was declared by the editor of the Richmond " Christian Advocate " to be " not only wise, but eminently conservative, and forming now the strongest, and it may be the only, link in the golden chain that binds our national confederacy in glorious union." And such, moreover, were the sentiments of some Methodists at the North. And on these lines antagonist forces were arrayed in ecclesiastical and political organizations all through the North. At the South all were clamorous for obedience to the bill of 1850, and their pulpits and press, with much assurance, quoted St. Paul's exhortation, "Let every soul be subject to the higher powers: the powers that be are ordained of God;" and also Peter's admonition, "Submit yourselves to every ordinance of man for the Lord's sake."

And so the line of battle was removed from moral to political stand-points, but the warfare was waged more fiercely than ever. As the members and ministers of the Methodist Episcopal Church entered largely into this field of strife, it became essential to the object of this history to give one chapter on the correlated political action of the period noted.

CHAPTER XX.

THE GENERAL CONFERENCE OF 1852.

THE absorbing question at the Boston General Conference was lay delegation. That had a special committee and a patient and prolonged investigation. Slavery was referred to the Committee on Revisals, with every other question that proposed a change of the Discipline. Each had its subcommittee. The subcommittee on Slavery reported at the last meeting of the general committee, only three days before the adjournment of the Conference. The chairman presented that report on the morning of the adjournment, and called the Bishop's attention to it several times. But the pressure of unfinished business and the impatience and anxiety to adjourn prevented any consideration of or action upon it. Incidentally, slavery was briefly discussed on a proposition to form the Kentucky Annual Conference. That was the only opportunity afforded for any testimony against slavery.

Heman Bangs said: "What do you want to go there for? Have they not Methodist doctrine and Methodist discipline and Methodist institutions already? What do you want to go there for? If it is to preach against slavery, I have no objections to it; but if it is to get more of these miserable slaveholders into our Church, then I am opposed to it. Haven't we enough of them already?"—*Matlack's* "*Debates of General Conference of 1852.*"

John A. Collins said he was sorry that Mr. Bangs had made such remarks about "miserable slave-holders," because he believed that slave-holders were better off, better provided for, better taken care of, in the Methodist Episcopal Church than they would be anywhere else. And he would say, furthermore, that the servants held by Methodists were better cared for, and their condition in every sense better, than those held by any other class in the community. He could have no fellowship with the cant that had been uttered there about "these miserable slave-holders." No; he would bring them in and make them members of our body, and their servants too. It would make them better masters and better servants.

James Porter said he had listened to sentiments which he was persuaded were antimethodistic, and which would astonish this listening multitude by placing the Methodist Episcopal Church in a false light. To hear a member of this Conference say that he would have slave-holders drawn into the Church— that he would throw the arms of the Church around them for the reason that we can do them more good than others—to see the effort which the brother had made there to obtain fellowship and association with slave-holders, would be a source of astonishment to the people. Many here are not accustomed to regard slave-holders in any other light than as men-stealers, or slave-holding as any thing better than the sum of all villainies, and, of course, they could not consistently desire to throw their arms around the slave-holder. He repudiated that sentiment, and he believed that the General Conference repudiated it. They had slave-holders enough now. God forbid they should ever add one to the number!

Said Mr. Porter: "Those slave-holders who are in the Church were understood to be there by toleration rather than by right. It was matter of grievance, matter of profound regret, that there was one in the Church, and that our antislavery friends were under the necessity every four years of praying us to put a stop to slavery. They were retained in the Church only from the hope, presumed to be well grounded, that slavery was dying out, and that no slave-holders were among us, except a few who had fragments of old families left, to which they owed responsibilities and duties. Is it true that we are trying to tow others into our body? God forbid! We have had enough of them, and those who left us made us trouble enough, and I hope that we will try to add no more to our number. These are the sentiments of New England; and I believe I am not mistaken in saying these are the sentiments of the great West and of the Church at large." [Favorable responses were heard from New England men, but some Western men dissented at this point.]

Mr. Porter continued: "The Kentuckians are suspicious of us, it is said. They say we do not belong there, and that they must have a Conference of their own. What next? Why, we must admit slave-holders, for we shall be unpopular if we do not. What next? We must admit slave-holding ministers in the Church, or else we shall not be successful. What next? We must go the full length of the Church South, or we shall not be popular. Were we prepared to buy Methodists at such a price? He thought not. Do not let us compromise our principles by encroaching upon the territory of slavery, and succumbing to its terrible influence."

Mr. Porter's remarks produced great excitement in and out of the Conference, and fruitless efforts were made by leading Conservatives to induce a retraction or modification of his radical utterances.

This opposition did not prevent the organization of a Kentucky Conference, which was authorized by a vote of 77 yeas to 66 nays. Subsequently an Arkansas Conference also was organized. During the discussion on the boundaries of the latter, Rev. J. C. Houts, of the Missouri Conference, said: "It has been questioned on the floor of this Conference whether there was not a liability to yield to the prevailing influence of slavery and form an alliance with it." If he did not believe our Church was destined to exercise an antislavery influence, he would never raise his voice there again, he said. Their position was of the conservative antislavery character, which distinguished the Methodist Episcopal Church in its earlier days. "There were," he said, "two classes of slave-holders there. One received and held slaves from mercenary motives alone, making them work solely that they might accumulate money. This class was, strictly speaking, in a servile condition. The other was a class which received and held their slaves solely from the force of circumstances, whose servitude was of a domestic nature. The former affiliated with the pro-slavery party of the State, while the latter would gladly free their slaves if they could. Occasionally, members of this latter class were received into the Churches, the body of the membership, however, being those who do not hold slaves."

Mr. Houts informed the writer at the time that the membership of the Missouri Conference was then about eight thousand, of which number one in twenty were slave-holders, and that they admitted all the slave-holders that asked to unite with the Church, believing that the Discipline was on their side in the matter. But he said that "the slave-holders of a violent character do not ask to join us; they go with the Church South."

On the last day of the session of the General Conference John A. Collins informed the body that telegraphic dispatches and a long memorial had come to his hands from Baltimore, which related to the discussion of a few days previous. This discussion, he said, has produced great commotion in some sections of our work; and is destined to produce still greater excitement. Our people who have servants understand that they are in the Church, not by sufferance but by right; and Mr. Collins wished to have the opposite sentiment disavowed by the Conference. But the hurry and multiplicity of business prevented even a patient consideration of the matter.

Three days before, on May 29, Calvin Kingsley, who had led off in presenting the antislavery memorials, which many were persuaded would not be heard from, took the initiative for direct action by the Conference in offering a resolution providing for a change in the section on slavery, which was laid on the table for one day under the rule. It read as follows, answering the question, "What shall be done for the extirpation of the evil of slavery?"

1. We declare that we are as much as ever convinced of the great evil of slavery; therefore, no slave-holder shall be eligible to membership in our Church hereafter, where emancipation can be effected without injury to the slave.

2. There shall be a fund raised, called the Extirpation Fund, to be constituted by annual collections in all our con-

gregations where the people are willing to contribute; which fund shall be under the control of commissioners appointed by the General Conference, and shall be appropriated by them in assisting our brethren who may be connected with slavery to remove their slaves to a free State, if necessary, in order that they may enjoy freedom; and, also, in purchasing, for the purpose of freeing them, such slaves as it may be necessary to purchase to prevent severing family relations where a portion of the family may be set free by being removed to a free State, or otherwise; and also in rendering such other pecuniary assistance to our brethren, who are desirous of emancipating their slaves, as such commissioners, under the direction of the General Conference, may think necessary.

3. If there be cases where the emancipation of the slaves cannot be effected without manifest injury to the slave himself, our preachers shall prudently enforce upon all our members in such circumstances the necessity of teaching their slaves to read the word of God, and of allowing them time to attend upon the public worship of God on our regular days of divine service.

Professor Kingsley made an earnest effort on the last day of the Conference to bring up the question involved in his resolution for at least a brief consideration, but failed, although in possession of the floor, through the disorderly opposition of many loud remonstrants. He took his seat, evidently aggrieved, saying, with his peculiar expression of calmness and firmness combined, " Very well; you shall hear from this matter again elsewhere." This personal purpose was also a general prophecy of what was amply fulfilled in the early future.

The fact that the few antislavery memorials from Annual Conferences, district associations, and circuits were never heard from after being referred to the Committee on Revisals, very plainly indicated the small measure of antislavery interest in the com-

mittee; but it was not an index of the mind of the
Conference, nor of the Church generally.   The statements of Mr. Collins and Mr. Houts, when published,
deepened the conviction, newly awakened, that there
was an imperative demand for such change in the
General Rule and the section on slavery as should
prevent the admission of slave-holders into the
Church, and provide for the freedom of Methodist
slaves and many others who were held in slavery by
members of the Methodist Episcopal Church.   And
the adjournment of the eleventh General Conference
was the close of a period of denominational inaction
which had continued for eight years, but it marked
the opening of a new era in the antislavery movement in the Church which continued with ever-growing power up to the doomsday of slavery.

The facts connected with the report on the subject of
slavery at the Boston General Conference are given in
the "Northern Christian Advocate" of July, 1852,
(Letter of William Reddy.)   "The petitions and
memorials on the subject of slavery were referred to
a subcommittee on slavery.   No report was made by
that subcommittee until the Friday or Saturday
night before the adjournment of Conference, which
occurred on Tuesday.   At that last meeting of the
Committee on Revisals the report of the subcommittee on slavery was submitted.   Exceptions were
taken to it in some of its aspects, and the subcommittee were permitted to take back their report, to
conform it to some of the suggestions made.   It was
not again submitted to the large committee, but was
to be presented to the Conference with the modifications promised.   On Tuesday morning, the day of
final adjournment, I asked our chairman, Dr. George

Peck, if the slavery report was not to be presented.
He answered, Yes; he should not suffer any business
to take the place of the order of the day—presenting
of reports from standing committees. But the report
was not presented. The chairman laid that report on
the Bishop's table, and called his attention to it three
or four times. The Conference had requested the
Bishop to prepare a list of the most important items
of business, and he kept to the list he had previously
prepared. Thus the matter passed off. So the fer-
mentation must go on for the next four years. The
Church must endure the reproach that will be laid
upon her."

CHAPTER XXI.

IS ALL SLAVE-HOLDING SINFUL?

THE quadrennium following the Boston General Conference was distinguished by an unusually vigorous and extensive discussion of the character of slavery, or of the moral standing of the slave-holders. Dr. Bond, editor of the "Christian Advocate" at New York, while he antagonized the violent pro-slavery sentiments of the South, yet maintained the right of slave-holders to a place in the Church for the present, and therefore opposed all efforts to exclude or expel them. Dr. Elliott, of the "Western Christian Advocate" at Cincinnati, took the same position, and so also did Dr. Homer J. Clarke, editor of the "Pittsburgh Christian Advocate." These two papers were open, however, to a full discussion of the questions involved.

On the other hand, "Zion's Herald," Rev. D. Wise, editor; the "Northern Advocate," Rev. W. Hosmer, editor, and the "North-western Advocate," Rev. J. V. Watson, editor, were agreed in condemning the system of slavery, the traffic in slaves, and all slave-holding as well. Allowing as innocent the legal relation of slave-holder to any who had slaves bequeathed to them, or who might buy slaves to free them, these editors favored such a change in the Discipline as would prohibit all slave-holding for mercenary purposes. The conflicting views thus represented were the occasion of a controversy that called forth the

utmost strength of able correspondents and editors
as well.

Within a month after the adjournment of the General Conference Dr. Calvin Kingsley published in the
"Christian Advocate and Journal" the changes he
had proposed in the chapter on slavery, but had failed
to get fully before that body, with an elaborate argument accompanying them. These changes tolerated
slave-holding where "emancipation would be a manifest injury to the slave," and provided an extirpation
fund for purchasing slaves to free them. He, therefore, did not awaken any opposition from the conservatives in the Church. These views were partially indorsed, moreover, by Dr. Bond and Dr. H. J. Clarke,
editor of the "Pittsburgh Advocate," who both objected to making "injury to the slave" the sole consideration. They would associate "the interests of
the master," or qualify by the words "manifest injustice to the master."

Dr. Bond's view of the question, "Ought all slaveholders to be excluded from the Church?" are given
in brief, editorially, December 15, 1853. These sentiments controlled his action as the conductor of the
leading official organ of the Church, and were unchanged during his connection with that paper. He
says: "It is admitted that many of our members who
hold slaves cannot make them free, because the laws
under which they live do not allow emancipation and
residence in the State. To discharge from service, or
to renounce ownership, is, therefore, only to turn the
slave over to the sheriff to be sold at public auction,
with the certainty that the purchaser will be a merciless slave-trader; or, to remove them to a free State,
with or without their consent, which may involve the

separation of husband and wife, parents and children. In vain we plead that both the one and the other would be a violation of the law of God—the golden rule itself. The only answer is, 'Slavery is a sin under all circumstances, and the Church cannot tolerate sin.' But we deny the premises. Sin is a transgression of the law, and therefore a fulfillment of the law cannot be sin. If, then, the premises are false, the conclusion from them is necessary erroneous. Indeed, if we admit the premises, we accuse the apostles of our Lord of conniving at and tolerating sin; for nothing can be clearer from Scripture than that the emancipation of slaves was not made a condition of membership in the primitive Church, simply because it was impracticable under the laws of the Roman Empire. . . . Most of the slave States have copied the slavery code of heathen Rome, and prohibit emancipation, and hence our members who own slaves are placed under similar circumstances with those who professed Christ under the ministry of the apostles; and the practice of the first heralds of salvation shows that slave-holding is not sin under all circumstances, and therefore circumstances must now, as then, govern the action of the Church in regard to it."

The leading position in favor of excluding all slave-holders was occupied by the "Northern Christian Advocate." Mr. Hosmer, the editor, maintained with great energy the sentiment that Christianity is so utterly irreconcilable with slavery that neither the master nor the slave could be Christians. He said, August 4, 1852: "No Christian can, by any possibility, either be a slave or a slave-holder, in any proper sense of these words; . . . because no man can serve two masters—that is, two supreme masters. If the slave must obey man, whatever he may command, he cannot obey God ; . . . because no Christian can exercise unlimited control over another human being ; . . . because slavery is an unholy invasion of another's rights ; . . . because a Christian must love the colored man as himself. . . . But we go one step further, and affirm that a man cannot be a man, in any proper sense of the word, and be a slave. The same is true of the slave-holder. To be a slave is to sink below the order of humanity into that of brutes. The slave-holder descends not only below religion, but below all the more honorable principles of humanity."

All who favored the exclusion of slave-holders from the Church, whether editors or correspondents of other Methodist official papers, were designated "Hosmerites" by the New York "Christian Advocate." "The Hosmerite movement" was noticed and censured and deprecated as every way inimical to the interests of the Church and to the cause of religion by Dr. Bond, its editor. The controversy between the two editors occupied many columns and became severely personal. The doctor's personal published criticisms of the correspondents in Mr. Hosmer's paper provoked elaborate rejoinders in the " Northern Advocate," in which the critic received as many sharp words as he gave. Besides this the correspondents of Mr. Hosmer's paper furnished an able and exhaustive discussion of the whole subject of slavery and of the relation and duty of the Church on that question.

"Zion's Herald," of Boston, prior to 1852, had been edited by Rev. Abel Stevens, whose entrance upon that work in 1840 had been inaugurated under peculiar circumstances of embarrassment from the timidity of the Wesleyan Association on the slavery

question. A letter to Mr. Stevens, published in 1856
by him, from one of the directors, Dr. Snow, states:
"It was distinctly agreed between you and the directors of the Association, that the discussion of the
slavery question should be limited to correspondents,
and as much as possible curtailed. . . . Editorially the
paper was to occupy a neutral position so far as related to colonization and abolition. . . . It was true
the editor was not denied the privilege of expressing
a strong antislavery sentiment; but he was to take no
sides with the parties that then existed, except to discountenance ultraism, schism, and secession." But,
before Mr. Stevens was taken from that position by
the General Conference of 1852, the "Herald" had
been long recognized as among the prominent antislavery papers of the country.

The Rev. D. Wise succeeded Mr. Stevens, and, being a radical Abolitionist, made the "Herald" more
aggressive in its antislavery character, and advocated
the exclusion of all slave-holders from the Church.
Toward the editor of the "Herald," therefore, also,
the attention of Dr. Bond was directed, and he was
classed with Mr. Hosmer, whose "most ultra opinions" he is declared to have indorsed, the doctor
adding, "We had no doubt of the 'Herald's' position.
It has been explicitly given; and all that remained
was to consider that paper as enlisted in the crusade
against the peace and integrity of the Church."

The "North-western Christian Advocate" put
forth, as an "olive-branch to the Church," its position
on slavery thus: "Let no more holders of slaves be
admitted into the Church. While we contend for
this inhibition in the Discipline we are not to be understood as contending for its *ex post facto* action.

We speak of those who sustain the *relation* of slave-holders in the Church. We allude not to those who are slave-holders *con amore*, or for the love of the thing—for what it is in itself. The latter should at once be expelled the Church, while forbearance with the former is to be determined by circumstances. . . . The present position of Methodism in slave territory is just such as must forever deprive her of that social respect and popular confidence which it is contended are necessary to her success. At present, as respects slavery, she is a perfect *tertium quid*—neither hot nor cold—neither fish nor fowl. Claiming to be opposed to slavery, she invites and woos it to the protection of her altars. Denouncing slavery extirpationists, she points to her Discipline, which avows slavery extirpation to be one of the ends sought by Methodism. Denouncing her younger sister—the Church South—she wipes her lips and turns round and practices just as the Church South does."—*Editorial, July 5,* 1855.

Dr. Elliot freely criticised and condemned the utterances and the course of the "North-western," and vindicated opposite views with greater energy than logical consistency, having committed himself by the most radical and unqualified denunciations of slavery in two volumes published in 1850, which were used with great force in a reply by Professor W. L. Harris in the columns of the "Western," as also by his editorial antagonists, and others. But his consistent maintenance of the following proposition was unchallenged: "We propose to defend the Methodist Episcopal Church to the last, believing firmly that she has been always right on slavery, both theoretically and practically, as a whole, and we believe

she is now right in all material points." What the
position of the Church was in his opinion is thus set
forth : " The principle that the apostles admitted
legal slave-holders into the Church who repented of
their sins and forsook them—without countenancing
slavery—but rather to its subversion, is a leading
doctrine of the Methodist Episcopal Church, taught
by St. Paul, and on which our Discipline is based
since the origin of the Church in 1784."—*Editorial,
January* 23, 1856.

Dr. H. J. Clarke, of the "Pittsburgh Christian
Advocate," favored none of the changes proposed.
He said : "The actual relation of the Church to the
system of slavery is that authorized by the teachings
of the Gospel and the example of the primitive
Church. She condemns it, she opposes it, she toler-
ates its existence within her pale only in those cases
in which an entire exclusion of it would inflict additional injury upon its subjects."—*Editorial, September* 18, 1855.

Dr. John P. Durbin wrote on "Slavery and the
Church," affirming : "1. When the Apostolic Churches
arose they found slavery existing in the State. So,
also, when the Methodist Episcopal Church sprang up
in the midst of the people she found slavery existing
in the State. 2. In the Apostolic Churches masters
and slaves were converted and came into her bosom.
In like manner masters and slaves were converted
and came into the Methodist Episcopal Church.
3. Neither the Apostolic Churches nor the Methodist Episcopal Church made the mere relation of master and slave a bar to Church membership. 4. Both
claimed and exercised the right to enforce upon
masters and slaves, as such, their duties respectively,

considered as between themselves and between them and the Church. 5. In this Discipline it was clearly manifested that they disapproved of slavery as a condition of society and of the individual, and sought its extinction."—"*Christian Advocate*," *July* 26, 1855.

Dr. Durbin further indicated five particulars which should enter into the Discipline of the Church in regard to slavery within her bosom: 1. Recognize marriage between slaves as existing by the laws of God. 2. Recognize the relation of slave parents and children, and prevent their separation. 3. Require masters to provide religious instruction for their slaves. 4. Require masters to make reasonable provision for the physical wants of their slaves. 5. Forbid buying and selling slaves, except when the slave can be benefited." And he added: "If the Methodist Episcopal Church shall judge that the conditions of slavery in her communion call for further action, we respectfully commend what is written above for her candid consideration."

Subsequently, in the "Western Christian Advocate," (December 19, 1855,) Dr. Durbin vindicated the propositions first named very elaborately, by numerous quotations from the New Testament, touching masters and servants, with the expositions of the most learned commentators and scholars, in support of the view "that the apostles admitted slave-holders into the Church." Replies were made at length denying this affirmation by the editors of "Zion's Herald," the "Northern Advocate," and the "North-western Christian Advocate." Their ablest correspondents, also, made these propositions and arguments the text for an extended discussion on the negative side of this question.

The doctor's views were supported by the editors of the Christian Advocates at New York, Pittsburgh, and Cincinnati. Their columns were open also for opposite views, which were ably maintained. The controversy was prolonged and covered a wide field. The best scholars and writers were engaged in this discussion on each side. What the apostolic Churches allowed or disallowed had a direct bearing upon the issue, for or against a new rule or no rule on slavery. And the Annual Conferences were largely occupied near the close of the quadrennium with reports on slavery, and with the practical question, Who shall be our representatives in the General Conference of 1856?

The conflicting views entertained on the subject of slave-holding in the Methodist Episcopal Church, as represented by the action of the Annual Conferences, were supported by four parties: First, Those who were satisfied with the Discipline unchanged; Second, Those who were in favor of only a slight change; Third, Those who desired an important change of the chapter on slavery; Fourth, Those who were for a new rule, excluding slave-holders from the Church. The two last were most numerous.

Having failed to prevent the advance of antislavery sentiments in the Church, and finding that the ensuing General Conference would be made up largely of men in favor of change, the conservative element made a strong point of the peril to the unity of the Church on the "border" to prevent any change; and the Church, for the first time in its history, read words of deliberate counsel in favor of nullifying Church law in the columns of its leading newspaper: "We did intimate that if the next, or any subsequent

General Conference, should enact a rule of discipline excluding all slave-holders from the Church, whatever be their character or circumstances, it would become the duty of the border Conferences to disregard the rule."—" *Christian Advocate*," *Dr. Bond, editor.* "They must disobey the authority of the General Conference, and refuse to execute the rule."

CHAPTER XXII.

THE GENERAL CONFERENCE OF 1856.

THE four years preceding the session of this body, which was held in Indianapolis, had been occupied, as already noted, with a thorough discussion, through the official press and in the Annual Conferences, of the enormity of the evil of American slavery, the responsibility of the Church, and the duty of immediate action condemnatory of all slave-holding by its membership. Twenty-nine Annual Conferences, of thirty-eight, memorialized the General Conference of 1856 in favor of antislavery action; and the very large majority of antislavery delegates in that body, and the numerous memorials from all parts of the Church which they brought with them, expressed unequivocally the voice of the Church against slavery. The Secretary, Professor W. L. Harris, who was chosen on the first ballot, was the representative of the New-Rule party.

The Address of the Bishops stated that " in compliance with the request of the Troy, Erie, North Ohio, and Wisconsin Conferences, different resolutions asking a change in the General Rule on Slavery were laid before all the Annual Conferences for their concurrence. We believe no one of these resolutions received the constitutional majority of the members of the Annual Conferences. In view of this fact, the question may arise whether this body has authority to change the Discipline upon this subject so as to affect membership in the Church. We are aware that it is difficult to separate the consideration of the desirableness of any measure from its constitutionality, and especially where deep feeling on the subject may exist. Yet we think it to be our duty to express our strong doubts whether, in view of the restricted powers of a delegated General Conference, any measure equivalent to a change in the General Rules can be constitutionally adopted without the concurrence of the Annual Conferences. As to the propriety of any modifications, not of such a character as to conflict with the constitutional economy of the Church, while opinions and views may be various, we can fully confide in the wisdom of this General Conference as the supreme council of the Church.

"In our administration in the territory where slavery exists we have been careful not to transcend in any instance or in any respect what we understood to be the will and direction of the General Conference. That body having retained its jurisdiction over Conferences previously existing in such territory, and having directed the organization of additional Conferences, it became our duty to arrange the districts, circuits, and stations, and to superintend them as an integral part of the Church. As the result, we have six Annual Conferences which are wholly or in part in slave territory. These Conferences have a white Church membership, including probationers, of more than 143,000; with the attendants upon our ministry making a probable population of between 500,000 and 600,000. They have a colored membership, including probationers, of more than 28,000, with the attendants upon our ministry making a probable population of upward of 100,000. A portion of this population are slaves; the others are mostly poor. They are generally strongly attached to the Church of their choice, and look to it confidingly for ministerial services, religious sympathy, and all the offices of Christian kindness. The white membership in these Conferences, in respect to intelligence, piety, and attachment to Methodist discipline and economy, will compare favorably with other portions of the Church. In our judgment the existence of these Conferences and Churches does not tend to extend or perpetuate slavery."

A committee on slavery had been appointed on the first day of the session, on the motion, first, of James Porter, of New England, who accepted a substitute providing for several other committees, each consisting of thirty-eight members. The Bishops' statements, above quoted, were referred to the Committee on Slavery, with all memorials, resolutions, and Conference action thereon. And this committee occupied several weeks in discussion before agreeing upon a report, which marked attention was a confession of the strange indifference of the two preceding General Conferences. And their report recommended for adoption the following resolutions:

1. That we recommend the Annual Conferences so to amend our General Rule on Slavery as to read: "The buying, selling, or holding a human being as property."

2. That the following be, and hereby is, substituted in the place of the present Seventh Chapter of our Book of Discipline, to wit:

What shall be done for the extirpation of the evil of slavery?

Answer 1. We declare we are as much as ever convinced of the great evil of slavery. We believe that all men by nature have an equal right to freedom, and that no man has a moral right to hold a fellow-being as property. Therefore, no slave-holder shall be eligible to membership in our Church here-after where emancipation can be effected without injury to the slave. But, inasmuch as persons may be brought into the legal relations of slave-holders, voluntarily or involuntarily, by purchasing slaves in order to free them; therefore, the merely legal relation shall not be considered, of itself, suffi-cient to exclude a person who may thus sustain it from the fellowship of the Church.

Answer 2. Whenever a member of our Church by any means becomes the owner of a slave, it shall be the duty of the preacher in charge to call together a committee, of at least three members, who shall investigate the case, and determine the time in which such slave shall be free; and on his refusal or neglect to abide by the decision of said committee, he shall be dealt with as in case of immorality.

Answer 3. It shall be the duty of all our members and pro-bationers who may sustain the legal relation of slave-holder, to teach their servants to read the word of God; to allow them to attend the public worship of God on our regular days of divine service; to protect them in the observance of the duties of the conjugal and parental relations; to give them such compensation for their services as may, under the cir-cumstances, be just and equal; to make such provisions as may be legally practicable to prevent them and their posterity from passing into perpetual slavery, and to treat them in all respects as required by the law of love.

Answer 4. It shall be the duty of our preachers prudently to enforce the above rules.

All of which is respectfully submitted.

M. RAYMOND, *Chairman.*

A minority report was presented by John A. Col-lins, as chairman, which embodied an argument against the majority report, and which concluded briefly: "*Resolved*, That we non-concur in the action of the majority." The majority and minority reports were supported, respectively, by seventeen and six-teen members of the committee.

Two days after the first report was presented the discussion was commenced, (May 23,) and continued several days, ending May 29. It was a memorable debate. The advocates of the majority report were some of the ablest ministers of the Church, who met their equals, of the minority, in the first great anti-slavery contest on the General Conference floor. The relation of that debate to the ultimate extirpation of slavery from the Church made it historic. The authorized report of the speeches constitutes the basis of the record here made. Being in attendance as a reporter the writer can vouch for their faithfulness, and quotes therefrom largely, because thus authenticated.

Mr. Raymond, of New England Conference, said:

When I consider the character of the body here assembled, ministers of the Lord Jesus Christ—men who are renewed by the Holy Ghost, called to preach the everlasting Gospel to perishing millions — by consecration devoted to that work, with an eye single to the glory of God, and drawing all the motives for their action from the retributions of eternity; and when I consider the nature of the business which now engages us, that of legislating for the Church of God, which is organized in all its arrangements to this intent that now "unto principalities and powers," etc., might be known to the Church the manifold wisdom of God; when, also, I consider the results of our discussions — results connected with the temporal and eternal happiness of the flocks committed to our care — results to our children and children's children through all time to come — results that no finite mind can anticipate, I cannot allow myself for a moment to believe that any other than the one question will be permitted to engage the attention of any one of us in the discussion of any matter that shall come before us.

In the discussion of this question the character of the men comprising this body, the nature of the work in which we are engaged, and the inconceivable results of our action, force upon me the conviction that but one question will be considered, but one principle will influence us. That one question decided, all others are decided, and that one question is, Are the measures proposed in this report *right?*

I cannot believe for a moment that any one of these men will allow himself to give attention to any other than this one question, Is the measure right? Is it just and equal? Is it well-pleasing in the sight of God? This question never pressed on my own consciousness of obligation as it does on this blessed, bright morning! Never has my position, as a being responsible at the bar of God and a candidate for eternity, made a deeper impression upon me of the importance of having a single eye to the truth and glory of God!

The question is, Are the doctrines of this report true? Its doctrines are two. First, that the reduction of a human being to the condition of property is wrong; and, secondly, that individuals may be connected with the system innocently, and even virtuously; that men may purchase and hold slaves for benevolent purposes, and may claim in doing so the fulfillment of that promise that a cup of cold water given in the name of a disciple shall not lose its reward.

We recur to the question, Are these doctrines true? Is slavery in this sense wrong? May a man own a slave in this sense, and be an innocent man?

The only consistent opponents to this report are of two classes — those who hold slavery to be right, to be a divine institution, founded on the philosophy of society, sanctioned by the Bible, a thing for which we should be thankful to God. Those who hold this view must conscientiously oppose our report. On the other hand, the report is consistently opposed only by those who hold that the relation cannot innocently exist under any circumstances. But, in the language of the report, no such doctrine is taught, no such design is apparent. No such position has been taken by our Discipline in the history of Methodism. If the measures proposed in the report indicate such a sentiment, I have been unable to understand it.

The measures proposed are in perfect parallelism to the doctrines I have stated. If I supposed they were not, I would be willing to stay here twelve months and discuss them. I never would make the door of the Church narrower than the gate to heaven. I do believe Christian men, children of God and heirs of glory, may innocently sustain the relation. These are the doctrines of the Church, if we understand language. In the minority report the only points raised are not those of the rightfulness or otherwise, but of expediency.

What a contrast is here presented between the moral sublimity of the subject and the argument! A question of personal liberty, involving the moral and eternal interests of millions created in the image of God, purchased by the blood of the incarnate Deity, moved upon by the Holy Ghost, capable of the highest glory; on such a question men descend from considerations of righteousness and truth to discuss questions of expediency. On what times have we fallen, in what an age, when we, the strongest Church in the world, followers of Him who was spit upon, scourged, derided, whose disciples in other ages wandered about in sheepskins and goatskins, who subdued kingdoms, wrought righteousness, stopped the mouths of lions, quenched the violence of fire, of whom the world was not worthy; that we, their followers, should descend from the sublimity of this question of truth and righteousness to deliberate on the questions of expediency!

It is said the provisions of this chapter are in conflict with the General Rule, and that to adopt this chapter or to do any thing at all will close up all access to the slaves. The questions are those of constitutionality and usefulness.

For the sake of the argument, let it be admitted that the chapter proposed is unconstitutional. Then remember it is not denied that the doctrines of this report are true and its measures right. It is right, but not constitutional. Shall we, therefore, reject that which is right because unconstitutional ? Is this good logic ? Is it not a *non sequitur ?*

Those who raise the question of the unconstitutionality of the new chapter proposed are bound to put their hands to the removal of the constitutional difficulty. The doctrines of the report being true, admitting that the chapter may not be constitutionally adopted, what is the inference ? It is that every good man should put his hand and his heart to the removal

of the constitutional difficulty, should let it go to the Annual
Conferences, and thus remove the constitutional difficulty of
doing what we believe is *right*.

We admit the unconstitutionality of the chapter only for
the sake of the argument. We deny that it is so. It does
not contain a new term of membership. It recognizes slave-
holding as in the Church. In nearly every passage of the
chapter proposed it is contemplated that persons may sustain
the relation for purposes that are laudable. I beg attention
to the fact that in the chapter, from Alpha to Omega, every
provision but one, which I do not wish to leave out, does con-
template the existence of slavery among members, even
among probationers, in the Church. It cannot be made out
by any fair argument, by any reasonable construction of the
chapter proposed, that non-slaveholding is, in all cases, a bar
to Church membership. It simply indicates that mercenary
slave-holding is sinful, and ought to be subjected to Church
discipline.

Mr. Coombe, of Philadelphia Conference, said:

I wish to say to Dr. Raymond that the simple question with
me is, Is this action proposed by the majority right? My
conclusion is, it is wrong. My conclusion is drawn from the
report, and from the report alone. The report proves two
things. First, that this General Conference has no power to
make the change proposed; secondly, the report shows as
clear as sunlight that if it had the power there is no necessity
to make the change. So whether it has or has not the power,
it would be wrong to make that change, seeing there is no
necessity for it. Now I proceed to prove these two propositions. That it has no power: I want to call your attention
to this report, for from this alone I draw my argument.

This report was written and adopted by Northern antislavery men. I say this to distinguish them from Southern
antislavery men. And those who have written and presented
this report desire a change in our Discipline. Now, what
their report teaches they ought to be willing to abide by.
What does the report admit? First, that this General Conference has no power to alter the General Rule. Not only is

this admitted, but this report asks that we recommend the Annual Conferences to change this rule. If the General Conference had the power it would not ask the Annual Conferences to do it. If this General Conference has no power to change the *rule*, it has no power to do the same thing in the chapter.

This report admits that it has no power to change the rule, and therefore it has no power to do it in any other part of the book. I want to ask the friends of that report if this new rule were in the book what explanation would the advocates of this report give to that new rule ? This question has not been touched. The explanation would be precisely the same that is contained in this new chapter, and no other.

This report declares that the relation may exist innocently; that the merely legal relation shall not prevent persons from Church membership. Therefore, if this new rule were in the book it would do no more than is proposed to be done in this chapter. As Dr. Raymond has well and beautifully argued here, they would not propose to exclude the innocent. Now, then, I ask you to go back. Suppose this new rule was in the book, and we were acting under it, would the chapter proposed give any higher expression or greater force to that rule ? The exposition of that new rule, which they admit they have not the power to put in, would be the same explanation they give it in this new chapter. Now, if that new rule would authorize no more or higher action, but the same that this chapter proposes, and they have not power to change the rule, have they the power to put in the new chapter ? But they say they have not the power to change the rule so as to punish the guilty and protect the innocent.

Again, this report, according to its own showing—and I am judging them by their own document—proves conclusively and clearly that if the General Conference had the power there is no necessity for its exercise, because every claim they make is met.

1. The new chapter is not necessary to change the position of the Church.

That report teaches that the Methodist Episcopal Church has, in good faith, in all the periods of its history, proposed to itself the question, " What shall be done for the extirpation of slavery?" and it has never ceased, openly and before the world, to bear its testimony against the sin, and to exercise its disciplinary powers to the end that its members might be kept unspotted from criminal connection with the system, and that the evil itself be removed from among men.

The report says the Methodist Episcopal Church has ever maintained an unmistakable antislavery position. If this is so, where is the necessity of any change in any part of our Discipline? Our brethren of the majority must either annul their report or abandon the proposed change. I call your attention to the peculiarly strong language used by the chairman of the committee on the floor and in this house. The chairman knows the use of language. The Methodist Episcopal Church ever—ever what? maintained—maintained *what?* an unmistakable antislavery position. Can any thing be stronger than that? and that position was antislavery.

2. This report proves that there is no necessity of any change in the Discipline to change the doctrines of the Methodist Episcopal Church. That Church has ever proposed to itself the question, "What shall be done," etc.

Here, then, is the testimony of our Northern antislavery friends—intelligent men, men of God, men of piety, men of honesty—who went into the investigation of this subject to come out and tell us that the doctrine of this Church is sound and scriptural; and if this is so, in the name of God, of humanity, where is•the propriety of changing what is sound, scriptural? Is it right to change what is right?

3. There is no necessity of changing the Discipline on slavery to change the *influence* of the Church. What does the report say? "It is affirmed and believed that the Methodist Episcopal Church has done more to diffuse the antislavery sentiment, to mitigate the evils of the system, and to abolish the institution from civil society than any other organization, either political, social, or religious." Why, sir, when I read that I had liked to have said, Glory to God! It was such an indorsement of our course by our Northern antislavery brethren.

If that is the position; if we have stood high, head and shoulders, above all other organizations in diffusing antislavery sentiments, and to abolish the institution from civil society, in the name of humanity why do any thing to jeopardize even that tremendous instrumentality ?

4. The report proves that there is no necessity of changing the Discipline to change the practice and action of the Church on slavery. "It is also affirmed and believed that the administrators of Discipline in our Church, within the bound of slave territory, have faithfully done all that, under their circumstances, they have conscientiously judged to be in their power *to answer the ends of the Discipline in terminating that great evil.*"

Now, here is testimony to the practice and action of the Church; not in non-slave-holding territory, not in the North, not in the East, where the evil does not exist, but in slave territory. Now these points are sustained by the testimony of our brethren themselves. I ask, then, in the name of humanity, what more can they ask or desire ? These brethren say that we have not only done *well*, but have faithfully done all that could be done to carry out the views of the majority report, and to ensure the end of the Discipline—the extermination of this great evil. If they had said " enter thou into the joys of thy Lord," it had been happy; but they come up and say " Well done," and then, instead of saying "enter thou into the joys of thy Lord," they send us back to the South, and take away our only means of doing the great work assigned us.

Let us review this argument. First, from the report, we learn that the position of the Church is unmistakably anti-slavery, her doctrines are plain and sound, her influence wholesome and strong, and that her discipline has been faithfully administered in slave-holding territory. Now, sir, if that is the opinion of these brethren, I ask again, What more do they want ? I ask them to stay their hands. If it is not necessary, then, from this showing, is it not wrong to attempt this change ? It is not a question of expediency, but of right and wrong. If the brethren of the majority will let us alone we will go on breaking the chains of the oppressed; but if they chain us we can unchain no one else.

Hiram Mattison, of the Black River Conference, said :

I am in favor of the report of the majority as it is, and cannot see the force of the objections urged against it by the last speaker. If I understand him it is this: The report admits that the Church has all along borne a testimony against slavery quite as strong as this proposed new chapter, and that this new chapter is wholly unnecessary. This argument will apply both ways. If the assumption of the report is false, then further expression may be necessary, and Brother Coomb's argument falls to the ground; but if, on the other hand, the assumption of the report is true, as I firmly believe, then the proposed new chapter is perfectly in harmony with the testimony of the Church against slavery from first to last, and cannot, therefore, be unconstitutional.

This is my position: that the General Rule on slavery was designed to shut all slave-holding out of the Church, and that, consequently, the proposed new chapter is not in conflict with, and does not go beyond, the General Rule, but is in perfect harmony with it.

That the paragraph relating to slavery in the General Rules was put there to prohibit the admission of slave-holders into the Church is evident from the circumstances of its introduction into the General Rules and from the whole history of our Church, so far as this slavery is concerned, from first to last.

Which history the speaker quoted, as we have it already noted in former chapters. He then said:

In 1808 provision was made for a delegated General Conference to be held in 1812; and in defining the power of the General Conference it was said, "They shall not revoke or change the General Rules of the United Societies." So the restriction has stood ever since; and now it is argued that to restore the chapter on slavery, so far as to prohibit the future admission of slave-holders into the Church, is to change the General Rule; and, therefore, we cannot do it without a vote of two thirds of the General Conference and three fourths of all the Annual Conferences!

But has not that chapter been altered by the General Conference so as to nullify the General Rule, even since the

restrictive rule was adopted ? In 1812 the following alteration was made: "Whereas the laws of some of the States do
not admit the emancipation of slaves without a special act
of the Legislature, the General Conference authorizes each Annual Conference to form their own regulations relative to
buying and selling slaves."—"*History of the Discipline*," p. 278.

Here "the laws of the States"—slave States—are installed
in place of God's word; and even the "buying and selling
of slaves" is taken from under the operation of the General
Rule forbidding them, and handed over to the Conferences in
slave-holding territory.   Was not this virtually changing the
General Rule ? And was this proposed change sent around
to the Annual Conferences ? No, indeed.   And the modern
cry of "unconstitutionality," first uttered here, I am sorry to
say, by our venerated, beloved Bishops, was not then heard
of.   It was all well enough when the legislation looked toward the widening of the door of the Church for the ingath-
ering of slave-holders, but the moment the slightest modification is proposed, looking for the elevation of the antislavery
standard of our Church to where it stood in the beginning,
we are to be frightened out of our wits by the cry of "unconstitutionality." This very chapter has been altered four times
since the restrictive rule became fundamental law with us; by
one of these changes the terms of membership in the Church
were changed from non-slaveholding according to the General Rule, and the chapter itself, to whatever an Annual Conference in slave territory might determine.   In 1816 the General
Rule was made to merely prohibit slave-holders from holding
office in the Church; and in 1820 the rule which allowed Annual Conferences to legislate upon the subject was stricken
out.   It remained just long enough, and, I think, purposely,
to fill the Church with slave-holders.   In 1824 the last four
paragraphs of the chapter were added.   "*History of the
Discipline*," p. 27.

Thus we have had this chapter modified four times, under
the same general rule and restrictive rule that now exist,
but now we are warned not to touch it, lest we violate the
"Constitution!"

There was no word of remonstrance from the bench of
Bishops against the change as unconstitutional.   The fa-

thers, sir, have been backsliding on this question from the first prohibition.

I conclude by re-affirming what I think I have proved—that the General Rules are both antislavery and prohibitory; that therefore all tampering with this chapter for the last forty years, to lower its antislavery tone, has been in violation of the General Rule, and unconstitutional ; while the section proposed in the report is in perfect harmony with the General Rule, and perfectly constitutional. Let us adopt it, then, as it is, and forever prohibit what is admitted on all hands to be sinful slave-holding from the Methodist Episcopal Church.

George R. Crooks, Philadelphia Conference, submitted, that in this discussion we have on one side facts, and on the other side theories ; on the one side abstractions, on the other constitutional realities ; on the one side the vagaries of ultraism, on the other side the matured opinions and experience of the fathers. He then reviewed Mr. Mattison's quotations in the light of other portions of their sayings and doings. He said that while it was true that the fathers did promulgate theories akin to those now entertained, it was equally true that, after testing their theories by the stern realities of fact, they found that the widely-opening doors that had met them everywhere in the South were closed one after another. And they had wisely receded from their impracticable schemes. They chose to give prominence to the salvation of the souls of men, and make the amelioration of their social condition a subordinate matter. To all the constructions by which the Discipline was made to prohibit all slave-holding, Mr. Crooks said : "The fathers understood the English language, and if they meant that they would have said that. But they had not said that, and therefore they did not mean that."

A glowing eulogy was passed upon Asbury and the fathers. The intimation that they had backslidden in their testimonies was repudiated with great feeling and some indignation. After various comments upon quotations from Asbury's "Journal," Mr. Crooks closed with one of special interest, the last words of which were: "What is the personal liberty of the African, which he may abuse, to the salvation of his soul? How may it be compared?"

Gordon Battelle, of Virginia, said:

This body is not invested with the power to legislate upon and settle great questions of a purely civil and national import. For one, I am here, a plain Methodist preacher, as a member of this General Conference, to aid, to the extent of my feeble powers, in making rules and regulations, not for the nation, but for the Methodist Episcopal Church. In the opening of this debate the real question for determination was fairly stated to be: Are the measures proposed in the report of the majority of the Committee on Slavery right? There is one source only to which we can look for authoritative decisions on all questions relating to the proper tests of membership; and that is the New Testament. Without arguing the point Mr. Batelle assumed, further, that slaves and slave-holders were both admitted to the apostolic Churches. There is not, said he, in the New Testament, one verse, line, or word even, that imposes any such obligation or test like that which this new chapter seeks to establish. The New Testament establishes no restriction at all with regard to the admission of slave-holders into the Christian Church. And no such restriction had ever been established by Wesley nor the English Wesleyans; and it is entirely opposed to the fundamental law of the Methodist Episcopal Church.

I am opposed to the measures of this report as practically inaugurating a new and restricted commission for the Church, unauthorized by the only Head of the Church. They tend virtually to seal up that message, so far as our publication of it is concerned, in reference to sections and Conferences of the Church; even where, as is the fact in my own Conference, the proportion of those in the Church connected with slavery, is, to those who are not, scarcely as one to five hundred. I object further, that this restricted message, if it ever reach the master or slave at all, offers him salvation, not now, but some time hence, when certain technical processes are pondered and consummated; it may be a year, or ten years— when, in short, it may be forever too late.

Brethren ask us, Why not take a step in advance? I answer, We are now standing on the only solid foundation. The right to go one step beyond it implies the right to go any length in any direction. Here is firm ground; "all else is sea besides." Our people who are not here to-day have confidence in our abiding by the safeguards to a precipitate action, which we ourselves have long since pledged to them.

Israel Chamberlayne, of Genesee Conference, said:

Slavery can never regenerate itself. Its native tendencies are all in the opposite direction. The truth of this assumption appeared in a rapid survey of its general history. But of slavery in the Church—for, unhappily, slavery in the Church has its history also; not Abrahamic and Jewish slavery, but, as is pleaded, Gospel slavery; not post-apostolic, but co-apostolic; not patristic, nor mediæval, nor papal, but Wesleyan —Wesleyanly Methodistic—Episcopally Methodistic slavery ; you must have noticed, sir, that our contestants for apostolic slavery apologize for it on the ground that, being underlaid with the principles of equity and love, it was expected that those principles would soon obliterate it by obliterating the distinction between the master and the slave; and that, until that result was reached, the former, as well as the latter, was admitted to the Church, that its meliorating associations, by making the master a better man, might prepare a better master for the slave.

Supposing so much of this assumption to be true as regards the idea that the principles of the Gospel were expected by the apostles to operate the gradual, if not the speedy, extirpation of slavery, I shall only express our common regret that, according to these annalists of slavery in the Church, the apostles' expectation has never yet been realized —not quite. But Methodism is now its antagonist. Methodism,

which is not particularly displeased by being considered the
purest, most just, most benevolent, and the mightiest of all
post-apostolic organizations — this is the power by which
slavery was grappled seventy-six years ago. Moved by the
utter abhorrence of slave-holding, so freely uttered by their
founder, the first Methodist preachers went straight to the
conscience of the oppressor with—"Thus saith the Lord, Let
my people go." Slavery—I speak of it as then existing in
our Societies—slavery, having some conscience then, and
writhing and alarmed by the energetic utterances of these
men of God, half-relaxed her grasp upon her victims, and
only pleaded that time might be allowed her to consummate
her repentant purposes, by preparing the exodus of her sable
captives.

In her next phase she appears to have half-repented of her
partial repentance, and repulsed the message of emancipation
with—"Why do ye," fanatical intermeddlers, "let the people
from their work ?" till at length, waxing bold in her impiety,
and emulating the audacity of her Egyptian prototype, she
puts down her queenly foot as a final period to all negotia-
tion on the subject, by virtually saying, "I know not the
Lord ; neither will I let the people go." Then it was that
the voice which pealed upon the ear of Freeborn Garrettson
—the voice which cried, "Let the oppressed go free!"—the
voice which pursued him till his last vassal was emancipated—
then it was, I say, that that voice began to die away upon the
ear of the Methodist slave-holding conscience. True, we have
been saying our Catechism on the "extirpation" of slavery
from that day to this; and it must be admitted that some of
us who were at a safe distance have not only said it according to the book, but have, now and then, edified each other
and eased ourselves of some pent-up indignation by impro-
vising some hard epithets which were not in the book. But
what answer can we give as to what else we have done ?
Shall we point to the existing separation between us and a
half million of slave-holding Methodists in the South ? To
this candor demands we should admit that it came without
our choice, and that it was submitted to as a great calamity,
and with many a fraternal pang.

And it must be further admitted, that, while the Southern

secession has expunged the chapter on slavery, and declared that the General Rule is innocent of any hostility to such common slavery practices as do not involve the outlawed African slave-trade—and while buying, selling, and holding human beings as chattels is perfectly free, as well to every grade of her ministry (including Bishops) as to her private members—it must be further admitted, I say, that while this is the case, there is not wanting, on both sides of the line, a confraternal feeling, not only inducing the interchange of kindly social offices—an object greatly to be desired—but also of mutual recognition in acts of public worship, in sacraments and ordinances, at the altar and in the pulpit, by our laymen and by our ministers.

That we can claim no merit for the sloughing off the Southern slaveryism, other than inflexibly maintaining the inexpediency—not the sin, but the mere inexpediency—of episcopal complicity with it, is further obvious from the fact, not that our Methodism, with John Wesley's ideas of it and the ideas of our cis-Atlantic fathers, has been carried into slave territory, and established and extended there; but from the fact that it is there as much a slave-holding Methodism, so far as private membership is concerned, as the Methodist Episcopal Church, South. And it is obvious from the further fact, that it is not only there as a receptacle for those who live on compelled and unrequited labor, in violation of natural justice and the word of God, but that it is in course of extension, by building churches, organizing circuits and districts and conferences and missions ; and that moneys collected for the general missionary purposes are appropriated, in part, for this purpose—the maintenance and extension of a status which invites to our communion those who hold in cattlehood their own blood, their own brethren! These references to slavery, its developments and operations in our country and in our Church, will at least suffice to show that slavery, because it is intrinsically evil, can never exhibit and never has exhibited, any tendency to self-correction—self-extirpation. On the contrary, as the above references show, the whole history of slavery, whether in Church or State, presents it as the antagonist to all that is sacred in natural justice and the inalienable rights of man; to all that is sa-

cred in the relations of husband and wife, parents and children; to all that is distinctive in ethical Christianity and
Methodism, from "the most execrable villainy that ever saw
the sun." And it not only exhibits these points of antagonism to natural justice and human rights and preceptive
Christianity, but in the nature of things, as well as in point
of fact, it has been, is, and ever must be, actively aggressive
upon all these interests. So that the question now forced
upon us, as to what shall be done—not what shall be *said*,
merely, but as to what shall be done—for the extirpation of
slavery, is a question which appeals directly to the instincts
of self-preservation. For he must be a dull interpreter of
history and the signs of the times who does not see that if
freedom does not extirpate slavery, slavery will extirpate
freedom; that if Methodism does not extirpate it, it will extirpate Methodism; and, finally, that if we do not extirpate
slavery, slavery will extirpate us.

Sir, we are admonished to "*let well enough alone*." But we
must decline this advice, because, for the life of us, we cannot
agree that slave-holding, especially the everlasting influx of
it into the Church, *is* quite well enough.

And now for a few words more immediately to the report before us. I am in favor of it: 1. Not because it
contains so little of what we believe ourselves entitled to
claim, but because it contains any thing; not because it
waives so much that is material to our principles and
aims, but simply because it does involve the principle of prohibition. .

I am in favor of it: 2. Because this prospective prohibition
is covered by the ægis of undisputed precedent. The fourth
restriction is, "*that they*"—the General Conference—"*shall
not revoke or change the General Rules;*" that is, they shall not
strike out or change the *sense* of either of those rules. Neither
of these two things is contemplated in this report so far as
relates to the chapter on slavery. But the General Conference has ever held, and on various occasions exercised,
the right of interpreting and constructing these same General
Rules. They have this right, and exercised it in 1836 and
1840, by making baptism and a correct faith conditions of
membership.

By way of corollary he added :

1. The General Conference ought to have the right of declaring the true construction of the General Rules.

2. That right involves the right of correcting a defective or false construction.

3. It has that right.

4. It has exercised that right.

5. It has exercised it freely and repeatedly.

6. It has exercised it in cases, one at least, exactly analogous to that in which this report proposes its exercise.

I conclude by remarking: That, for the mere exercise of such a right of construction as does not disfranchise our existing membership, nor abridge any of their chartered or just rights, this General Conference is amenable to no earthly tribunal whatever. And that, as to those who, claiming and exercising the right of property in their fellow-men, propose themselves as members of our Church hereafter, they cannot justly complain of the action proposed by this report as violative of their rights, for the simple reason that they have no such rights.

CHAPTER XXIII.

DEBATE ON SLAVERY—CONTINUED.

DURING the debate able speeches were made in favor of antislavery action by C. N. Smith, of New Hampshire; J. Dodge, of East Genesee; William Reddy, of Oneida; and W. C. Hoyt, of New York East; and also speeches against any action by J. Drummond, of Western Virginia, and G. W. Walker, of Cincinnati, which have been omitted only because of the space they would occupy, and because not necessary to a complete exhibit of the main line of arguments *pro* and *con*.

Dr. Edward Thomson, of North Ohio, said:

I am very happy that this discussion has commenced, and hope it will continue until every brother shall have had an opportunity to be heard. I hope it will be conducted in a spirit of charity. Any person may become charitable on this subject if he will exercise a little patient thought. Take the map: on a certain latitude men are pro-slavery, on another antislavery, and those between the two are conservative. The reason is, man is frail, and the circumstances around him influence him. The question before us is twofold. First, Ought slave-holding to be tolerated? And, secondly, Is the plan in the report the proper plan? When I say slave-holding, I do not mean ante-apostolic, apostolic, or post-apostolic slave-holding, but slave-holding in 'fifty-six in these United States. When I speak of the theater, I do not speak of the theater set up by Gregory Nazianzen, but as it exists in these United States, with its associations and tendencies. And when I speak of slave-holding, I speak of it as our own and nothing else. Let me abridge the argument by making con-

cessions. Concede, for the sake of the argument, that the
negro is an inferior variety of the race; that in his native
home he is a degraded, wretched being; that in his bondage in
the United States his is a condition of comfort; that there
are no three millions and a half of colored persons better
housed, fed, and clothed; that they are contented with their
lot; that their masters had them, not from choice, but by inheritance; that there are difficulties connected with their
emancipation; that the North is equally involved with the
South in the sin and profits of slavery. Let it be conceded,
also, that God will bring good out of their bondage, etc.
Take these propositions separately or collectively, they do not
afford any justification for the holding of men in slavery.

Is slave-holding to be tolerated in the Church of God?
Holding men as property is what I mean by slave-holding.
This is the law: it chattelizes men. The slave may be sold
for his master's debts, or mortgaged. Is that right? Is it to
be tolerated in the Church of God? Ask reason. Is it right
that one man should hold another man as property? What
is a man? A moral, rational, immortal, accountable being—
capable of moral discernment—acting under a moral law—with
a moral nature—capable of moral enjoyment. If he is accountable to God for his conduct, should he be controlled
as an ox or an ass? You may acquire property by possession
which was not originally rightfully acquired, but not when
the original owner is present; and where the slave is, there
is the owner. Knock at his breast, and ask him if he
has no right to his limbs, his eyes, his ears. We see how
some men reason, and throw the sin upon God, that God authorizes it. When a man tells me that, I say as Marshall
said, I have too much respect for Almighty God to defend
him against such an accusation. Go to the Bible. I would
not refer to it, but it has been alluded to. The venerable
Bishop Soule once said to me, "Abraham had slaves bought
with his money, and born in his house." I respond, these
slaves were not American slaves—were not held as property.
And I think I can convince him. Abraham armed his slaves,
three hundred strong, and marched them into a hostile territory, and then marched them back. In the name of sense
how could he have found his way back a slave-holder? Sup-

pose he had had slaves such as the Southern slave-holders had, could he have done this?

Now to the Mosaic dispensation. I mention two principles: First, the fugitive slave law of the Hebrews; it was, that if a fugitive slave came into the country, the commonwealth was pledged to prevent him from being recaptured. On what principle was this practicable if the right of property was admitted? What would be the effect of that slavery? Here was little Palestine surrounded by pagan states, and if the commonwealth would not let the fugitives go back, these pagan nations would not let the Hebrew slave that escaped to them go back. Again, they had an emancipation statute. To buy a pagan slave was to put him into a process of emancipation; for a jubilee was proclaimed every seven years for Hebrew slaves, and every fifty for all the inhabitants.

The New Testament is not pro-slavery—is not even tolerant of slavery. The law of love and the principle of redemption run all through the world of revelation, underlie its surface, overtop its mountains, crop out of its hill-sides, etc. Not so with those passages which are sometimes quoted on the subject of slavery. I could as well prove that Lake Erie is medicated because a chest of medicine had sometime fallen into it. If the New Testament is pro-slavery the apostles were moral homœopathists! Do you believe that Onesimus was a slave? [Cries of "Yes," "No!"] If so, how did the apostle get him back? A little girl was asked how the Lord made heaven and earth? She answered, "He just said it!" Not so with apostles; they had not the same power. If Paul was a supreme judge, with marshals at his back and secret service money at his command, he might get him back. But to just *say* him back—tell him to go back—would be vain. Bring the fugitive here, and let these Bishops and this Conference say go back. Should we do so, who would venture to send a letter back by him to his master?

We are to judge by general principles. Minor principles are not to bend to general principles. What are they? "God hath made of one blood," etc. Suppose you go to New Orleans, and see a man on the auction block. You find him to be your brother, from the same womb, the same loins, the same breasts. Would you hold him in slavery? If you did, what would your father say? "Thou shalt love," etc. "Whatsoever ye would," etc. Does that law measure out your obligation, so that you can hold your fellow-man in bondage? This law has its guards. The ten commandments are its guards. If you measure up to adultery, you have made a mistake. So of stealing, so of idolatry, and it is in view of these general principles that we are to interpret minor principles.

If there is any thing tolerant of slavery in the Bible, then the two revelations are in conflict—that of the New Testament and that of nature. Even the South admits slavery to be an evil to the body, the soul, the slave, the master, to the soil, even. If God in nature and providence has pronounced it cursed, has he in his word pronounced it blessed! Arguments multiply as we advance. Look at the tendency of the New Testament. What has produced emancipation in Europe—in the Northern States? Not infidelity, but Christianity. And what has produced throughout the North the long, universal cry for emancipation? The New Testament. If it could be maintained that any thing in the New Testament tended to perpetuate slavery, why then the South ought to make their slaves read the word of God.

But there are objections to passing a rule by which all men who hold slaves shall be excluded from the Church:

1. "That it cuts asunder the great commission to go and disciple all nations." I do not so understand it. If men are willing we should go to the South with the whole Gospel, and not an emasculated Gospel, we are ready to go, but not otherwise; and we justify ourselves by our Lord's words: "If they persecute you in one city, flee into another." I honor the fathers, living or dead, and yet I have not been taught adulation or adoration of mortal man. The mistake made by Bishop Asbury, when he lowered the standard of the Discipline to establish the Church in the South, was one of the greatest ever made by a mortal man. Would you go to Utah and write in your Discipline that no man might have more than three wives? [Several voices, "No."]

If Asbury could see the results of his course, he would weep. Let the whole Gospel go there to work as the leaven, and leaven the whole lump. Is the Gospel antislavery? If so, then, sir, it has never been properly applied in the Southern States. Slavery has existed three hundred years in these United States, and is stronger to-day than it ever was before. Now, I ask at what rate is the Gospel accomplishing its work, if after three hundred years slavery is stronger than it ever was? This is important. There are now three and a half millions slaves, and after a comparatively short period we shall have forty millions, or a hundred millions. What is to accomplish their deliverance? Politics? I have no hope here. The sword? I pray God not—and another thought, we have no example of successful servile war; though the blood of blacks and whites should redden the Mississippi, it would not result in emancipation of the enslaved. I had hoped that, as the slaves increased, their value would diminish. But the opening of immense territories to slave labor has cut off that hope. My hope is in God—in the Church of God. Will the Church in the South ever rise and take her stand in favor of emancipation, while there are ministers, bishops, and archbishops who are justifying slavery? Never until the Church at the North arises to a correct position is there any hope of success.

I have my doubts whether the new chapter is consistent with the General Rule. I will indicate the reasons of these doubts, but shall not now elaborate my views on this question:

First. The antislavery action of the Church was less and less stringent, up to the time of the adoption of the General Rule.

Second. The purpose of the rule evidently was to open the Southern States to the preaching of the Methodists.

Third. The interpretation given to the rule on slavery by contemporaneous action must fix the meaning of the General Rule, as designed to allow of slave-holding by members of the Church.

Fourth. The proposition to change the General Rule shows a doubt of the propriety of the provisions of the new chapter while it remains as it is. I propose to go to the root of the difficulty—to change the General Rule. It is wrong to attempt to compass in the chapter what you cannot do in the constitution. I say, honor bright, I nail my colors to the mast-head, and would rather sink fifty fathoms with my colors in the right place, than to succeed by equivocal methods.

John A. Collins, of Baltimore, referred to the kind words spoken of him by Dr. Thomson, and reciprocated in glowing terms of eulogy personally, but regretted the necessity of dissenting very positively from his sentiments on the subject of legislating against slavery. A brief of his argument only is given:

I wish it understood in the outset that there are not two parties here, as existed in 1844, a genuine Southern party and an adverse party.

I am not here to defend slavery from the Bible or any other source. I am not here to make that issue. Not at all, sir. The brethren representing the Baltimore Conference are not pro-slavery. My honored people, which I in part represent on this floor, are not pro-slavery. And we have given the strongest possible proof of that fact. Why does Baltimore stand where she does? Why did she not go off with the Church South? Why maintain her allegiance to the Methodist Episcopal Church in these United States?

What is the reason? But one reason can be given. We do not believe in the sentiments of that Church. The section of the country with which I am not most familiar was passed through by an able man, proclaiming slavery to be a divine institution, a divine right, running it out into all the ramifications of society. Another followed him on the same strain. I stood up and met him on these issues. Our people did not go with the South. Why is she where she is?

If we had chosen to affiliate with the Church South stars and garters awaited us. Baltimore would, in that case, have been the emporium of Southern commerce. Baltimore would have had the Book Concern of the Church South, and would have concentrated the publishing interests of that Church. Yet she did not go; and why did she not go?

Dr. Thomson says that slavery is on the increase, that it

has more power now than it formerly had. If this be the
fact, the Methodist Episcopal Church is not responsible for
it. Religion never made slavery. The Church never made
slavery. However true the remark may be as to the increase
of slave-power in certain places—and I admit the force of his
remark in some respects—however true it may be in other
parts, it is a great mistake in regard to that part of slave territory within our bounds. It is not on the increase there.
Perhaps you will be surprised to learn that in the whole of
Baltimore City Station, according to testimony of brethren
well informed on the subject, there is but one single slave-
holder, and it is doubtful that there is even one.

We have a colored membership of from 15,000 to 20,000.
They have good churches there; they sing more sweetly and
pray more powerfully than any people I have ever seen. I
would rather preach to them than to any other people. They
have their Sabbath and day-schools. You may thread the
streets of Baltimore, and you will not meet with a single colored beggar. We do meet with beggars there, but they do
not come from the descendants of Africa. Slavery is not on
the increase there. Brother Griffith says it is on the decrease.
[Several voices, "True."] Our people there have some sense.
They know they can hire labor cheaper than they can buy it
and become responsible for the clothing, feeding, and sustaining of the slaves when unable to labor. Slavery is on the
decrease there, and if the Discipline be permitted to remain
as it is, and operate as it has been doing, it will still decrease.

The new test of membership contained in the new
section proposed, and the unconstitutionality of such
a method, were elaborately argued by Mr. Collins,
who also objected to such a change of the constitution as would introduce a new rule on slavery. The
parable of the tares he interpreted to mean: Some
evils are such that it will do more harm to meddle
than to desist, and such he believed to be the fact in
regard to this question. "Let both grow until the
harvest," was Christ's advice.

A. J. Phelps, of Black River Conference, said :

It appears to me almost every feature bearing against this measure is greatly overdrawn; the numerous membership to be affected; the vast interests jeopardized in Conferences of recent creation in slave territory; our obligations to support these Conferences, to which we are said to be solemnly and sacredly pledged; the sacrifice and hazard of self-denying men of God, and the interests of poor slaves themselves—are all impressed upon us to teach us the inexpediency of this measure.

But let us look at a few statistics bearing upon these aspects of the subject.

An impression prevails to a considerable extent that a white membership of 143,000 is to be directly affected by any action on this subject. Whereas, the General Minutes of 1855 show a white membership of only 136,332 in the six Conferences, in whole or in part, in slave territory; while nearly one third of Baltimore Conference, and more than half of Philadelphia, besides small portions of other Conferences, lie in the free States. In Baltimore and Philadelphia Confer ences alone we have 43,967 members in free territory, which, deducted from the total white membership of the six Conferences, leave 92,363. Of this showing, however, 865 are local preachers already under restriction, and therefore not capable of being personally affected by any proposed change; and 11,946 are only on trial; deduct these two classes, making 12,811, from the 92,363 situated in slave territory, and we have a membership in full connection within those limits of 79,552, instead of 143,000—a large discount; nearly fifty per cent. From this footing deduct one third for minors, and one third for married ladies, and we find remaining 26,517, the highest probable number who are capable of holding slaves. This, therefore, is the largest number who can be personally affected by the proposed measure, provided every one capable of holding a slave is an actual slave-holder. But how is this? The census of 1850 shows that only one third of the families of the white population hold slaves. Then, provided our members are no better than the masses, the probable number of slave-holders among us would be 8,834. But if all our members in that region are superior

Methodists, possessing good, tender hearts, and only hold slaves for the good of the enslaved, as presented by their apologists, then the rule hurts no one. But suppose they are only comparatively good, and have some conscience, such as the climate will allow, and only wish to make gain out of human bones and sinews and souls, with moderation and modesty, then the proportion of slave-holders in the Church must be less than in the masses. What, then, is the probability? How many slave-holders have we in the Methodist Episcopal Church? Have we 5,000 or 1,000? Dr. Durbin, who is well posted about every thing, has expressed the opinion that we have not less than 1,000 slave-holders in the Church, and we set this down as good authority.

If this basis be correct, we have 1,000 slave-holders in the Church whose connection with us exposes 700,000 Methodists in the free States to taunts and jeers from their enemies, to the most excruciating tortures in their own bosoms; while more than 4,000 ministers are hindered in the great work of saving souls. The old doctrine is reversed. Our fathers taught, "better one suffer than many." But now the sentiment is better 700,000 than 1,000.

But this inferior minority of one to seven hundred must be sustained at any expense. The moral force of the whole Church must defend oppressors. Church authorities and Church papers must apologize for the nefarious villainy. The press must be muzzled, and every possible expedient seized upon, to hold the seven hundred in check and give the one ascendency.

It is earnestly pleaded that we are under solemn obligations to the three newly-created Conferences in slave territory. Let us look at this matter a moment. These Conferences—Kentucky, Arkansas, and Missouri—taken together number fifty-two effective preachers in full connection, with a white membership of 10,679, making a proportion of 205 members to each effective minister in the three Conferences; and yet it has cost the Missionary Society to carry forward this work for two years, 1855 and 1856, $16,200; and taking for granted that like appropriations were made for 1853 and 1854, it has drawn from our missionary funds to support these three Conferences, consisting of fifty-two members, all told, the round sum of $32,400. Appropriations in the same ratio for the work in the United States alone, leaving out of account Kansas and Nebraska and other distant fields, would require an outlay of more than $2,000,000 for domestic missions only.

One of the strong arguments for the institution of these Conferences was based upon the salutary influence they might exert upon the poor slave; and now we listen to the most heart-stirring appeals to our sympathy on the same subject. If their hands are tied, who is to minister to the poor slave? If they are crippled, who is to come near to lift up the poor wretches and minister to their famishing souls? All this sounds well, but let us see how it applies to these Conferences. How many colored people, bond and free, have been gathered into the Church within the limits of these three Conferences? The vast number of three hundred and sixty-five, all told; and could such as are slaves among them be here, and be allowed to speak, what would they be likely to say? Would they caution you, as their friends do this day, Be sure not to put any thing in the book against slavery, for it will do us harm? No, never!

The doctrine that a lax faith and easy morals are promotive of true godliness, that to indorse a grievous sin is the best means of removing that sin, can hardly be a question in morals.

It is further alleged that our antislavery Discipline will do much toward extirpating this great evil.

We submit, When and how? This excellent little book has long lived in the land of oppression. Has it advanced in the direction of freedom? Has it made inroads upon slavery, or has slavery made inroads upon the book? Has it ever purged the Church of slavery in its most offensive forms? Nay, verily; but, where left to Southern management, slavery has wrung out the last drop of its heart's blood, and left it a speechless ghost.

Allow me to say, before taking my seat, I favor the report of the Committee on Slavery not because it comes up to my views of what should be enacted on this subject. Nor would my sense of responsibility allow me to go for any measure as a compromise where so much of principle is involved. I take this weak solution, sir, just as in extremity I would take greatly diluted aliment as the best means at hand for prolonging life. My vote will be in favor of this report because there is no present hope of enacting a more stringent and less incumbered rule, and because I think this a small advance toward liberty. I go for it, so far as constitutionality is concerned, with a whole heart and a good conscience, believing most sincerely that the General Rules neither require nor authorize the holding of human beings as property.

Father Young, of the Ohio Conference, advised against so radical a change, and offered as a substitute for the new chapter proposed the following resolutions, which were supported by Dr. E. Thomson:

1. That no man has a moral right to hold a fellow-being as property.
2. That it is the duty of all our members and probationers who may sustain the legal relation of slave-holder to teach their servants to read the word of God; to allow them to attend the public worship of God on our regular days of divine service; to protect them in the discharge of the duties of the conjugal, parental, and filial relations; to give them such compensation for their service as may be just and equal; to make such provision as may be legally practicable to prevent them and their posterity from passing into perpetual slavery; and to treat them in all respects as required by the Ten Commandments and the law of love.
3. That we recommend all our membership and ministry to make the condition of the Africans in bondage upon our shores a prominent subject of prayer; beseeching God to deliver them from this bondage without servile or civil wars, the dissolution of our Union, or any other judgment, and to incline the hearts of the American people to repent of all their oppression, and by all possible means atone for the wrongs they have done to the helpless.
4. That we advise our people to memorialize Congress to provide by law that whenever any slave State shall signify her willingness to emancipate her slaves, such State shall re-

ceive for her slaves a reasonable compensation from the national treasury for the slaves so emancipated.

The only action had upon these resolutions was, after one speech, to lay them on the table to be printed.

W. B. Disbro, of North Ohio Conference, in concluding an elaborate speech, said :

What shall this General Conference do to extirpate the evil of slavery ? This is the great question. Will she do any thing ? We answer, Let something be done, some advanced step be taken, or send us not back to our people. If nothing is done our hearts shall mourn and our heads hang down as we go to the people again. Let us at least take one step. Let all be done that we have power to do to put the Church right before the world on this subject.

1. We should adopt the preamble to the majority report. This would be a clear declaration of antislavery sentiment.

2. We should vote on a change in the General Rule. Let us have a constitutional majority here ; then the Annual Conferences will follow our example, and in a short time the work will be complete.

3. We should adopt the first declaration of the proposed chapter. It answers the question, " What shall be done for the extirpation of the evil of slavery ? " All men have an equal right to freedom, and no man has a moral right to hold his fellow-being as property.

4. We may interpret the present General Rule so as to make our understanding of it strictly antislavery. We may pass strong antislavery resolutions, so as to make our records place us right before the Church. Whatever we do let us do nothing to tighten the chains of the bondmen, nothing to increase slavery influence among us. The captive prays, the whole heart of the Church is raised in prayer to God that this General Conference may be guided by divine wisdom, and reach such conclusions as shall send hope to the downtrodden, save the Church from the reproach of her enemies, and secure to all her bounds purity, peace, unity, and prosperity evermore.

Mr. Clark, of Wyoming Conference, said:

I am in favor of a change; had no sympathy with those memorialists who came here crying, "No change!" They did not propose to do any thing, but contented themselves with crying, "No change!" He was in favor of the report for several reasons. It proposes to exercise a just discrimination; it is founded on principle. Our position heretofore has been founded on expediency. It is also constitutional and according to precedent. The General Rules of our Church are not properly a constitution; they have none of the distinguishing features of a constitution. He would show them that the General Conference had not so regarded it. In eight different instances it, of itself, has made changes affecting the condition of retaining membership in the Church, and six of which vary the terms upon which persons are to be received.

The speaker quoted largely from Emory's "History of the Discipline" to substantiate this position.

Dr. F. Hodgson, of Philadelphia Conference, objected to the majority report; that it was self-contradictory; that it allowed a man to assume a forbidden, an unlawful, relation to another for the sake of conferring a benefit; that it does not secure the object at which its friends aimed; that it proposes a judicial practice contrary to the most equitable and established maxims, in assuming the guilt of parties, and putting them upon proof of innocence; that it attempts to sit in judgment on men's motives; that it required what would not be for the good of the slave; that it had a political aspect. After an able speech in opposition to the majority report, he closed by saying:

We are in the midst of perilous times. The outside pressure has been spoken of. I know it is great, and we are in danger of being borne down by it. Be careful of making changes now; we do not know what will be the consequences. There is danger. The eyes of the world are upon us, it is

said; ah, yes! two sets of eyes are glaring fearfully upon us—
the eyes of the great political parties. Would to God they
would leave us alone, to prosecute our own appropriate work.
When the Church was weak politicians cared but little for
her; but now she has grown strong each is eager to make
her its tool. If the Church turns aside she will become
weak, like Samson. Her eyes will be put out. She will be
shorn of her strength; and when she feels for the pillars of
heathenism she will be unable to pull them down. He
would be ashamed of his brethren if he thought they had not
grace enough in their hearts to let political parties alone, and
pursue their one great work of saving souls.

John Dempster, of Rock River Conference, said:

My aim will be: First, To identify the character of slavery, which the report proposes to remove from our Church.
Slavery proper cannot imply something apart from the intentions and acts of the master, or from that coercive control in
whose grasp the slave is a tool. It cannot claim to partici-
pate in both good and evil, so as to be susceptible of either a
useful or perverted application. It is not that which the
force of events can change or modify, as though it were of a
mixed nature. It can pass no mutation, but by destruction;
can have no altered relations, but by perishing.

The evils of slavery have been referred to the abuse of the
system of slavery. Were the reference correct, the system
would be good; as when evil arises from the perversion of
principles, good is their legitimate operation. Christianity,
in its perverted application, has crowded dungeons with confessors, and fed the flames with martyrs. In its legitimate
application, the reverse must forever be its workings. So,
if slavery has only wrought evil to the extent of its perversion, its excellences need sustaining by no better evidence.
But is it impossible to abuse a system so far as it is only evil?
Let us test slavery by this rule at a single point. Beyond all
question, slavery divests its victim of every shadow of liberty, personal, domestic, and civil. It abolishes his right to
the appropriation of his faculties—his right to his wife, his
children, and to citizenship. What, then, has it left him?

Life? But does this wholesale robbery leave life any longer a boon? He has been plundered of all that last right of created mind—the right to himself—and, by losing this, he has lost all else which this comprehended—all which has been given from heaven—all which lay within the range of human acquisition on earth. It is true a few scattered beams of original truth may pierce that gloom which is indispensable to his continued thralldom; but those rather disclose his calamity than administer relief. He is shut out from the very God that made him by unavoidable ignorance of his revealed word; he is cut off from all communications with him through his speaking works. The light in which these can be read would show the unendurable horrors of his thralldom: it must, therefore, be shut out from his soul. What more has he to lose? Not his wife; she is torn from him, and dragged with shrieks to distant bondage. Not his children; bathed in tears, they are hurried away by a new master to another State. Not his own faculties; these his master has appropriated, and they must be so applied under the power of the lash.

There is no future within the limits of life on which kindled hope can cast a beam. Has not slavery consummated its ruin by its own legitimate workings? Is there one green spot in his desert-life which it has not blighted?

The proprietary principle, binding society in union, lies dead and in ruin in his soul. His master has usurped his Maker's throne—has made him property—a chattel, like the beast with which he toils—a thing, like the soil he digs—like the clod on which he treads. What, then, remains for him to fear, but the curse of protracted being? What to hope, but the utter unconsciousness of what he now is? What other language can the wild scream of his completed degradation utter, but that of defiance to all authority and all agents, to add another drop of agony to his overflowing cup? Let the inquiry be pressed with the deepest emphasis, whether any abuse of the system can make it worse? Whether it be possible to rob a man of more than himself? You ask, then, is not half starving a slave making his condition worse than to be well fed? Is not twenty lashes a day worse than an unwounded back? True; but does not slavery authorize both these? Though they are abuses of the slave, they are not abuses of the system. Does not this fully authorize the master to so treat his slave, if he judges it for his interest? It is alleged that, it being against his interest, the slave has an indemnity against it. But how readily does interest yield to passion? Does not the system expose the slave·to become the victim of it? Well, sir, would it be for our humanity, were interest—even perverted to selfishness—the paramount force acting on society. There is a more wasting agency in the fiery gust of passion. Whether this raves in revenge or lust, woe to the defenseless victim of its fury.

Ah, sir, there is a sense in which a person can be robbed of more than herself—her master may make her not his property only. He may outrage those delicate instincts which God has planted deepest in woman's mysterious nature. The daughter of the noble Roman found a deliverer from the brutal lust of lawless power in her father's hand, which fastened a javelin in her heart to prevent her purity from being spotted. But who shall protect from brutal pollution the enslaved negress? She is property, she must be appropriated, she must be an unresisting victim of that polluting act for which, by another woman, death would be a just infliction. But is this shocking crush of all that is most lovely in human form—of what the laws of men and the laws of God have continued to guard as forever inviolate—is this in the control of the master's passion, by the very law of that property which he has in his slave?

In the light of all truth, then, slavery must be pronounced a sin against God and against humanity; a sin to be classed with theft, robbing, falsehood, swearing, and licentiousness. If those guilty of any of this class of sins can be admitted to the sacraments of the Church, those guilty of all should be. The Scriptures class these together.

What is called slavery is capable of existing in two forms: that of mere legal relation, leaving the slave really invested with his rights and only nominally belonging to his master, and that which embraces the most malignant principles of slavery. Now, which of these did the apostles admit into the Church? Was it slavery both in its form and malignant principles? Then we demand why? You answer that the

Christianity inculcated in the Church might more effectually abolish the principles of slavery. In other words, there can be no mode of removing sin so effectually from the world as by taking it in the Church. This, then, is the position of the advocates for slavery in our Church. Now, let the principle be fairly tested. If it applies to the sin of slavery, let them inform us why it does not apply to all sins: to theft, robbery, lewdness, drunkenness, and the entire list of sins excluding men from God's kingdom. At this point we must irresistibly press them. The question must be distinctly answered, Why take this sin into the Church to cure it, and not all sins? Doubtless, the debauchee would, in the Church, be encompassed with influences far more favorable to his reform than in the brothel. Why not permit him to alternate between the bed of pollution and the table of the Lord? Why not reform the highway robber in the same manner? The Church is more favorable to that end than the banditti. Do you allege that the cases are not parallel? Then the robber's is less aggravating. He has filched your purse, but permitted you to escape in possession of your other rights. The slave-holder has filched your ownership in yourself, and thereby left no right possible. Why should not the robber, the less guilty, be admitted to equal advantages? If the Church can best remove the evil of slavery by having it in its bosom, the same reason should put all other sins there. Would this make the Church one vast receptacle of all that degrades humanity? But this is simply the application of the principle; will its advocates show us why it admits of application in one case and not in all others of the same kind? They cannot be allowed to apply it in this case and reject it in all similar cases without reasons of great cogency. The brief conclusion, then, which forces itself upon us is this : Either slavery, including its essential principles, is no sin, or it was never admitted by the apostles into the Church, or the Church should admit men into it practicing all kinds of sin. The first, that slavery, including all its malignant principles, is not a sin, not one present will affirm. The third, that sinners of every kind and degree, should be admitted into the Church, is just as universally rejected. But are such aware that the rejection of these two compels the adoption of the

---

other? That if they believe chattelizing slavery is a sin, and that sinners of all kinds should not be admitted to the Church, they cannot believe that the apostles admitted chattelizing slave-holders to the Church. . . .

What is there in the General Rule with which the proposed chapter in the majority report is in conflict? The chapter in the first and second answers in resolution second, proposes to terminate slavery in our Church. Now with what is this in conflict in the rule? The rule employs two classes of terms: the one general, the other particular. It employs two words. The first class of terms is found in these words, "avoiding evil of every kind." The second of these, "buying or selling men, women, and children, with the intention to enslave them." The connecting words are "such as." It is true these connecting words are but once used; but as it is palpable to all that they would connect the general term with every specification in the rule, were the ellipses supplied, their force is recognized at every step. The language of the rule is, then, "avoiding evil of every kind, such as buying and selling," etc., etc.

Now, if there be evil of any other form of slavery, as the general term recognizes every evil of it, it must be included with these two here expressed. Why must they, sir? Because it is an element of evil of every kind, and the avoidance of this is expressly required; because it is such as these two expressly prohibited. Is not that in the proposed change, namely, the prohibition of slave-holding in the Church; is not this slave-holding of the exact moral character of buying with an intention to enslave? Observe, sir, it is not buying or selling that the rule prohibits. What is it, then? "The intention to enslave." Well, sir, I inherit a slave and hold him in slavery; have I, in this, an intention to enslave? Most certainly. Is not this, then, the identical thing which the rule forbids? Is not this all that the proposed chapter forbids? Can they be out of harmony? Is not the guilty element just the same in one who holds the inherited slave as property as in him who sells the victim as such? Such as doubt this must show the moral incongruity in the two things: that my holding property in a man is not like enabling another to do it; that holding him as a slave myself, just as my neighbor would do it, is still a very unlikely thing to doing it; that intending to hold him as a chattel, and intending to sell him as a chattel, occupy in ethics by no means the same sphere.

Now, sir, if this distinction is a dream, and the acts are two only in name, then how can the chapter which forbids the one be repugnant to the rule which forbids the other? It is hoped none will confound the particulars expressed under this General Rule with exhaustive specifications which are intended to express every species which is contained in the genus. For the reasons submitted they can be intended merely as specimens, and, therefore, leave the fullest scope to include everything like them.

James B. Finley, of Cincinnati Conference, opposed all new tests, because now only those who forsake their sins are eligible to membership in the Church; and slavery is a sin that must be forsaken. The Bible is against it. The whole Discipline of the Church is against it, and the only thing necessary to keep slavery out of the Church was to administer faithfully under the one test of forsaking all sin in order to admission therein.

James Cunningham, of the Philadelphia Conference, opposing the majority report, criticised sharply some of the arguments used by its friends. The construction of the General Rule which made it prohibit all slave-holding, he declared, was an afterthought, and had its birth in the Slavery Committee or on the Conference floor. He had never heard of it until coming to this General Conference. "Absurd as it is, it became necessary to assume and maintain it in order to justify the report of the majority. But in all the border work we stand committed to antislavery principles, and our Church is exerting an influence that depends upon our Discipline remaining as it is. The petitioners for change numbered four thousand in all. But seven hundred thousand had not expressed their wishes." He had no doubt that three fourths of our entire membership desired the Discipline to remain as it is. "The only testimony borne against slavery in slave territory is borne by the Methodist Episcopal Church. And if our Church is anywhere a pillar of cloud by day and of fire by night it is such in our slave territory."

CHAPTER XXIV.

DEBATE ON SLAVERY—CONCLUDED.

ABEL STEVENS, of the Providence Conference, said :

The main points involved in this constitutional question are these :

First. We have a series of terms of membership called the "General Rules," which are a part of the constitutional law of the Church, and one of which prohibits "the buying or selling of men, women, and children, with an intention to enslave them."

Second. The report before us proposes, as we allege, to make non-slaveholding a term of membership, and would thereby violate not only the existing General Rule, which prohibits only the "buying and selling" of slaves, but also the "restrictive," by rejecting the only authorized process for such a change. It is, therefore, a double assault upon the constitution of the Church, and however desirable the change it proposes may be, if rightly procured and applied, it is, as now proposed, pregnant with evil and disaster—as defeating the end sought, by enabling the opposition to disdain and disobey it should they remain in the Church, or turn it upon us should they revolt; pointing to the violated constitution as a motive of sympathy and co-operation from all the intermediate strength of the Church between the "border" and the North; pointing to it in all litigations for the local or general property of the Church amid the confusions that may follow its enactments.

My objections to this report are twofold—the obvious constitutional defect referred to, and the peril of a measure so extraordinary to the unity of the Church, and, by consequence, to the cause of the slave himself.

There are two classes of thinkers among us respecting the right to make new terms of membership. First. Those who contend that we can make no new General Rules whatsoever, except by the process prescribed in the restrictive rules—the two-thirds majority here, the three-fourths majority in the Annual Conferences. To these brethren, of course, the document before us is inadmissible. It prescribes non-slavehold-ing as a condition of membership in the Church. Now, this must be a new rule, an old rule, or no rule. There is no other possibility for it. It certainly belongs not to the last category of being no rule. It prohibits the admission of slave-holders in our Church hereafter under given circum-stances. This is certainly a rule or condition of membership. Is it, then, an old or a new rule? Assuredly it is not an old one, for what then would be the use of re-enacting it by the chapter of this report? It results, then, that it must be a new one, and therefore inadmissible to all such as believe that we cannot adopt a new General Rule but by the provis-ion of the restrictive rules.

Second. The other class of thinkers are few among us, and cer-tainly very recent. I know not that they have ever appeared except in connection with this controversy. They contend that the restriction on the change of the General Rules interferes not with the adoption of new rules, provided the latter be not incompatible with the old ones; that it interferes only with the change of the old ones; not with an addition to the series of the rules, but with a change of individual rules.

The question then presents itself precisely here : Is this proposed rule incompatible with any existing one? I contend that it is, and my reply to the question will be equally ap-plicable to the many brethren here who consider the objec-tionable section of the report as only an explanatory declara-tion of the old rule. They will please to observe this fact.

1. The existing General Rule prohibits the acquisition of slave property by the slave traffic — that is, the "buying or selling of men, women, and children," etc. I use the word traffic, not because it is the best, but because it is the most convenient. Now I affirm that this prohibition of the acquisi-tion of slaves by purchase implies, by the peculiar circum-stances in which it was made, the right to hold them by

inheritance. Here is a law affecting the great fact of slavery; that fact is chiefly continued by inheritance; the traffic, enormous as it is, is but an incident of the system compared with the vast range of its transmission by inheritance. But with the latter are complicated the property, heirship, business, and domestic establishments of families. It could not, therefore, be treated as uncompromisingly as the traffic. The purchase of slaves is, therefore, prohibited, while the inheritance of them is left untouched. Slave-holding itself is therefore not prohibited; in other words, sad a fact as it may be to many of you, slave-holding itself is allowed by the General Rules, the organic law of the Church, and, therefore, the introduction of a new General Rule prohibiting it is in contravention of the present General Rule, and can be done only by constitutional process provided in the restrictive rule.

Such, I insist, is the only legitimate construction of the literal expression of the rule. No other view is possible when you look it thus deliberately in the face. You may lament it; I lament it; we might have been saved infinite evil had the policy of the Church been otherwise from the beginning; but such has it been, and the question is not now how to evade, but how to rectify it — whether by an infraction of your organic law you shall provide a dead-letter to be justly rejected and disdained by your opponents, should they continue with you, or to be fatally used against you should they be driven from you, and thus in either case defeat your own designs pushing the slave farther and farther from your helping reach, or overthrowing the unity and strength of the Church, and this for the sake of a measure which it is in your power fully to secure by the prescribed constitutional process.

2. I have said that the whole history of the Church in relation to slavery confirms this interpretation of the General Rule.

Let us now look more deliberately at its relation to that evil before, at the time of, and ever since the introduction of this General Rule.

Prior to the adoption of the restrictive rules—that is from 1784 to 1808—the General Conference had unrestricted power over the subject. Its enactments respecting it varied. It was intent upon doing something effective, but was confounded

at every point by the embarrassments of the question. At
the memorable "Christmas Conference," 1784, having yet unrestricted powers, it prohibited all slave-holding on the part
of our members; but, notwithstanding its plenary powers, it
announces this law with noticeable diffidence, being "deeply
conscious," it says, "of the impropriety of making new terms
of communion for a religious society already established, ex-
cepting on the most pressing occasion." Before this extreme
measure it had only ventured to denounce slavery, and to
"pass its disapprobation on all our friends who keep slaves,
and to advise their freedom." This prohibitory law of the
Christmas Conference was accompanied with numerous provisos, granting many delays and conveniences for emancipation, and subjecting the whole enactment to the supremacy of
the varying laws of the different slave-holding States.

But now note one most important fact just here, namely,
that under a distinct question appended to this law the "*buying or selling*" of slaves—the very subject of the present General Rule — is treated also, and all the delays and indulgent
conditions of the preceding law are avoided; the "buyers"
and the "sellers" are "immediately to be expelled, unless
they buy them on purpose to free them." So reads this second law. Here, then, we see conclusively how "the fathers"
discriminated the traffic, the "buying and selling," from the
holding of slaves, even while providing for the extirpation of
both, and the former is distinguished by the very terms which
are used in our present General Rule. Let this fact be carefully noticed, for it clinches our argument.

But this is not all. The agitation produced by this comprehensive action against not only slave "buying and selling," but "slave-holding" itself, was so violent that in a few
months it was deemed necessary to suspend the law, and in
1785 the suspension was announced, and a Nota Bene inserted
containing a more general declaration against the evil. And
now mark, sir, this conclusive fact, namely, that the very next
year, 1786, after the long, detailed law against all slave-holding was repealed, the other law, passed at the same time,
against buying and selling slaves, is retained in the Discipline. The prohibition of simple slave-holding, with all its
accommodating provisions, is abandoned because of the dis-

turbance it had produced by its bearing on families and their legalized property in slaves; but the absolute, unconditional, uncompromising law which accompanied it, and which was exclusively against "buying and selling" slaves, is retained. Why could this be kept and not the other? Because it evidently referred to the traffic; and the traffic, known and acknowledged every-where to be atrocious and infamous, could be less hazardously condemned. And now I repeat, this retained part of the law is identical in sense, and almost so in words, with our existing General Rule, the rule which the advocates of the report before you contend comprises "slave-holding" as well as slave-"buying;" a construction utterly fallacious, but without which they would be compelled to abandon the chapter of their report as unconstitutional. The only essential difference is that it prohibits the giving away of slaves as well as the buying and selling of them—an important fact to be recalled directly.

But this is not all. The retained part of the old law was the only statute on the subject till the present General Rule was inserted among our constitutional laws. Only three years elapsed before that change was made.

Here, then, we have four notable facts. First, The enactment of a law specifically against slave-holding, accompanied by a distinct law against slave "buying and selling." Second, The repeal of the first, owing to the hostility which was produced by its complication with recognized property and household establishment. Third, The retention of the second, made possible, notwithstanding all this hostility, by the fact that it was addressed to an atrocious and ignominious incident of slavery — the traffic. Fourth, The incorporation, a short time afterward, of this retained prohibition into the constitutional law of the Church, in language essentially identical in meaning, and nearly so in words, with the exception of a phrase against the giving away of slaves, which is omitted. Now, confronting these historical facts of the case, can we longer doubt the sense of the General Rule?

Every incident, every accident, of its history thus bears down irresistibly to my conclusion. Why even the omission of that phrase respecting the giving away of slaves? It had been retained while the ordinance remained only as a common statute, but now that this statute is to be exalted to the supreme importance of a constitutional law, it is omitted. Why? Evidently because slave-holding—the transmission of slaves in families—was not intended to be prohibited. The gift of slaves to children at marriage; the settlement of them by parents at death on other branches of the family, might seem to be embarrassed by the phrase. Hence in making the rule a constitutional law it was more carefully guarded. And thus it stands to-day, with all these historical incidents and exponents about it, defining and defending invincibly its literal sense.

And, still more than all this — for I have thus far only shown, first, what was our action on slavery prior to this General Rule, and, secondly, at its inception—what now does the subsequent course of the Church testify on the subject? It has been one unbroken demonstration of my interpretation of the law. Brethren who favor this report in order to introduce, without the constitutional process, a rule virtually against slave-holding itself, assert that the present General Rule is such. But where is a single historical fact that supports them? When the rule was enacted the Church included slave-holders in all parts of its slave territory; but was it applied then to a single case?

A few years afterward Coke and Asbury wrote their Notes on the Discipline. They commented on this very rule, but without a single intimation that it applied to any thing else than the "buying and selling" of slaves, though slavery was extensively extant in the Church.

The same year in which their Notes appear, appears also in the Discipline a long chapter making various provisions for the trial of those who may "buy or sell" slaves, and certain guards against the promotion of slave-holders themselves to official posts of example, but without one prohibitory word against the domestic possession of slaves. More than this, that very chapter contains a paragraph making the slave-holder admissible to the Church, on condition that "the preacher shall have spoken to him freely and faithfully on the subject of slavery," but without a word requiring emancipation.

In 1812 the General Conference, being then under the

restrictive rule, omitted all the chapter of ordinary statutes on slavery, but retained the constitutional or General Rule, which it could not change, and referred the mode of its administration to the Annual Conferences; but the act by which it was thus referred said not a word about slave-holding; it speaks of the "buying and selling" of slaves alone.

Laws have been repeatedly made keeping slave-holders from the official posts of the Church, but never from private membership.

Thus, during sixty-seven years, the action of the Church has been continued on the subject, and has uniformly shown that non-slaveholding has not been a condition of membership, except for a few agitated months before the adoption of the present General Rule, and never once since its adoption. How can we evade the long unbroken demonstration of these facts?

2. And now, I ask, does not this literal and historical construction of the rule accord with the best principles of legal interpretation?

It is a familiar maxim of the bar that the exception proves the law—*exceptio probat requeam*. The practical or virtual law of the Church being the admission of slave-holders, the exceptions are the exclusion of the "buyers" and "sellers" of slaves, and the specifications of these exceptions prove the virtual or practical law. "The force of the maxim," says Whateley, "the force of the maxim (which is not properly confined to the case of an *exception*, strictly so called) is this: 'that the mention of any circumstance introduced into the statement of either a definition or of a precept, law, remark, etc., is to be presumed *necessary* to be inserted, so that the precept, etc., would not hold good if this precept were absent.' In short, the word *only*, or some such expression, is supposed to be understood. If, *e. g.*, it be laid down that he who breaks into an *empty* house shall receive a certain punishment, it would be inferred that this punishment would not be incurred by breaking into an *occupied* house; if it were told us that some celestial phenomenon could not be seen by the naked eye, it might be inferred that it might be visible through a telescope," etc.

The existing General Rule is a negative law; it prohibits

slave-buying and selling, thereby authorizing or permitting
slave-holding by inheritance. Negative laws often authorize
infinitely more than they prohibit. A law prohibiting the
circulation of paper money under five dollars prohibits only
four denominations, but authorizes the circulation of any
numbers beyond, even to millions. A law prohibiting the sale
of ardent spirits in less quantities than a quart authorizes the
sale of a quart, a keg, a hogshead, or a thousand hogsheads.
Turn to the chapter of your Discipline on slavery, and you
will find another example: *Official* members are prohibited
from holding slaves—a fact that certainly implies that unoffi-
cial members may hold them—and so Abolitionists have always interpreted and always complained of the law. Such is
the true method, as I believe, of interpreting our actual law
on slavery, and such the inevitable result of its interpretation.
Metaphysics are seldom an aid to legal investigation; the enlightened judge on the bench will take one clear, literal criticism, one illustrative historical fact, as more decisive than a
thousand metaphysical subtleties. The whole literal showing
of the law, and all the facts of our connection, as a Church,
with slavery for nearly three quarters of a century confront
and confound any metaphysical construction of the present
case contrary to that which we have given.

The precepts of the General Rules, of "doing no harm," of
"doing good," etc., have been assumed as authorizing a new
law against slavery without the process of restrictive rule;
and examples have been quoted from our past legislation.
One or two such examples have occurred, but our best judges
of law would say, I think, that they were unconstitutionally
obtained, however they may be, otherwise, compatible with
the constitution. They are unimportant, however, I think, in
this controversy. If these vague precepts authorize any such
liberties with our constitutional rights of membership, such
liberties must certainly be limited to generally conceded
points; especially must they not interfere with matters already in the law by direct specification or equally inevitable
implication. But besides the general principle to "do no
harm," or to "do good," etc., we have the specific rule on
slavery, and this, as I have shown, has its clear, literal, and
historical meaning. No general precept can interfere with

this, for no general precept can contravene a specific law given in the same code or the same document.

The result is that the existing General Rule authorizes simple *slave-holding*. It does not discriminate the moral character of this slave-holding, though it does that of the traffic; the discrimination of the former is implied in the general moral signifiance of our organization; it is implied in our secondary laws on slavery, but it is not *specified* in the terms of the constitutional law. Let it come out, then, sir, for the sake of frankness, for the sake of repentance, for the sake of amendment, let it be acknowledged that historically, constitutionally, administratively, we have been a *slave-holding*, though an *antislavery*, Church. Not *pro-slavery*, mark, but *antislavery*, yet admitting slave-holders—not because slavery is right, not because the Church admits it to be right. On the contrary, she declares it to be a great evil, yet has always held that she could not refuse a man admission into her communion simply on the ground that he was a slave-holder. We cannot deny it. You deplore it; every man here from the "border" deplores it, even though he may deem it a necessary fact. We deplore it, but cannot deny it.

How shall we reform the stern and sad fact. That is the question, and should be the gist of all our present rambling debates. How? Not by overriding the constitution and all the unmistakable monuments of our history respecting it; not by rending the Church by the provocations of an unauthorized and, therefore, oppressive proceeding; not by shaking down the walls of its strength that now bear up so many guns pointed against the evil merely because a single angle of those walls defends it. Such violent measures might call forth the shouts of the thoughtless multitudes, or gratify our personal antislavery zeal; but we are here not as a mob nor as zealots, but as legislators. The highest religious responsibilities of this continent center in this hall to-day. Methodism, though once severed and shivered by this terrible evil, stands yet forth in its organic unity, solidity, and mightiness throughout these Middle and Northern States. Shall the giant genius of discord, Samson-like, shake down its remaining pillars, and lay its remaining strength in the dust? Another division of the Church could not, we all know, be

limited to the border. It would strike its desolating fract-
ures, like the rending of an earthquake, through all our solid
central strength to the very North itself. Our denominational history would close, sir, with another such a disaster.
Fragments of the stately structure might remain, but fragments which would themselves only crumble more and more
away. And shall we incur this peril at a day in which, by
social and political causes, as well as religious, every hour is
enlarging our antislavery field and facilitating the speedy, if
not peaceful conquest — the *self-conquest*, it may be — of the
very region where this unguarded blow must strike most
ruinously, and whence it must rebound most disastrously upon
ourselves ?

Two positions have I always maintained in my long editorial career, on this subject ; the first, that our antislavery action
must always bear with it the guarantee of the constitution ;
secondly, that it should be so guarded as never to lose its
most important fields, as I deem them—the fields of the Border Conferences, where no man who knows any thing about
them can doubt that its ultimate triumph is certain, though
it be slow.

Both for the good of the slave and the good of the Church,
then, do I plead here for a modification of this report. Let
us have action on slavery, and let us have it as far forward
as we can without breaking up the constitution and breaking
down the Church. These are my only restrictions. I send
forth this avowal to all my friends, to all my enemies, and
will stand by it or fall by it. Any other course must be fatal
to our own ends ; why, then, should we insist upon it ? Are
we contending only for phrases ? for speculative opinions ?
or for practical results ? In any contingency whatever this
document must fail of practical advantage. If it fails here it
will fail because of the defect I have pointed out. If it fails
not here, yet will it fail elsewhere, on the same account ; it
will be decried and cast away as a dead letter because of its
alleged unconstitutionality. In either case, therefore, it will
fail, and fail, too, because brethren will persist in retaining
a form of words which many conscientious men cannot admit.
One only other result can follow : it may *not* fail in another
respect ; it may be the occasion of disunion, and in that case

its disastrous liabilities would affect every litigation, every title of local or general property, between the parties. Is, then, this the Christian-like, statesman-like measure that the exigencies of this hour demand at our hands? For the sake, then, of the slave, for the sake of the Church, admit, dear brethren, this feeble plea of one to whom both are as dear as to any of you.

B. F. Crary, of Indiana Conference, was in favor of a change of Discipline on the subject of slavery, because:

The regulations of the Discipline do not come up to the standard of public opinion in the Church since her organization, and the law of the Church ought to express her opinions on great moral questions. The law of the Church does not prohibit slave-holding nor extirpate slavery, although it commences boldly and nobly with the stirring question, "What shall be done for the extirpation of the evil of slavery?" Extirpation, from *ex* and *stirpo*, means, from the roots—taking out by the roots. And yet this earnest and solemn question is followed by the softest possible laws, provisos, and exceptions, which can only cut off the topmost branches of this tree we were determined to uproot. The law never reached the roots; they are green and vigorous, and have entwined themselves around the very heart of the Church. We might construct a statute of similar import on the subject of polygamy.

It is not my intention to reproach the fathers by contrasting this law on slavery with a like statute on polygamy, but with the utmost regard for them, and the sole intention of showing how much we need a change in this law, I will write it thus—Of Polygamy.

QUESTION—What shall be done for the extirpation of the great evil of polygamy?

ANSWER 1. We declare that we are as much as ever convinced of the great evil of polygamy; therefore, no man having two or more wives shall be eligible to any official station in our Church hereafter, where the laws of the State in which he lives will admit of divorce, and permit the divorced wife to enjoy good society.

Is that prohibitory?

ANS. 2. When any traveling preacher becomes the husband of more than one wife, by any means, he shall forfeit his ministerial character in our Church, unless he execute, if it be practicable, a legal divorcement of all his wives but one, conformably to the laws of the State in which he lives.

Is adequate punishment meted to the offender here? Does that law prohibit?

ANS. 3. All our preachers shall prudently enforce upon our members the necessity of teaching their wives to observe all the duties of the conjugal relation according to the word of God ; and husbands must treat their wives with equal kindness, permitting them to enjoy equal authority in the family, etc.

Is this a prohibitory or a license law? It is a regulating law, a law which does not attempt to strike the monster, but simply coaxes and lulls him.

We can come to no other conclusion than the sad one, that our disciplinary laws were never intended to prohibit mere slave-holding. It can and does exist under these *extirpating* provisions. The roots grew and flourished amid the wandering members of the Church; its branches, dark and deadly, overshadowed the ministry, and at last its bitter fruits were gladly caught and held by episcopal hands, and that venerable and honorable Board was vilely contaminated by the unhallowed contact. The Church was startled. A moral revolution was the result; convulsion followed convulsion on the border; desolation and grief went in their train. We leave the sickening details. We remember the opinions advanced by the members of the Methodist Episcopal Church, South, at the first General Conference after the division. They said, and truly said, we presume, that those laws on slavery were a dead-letter. They had not kept them; they did not intend to do so. The Methodist Episcopal Church, South, grew up under this peculiarly extirpating *régime.* They are bone of our bone, and flesh of our flesh, and with all their faults we love them still; our training made them.

We conclude that under the circumstances by which we were surrounded down to 1844 our rules did not do much toward the destruction of slavery. Private members, leaders, stewards, exhorters, preachers, traveling preachers, presiding elders, and bishops became slave-holders under this process. Is it not time to change? With sorrow and regret I must

acknowledge that our Discipline is liable to the charge of
being pro-slavery, and I call upon the toiling antislavery
men of the Church to change it. Let us endeavor to reach
the goal, if we have to change the constitution and the law.

C. Blakeslee, of Oneida Conference, said:

I do not believe that slavery has a constitutional existence
and right in the Church. In opposition to this notion I believe and maintain that it is in the Church, not by constitutional authority and power, but merely from the force of
necessitating circumstances; that it is in the Church by toleration and sufferance, as an evil, condemned and doomed
to extirpation. Slavery has no place in our constitution; it
is an incidental evil—an excrescence that may be cast off at
any time by General Conference enactment without touching
our constitution. In support of this position I beg leave, sir,
to adduce a few considerations:

1. The constitution of the Methodist Episcopal Church,
that is, the "Six Restrictive Rules and the General Rules," do
not deny the General Conference the power to determine
whether "slave-holders shall be eligible to membership" in
the Church; hence, as it originally had that power, and actually exercised it at the time of organizing the Church in 1784,
it must still have that right. Brethren of the other side will
not deny that the General Conference had the power to make
slavery a test of membership prior to the adoption of the
constitution in 1808. Then, as there is not a sentence or
word in her constitution taking from the General Conference this power, it now has it in all its original fullness and
strength.

2. The constitution nowhere says members ought to hold
slaves, or that they may hold slaves, or that we are under
any obligation whatever to hold slaves; hence, as to positive
requisition the constitution does not bind us, as a Church, to
slavery and to slave-holding.

3. The constitution does not say slave-holders, as such,
shall have a right in Church; hence, if they are in the Church
at all, it is, and must be, by mere tolerance.

4. The constitution does not forbid the exclusion of slave-
holders from the Church by the enactments of the General

Conference; hence this body may pass a rule making them ineligible to membership, without violating the constitution.

5. It cannot be put into the constitution of the Church by construction. A constitution, like a deed or charter, is virtually a sealed instrument, and, according to the fixed principles of judicial and legal equity and usage, its powers, limitations, and requisitions cannot be essentially altered or increased by implication.

6. It is not sanctified and established by our organic law, but it is condemned, labeled, and doomed to extirpation by the authoritative enactments and declarations of our highest legislative body, and judicial tribunal. It is said it has always been in the Church, therefore it is there by the power of the constitution.

Against this plea I further urge three objections:

1. It is an undeniable fact, that slavery is condemned by the great principles of civil law—of the common law of nations; and yet this plea assumes that it is established, maintained, and defended by the constitution of the Methodist Episcopal Church. It is an outlaw among the nations, but a legitimate child of our holy Church constitution. No, sir, it cannot be!

2. Then, if this plea be valid, wicked slave-holding in the Methodist Episcopal Church towers above the General Conference.

3. Then, if this plea be true and worthy, the whole dark, wicked system of slavery outside the Church has a broad, open, unobstructed highway into our Church. From the bottom of my heart I believe we have power to do all this majority report proposes — I believe we have full authority and power over slavery in the Church.

Samuel Y. Monroe, of New Jersey Conference, proposed to narrow the discussion to the proposition, Have we power to do what the majority report recommends, and if we have, ought we to do it? After indorsing Mr. Stevens' constitutional arguments Mr. Monroe dwelt with special emphasis on the point, that no necessity existed for any such legislation in order to remedy any existing wrong, or to condemn the principle of property in man, or to meet the case of offenders not now within the reach of existing law. Proofs were found, he thought, of the truth of these statements, from the testimony of the brethren of the border, from the unanimous sentiment of the Bishops in their address, and from the admissions found in the report before them. His conclusions were, that loyalty to Christ, loyalty to the Church, and non-interference with the political issues of the day, all combined to forbid any such legislation as was now contemplated.

Henry E. Pilcher, of North Ohio Conference, took the same position, arguing that the new chapter would interpose a barrier to the universal extension of the Gospel, and is in contravention of the organic law of the Church.

Henry Slicer, of Baltimore Conference, made an extended speech, severely criticising the arguments and the language employed by various speakers who wanted antislavery action. He dwelt with special emphasis upon the evil of having a bare majority override the constitutional restriction upon such important changes. Dr. Thomson's speech was largely reviewed. The alleged growth of the slave power was denied. Mr. Slicer said he did not believe a word of it. In 1789 twelve thirteenths of all the States had slaves in their borders. Instead of freedom going backward, six States of the original thirteen have become free, and in addition we have the free States formed from the North-western territory out of the soil ceded by Virginia. The population of the United States in 1790 was—whites, 3,172,464; free colored, 59,446; slaves, 697,897, or about five whites to one slave, and one free colored to eleven slaves. In 1850—whites, 19,558,068; free colored, 334,495; slaves 3,204,313, or about six whites to one slave and seven slaves to one free colored. The free colored people have increased to nearly half a million, and the disproportion of slaves to the white and free colored population is greatly increased since 1790. Emancipation has progressed from New England to the line of Delaware, where the slave population is sparse and slavery exists in its mildest form. Slavery is not destined to be perpetual in this country. He looked forward to the day when freedom should be universal, when Christianity will have worked out her legitimate results, and the clank of the last chain shall be heard, and the last groan of oppressed humanity die away.

After vindicating the fathers, the legislation, and the constitution of the Church as it is, Mr. Slicer said: "In conclusion, who ask for this change of Discipline? Who, of our 790,000 members? Have one in ten, or one in fifty? Upon examination it will be found that the Conferences whose delegates ask a change—if all their members did, instead of one in ten—are a minority of more than forty thousand, as compared with the Conferences whose delegates ask no change."

Dr. George Peck, of Wyoming Conference, reviewed the speeches of Dr. Dempster and Dr. Chamberlaine adversely, and, for reasons akin to those already reported at length, opposed all change or new legislation on the subject of slavery. The distinctive points of his speech were the special importance he attached to the fact that there are multitudes of our most pious and trustworthy people in Pennsylvania, New Jersey,

and in and about the city of New York, who are uncompromisingly opposed to any new rule on the subject of slavery.   They are in close sympathy with the
border :

If our brethren there should be disturbed by our action,
many of the most wealthy, pious, and influential of our members in the localities above referred to will be chafed and
disaffected—to say nothing more. We have intimations of
the state of feeling upon this subject in certain influential
quarters from the remonstrances which have been sent up to
this General Conference against change in Discipline on the
subject of slavery. The opinions of the men to whom I have
referred are well considered and are not likely to be easily
changed; and the feelings of such men are not to be trifled
with.   Should they be permanently disaffected, their influence
is lost to the Church and the Church will lose her power over
them.

And in concluding his remarks Dr. Peck opposed
the whole policy of the report now before the Conference, because it is regarded by its friends as a mere
" entering wedge," and not a finality :

If a hope might be entertained that the ceaseless agitation
on the subject of slavery would pause somewhere this side of
the total ruin of the work in the slave-holding States, there
would be some plausibility in a compromise measure; indeed,
almost any change in the law which would not absolutely
expel all slave-holders—if its enactment would set the question finally at rest—would be preferable to the irritations of
an endless controversy. Our progressive brethren are prepared to take all they can get, but with the frank avowal that
they will continue to press on toward the goal of a final separation of all slave-holders from the Church. This is what
they purpose to accomplish as soon as they can command the
votes; they will only pause upon intermediate points to take
breath for a brief period. The present measure, radical as it
is, is not a finality; it is not what our reformers ask for and

intend to have; agitation will go on, and the war upon our Southern border will continue to be pressed with increasing vigor, until our brethren there shall either be forced out of the Church or compelled to submit to legal enactments which are utterly impossible in the slave-holding States.

Dr. Raymond, by special vote of the Conference, because chairman of the Committee on Slavery, again presented the argument for the report, which is reproduced here in brief:

The report before us arranges slave-holders into three distinct classes: first, the mercenary slave-holder—the man who, under civil authority, coerces the obedience of his fellow-man for his (the slave-holder's) profit, pleasure, or convenience—the man who, for mercenary purposes, restrains the personal liberties of another man called his slave. The second class are termed innocent slave-holders—men who sustain the legal relation of master to slave involuntarily. It is a universally recognized principle in ethics, that what is done involuntarily has no moral character. It may in itself be beneficial or injurious; but in its relation to the agent it is morally neither good, bad, or indifferent. The agent is not by it rendered either blame or praise worthy. The third class contemplated by the report is composed of those who voluntarily enter the legal relation for benevolent purposes, as when one purchases a slave to save him from perpetual bondage—from separation from his wife and children and the graves of his fathers; a man who, by the payment of $500 or $1,000, secures the control of the personal liberties of a slave for his (the slave's) benefit, to save that slave from the terrors of banishment from home and of cruelty under the lash of distant task-masters, performs an act precisely the same in its moral character as if he had paid $5 or $10 to purchase clothing for the naked, or any other sum to purchase bread for the starving, in proportion to the amount of his sacrifice. The report thus contemplates three classes of slave-holders, not three kinds of slave-holding, but three classes of slave-holders, the mercenary, the innocent, and the virtuous. Is this classification exhaustive? If there be any others they are not recognized, they are utterly unknown, and of course are not included in the enumeration. . . .

Our opponents are of two classes: the first, those who contend for the Discipline as it is, who will admit no change; the second, those who desire some change, but oppose the one before us because of its alleged unconstitutionality. The position of the first is defined in the Minority Report, now on our table, the substance of which might be embodied in the following resolution:

Resolved, That it is inexpedient for this Conference to legislate on the subject of slavery.

The issue here is not between this document and another, but between something and nothing; the inquiry is not whether the doctrines of our report are truthful or erroneous, whether its measures are just or unjust, but whether we shall do something or do nothing. Were it proposed to substitute for the present chapter on slavery in our Book of Discipline the stereotyped declaration that "we are as much as ever convinced of the great evil of slavery," with our Saviour's golden rule appended, our brethren on the border, and those who sympathize with them, would be bound to oppose it for the same reason that they oppose what is now presented, namely, "We want no change, we go for the Discipline as it is." "The Discipline as it is," "the Discipline as it is," is the beginning and the ending of the homily read to us by the speakers to whom we now refer. Their real objection is not to the character of the thing proposed, but is an objection to any change whatever. . . .

We come now, to consider the constitutional objection. It is alleged that this report proposes a new term of membership not included within the general rules—more specifically it is alleged that non-slaveholding is by the report made a condition of membership—that the general rules interpreted by the facts of history do allow slave-holders in the Church, and that, therefore, the report proposes to do by a mere majority what the restrictive rules declare shall not be done, except by a vote of two thirds of the General Conference and three fourths of the members of the several Annual Conferences.

In reply to this, I beg to read again the extract already read twice in the course of these remarks: "The merely legal

relation shall not be considered of itself sufficient to exclude
a person from the fellowship of the Church."

I also call attention to the fact that every paragraph in this
proposed chapter, except the first, contemplates the existence
of slave-holders in the Church, even among probationers. I
affirm I am utterly unable to understand the meaning of
words, if this chapter, either in letter or spirit, in part or in
whole, gives the least possible occasion for the objection that
it makes absolute non-slaveholding a condition of membership. It excludes sinful slave-holders, and such only. What,
then, is the import of this constitutional objection? Evidently that wicked men are in the Church by its organic
law—by right, and not by sufferance. This assumption we
most solemnly deny; we can never be persuaded to admit
that the Methodist Episcopal Church ever, either by constitutional or statute law, sanctioned the enormity of mercenary
slave-holding, and since our report is opposed as unconstitutional, because, as is alleged, it excludes persons having constitutional rights to membership; and since it excludes none
but sinful slave-holders, we cannot retire from this report
without acknowledging the horrible doctrine that the vilest
of all enormities is sanctioned by the organic law of the
Church. But if the time ever was when we could have honorably accepted a substitute to avoid the alleged objection,
we cannot do it now, since in a speech prepared by one of
the ablest pens in our Church, pronounced by one of the most
eloquent tongues among us, listened to with the most profound attention, with almost a breathless silence—a silence
maintained by the fall of the chairman's hammer as oft as it
was disturbed by a rustle in the lobby, since in a speech
claiming and receiving such high consideration, a speech to
be circulated through all our borders, East West, North, and
South; powerful in its logic, beautiful in its rhetoric, rich in
its historical illustration, elevated in style, and, not the least
of all, sustained by the authority of its author with his
twenty years of official antislavery antecedents, it has been so
unqualifiedly asserted and maintained that the report proposes what is unconstitutional. Mark it well, Mr. President
and brethren: that speech, indorsed by the prominence given
it in its reception, maintains that our report is unconstitu-

tional, because it excludes persons having constitutional rights to membership. Now, mark again, our report excludes none but acknowledged sinful slave-holders. What is the *sequitur?* Can it be any thing else than that sinful slaveholders are in the Church by constitutional rights? Ask me, either by a vote or a refusal, to indorse such a doctrine! The rather take instruments of torture and sever that right arm, with a fierce finger pluck that right eye from its socket, or bathe a murderous dagger in this beating heart. No, no, I would sooner stand alone on the floor of this Conference in defense of the position I now maintain, and thus by my protest leave this an open question for the decisions of future time, than yield one moment under circumstances such as now press us to the assumption that the Church, which under God has been the mother of my salvation, was ever guilty of such an enormity as to confer by organic law the right to her immunities upon those guilty of "the vilest sin that ever saw the sun."

The doctrine we oppose admitted, and all that has been said under the promptings of Southern enmity about the injuries inflicted by us upon the Church South is true; all that has been said under the promptings of seceding proselytism among the Wesleyans of the North, about the corruptions and pro-slavery character of our Church, are verily yea and amen. Let this General Conference indorse this doctrine, and I venture to prophesy a storm will be thereby raised in public opinion that will lay the temple of our Zion low in irretrievable ruin.

Mr. President, this bill was put on its passage through this house under disabilities inconsistent with the processes of impartial legislation: a panic had been excited—a project had been discussed in some of our periodicals of introducing into the chapter on slavery, by a mere majority vote, an absolute prohibition; a measure which, as I judge, is not only in conflict with our organic law, but wrong in itself, since it would make the door of the Church narrower than the gates of heaven. This, I doubt not, was in part the occasion of the suggestion on this subject contained in the Episcopal Address; a suggestion of which I do not complain. By reason of these and similar concurrent circumstances, it has come to be a matter of real history that this persecuted report was pronounced unconstitutional before it was written. Threats of secession and division have been industriously circulated, all, as I believe, without competent authority, yet not the less effectual for want of authority, which have been sufficiently terrific to frighten even brave men from their self-possession; and, to crown the accumulation of unfortunate circumstances, the magnates of the Conference have been opposed to us.

James V. Watson, of Michigan Conference, spoke in favor of the earliest practicable prohibition of holding humanity as property by our Church members. He had not deemed it necessary to change the constitution in order to make a prohibitory statute in the chapter binding. He would now, however, favor commencing work upon the constitution, although his opinion was unchanged as to its necessity.

Dr. John M'Clintock, of New Jersey Conference, expressed a fear that a time "may come, in some future age, when the historian shall give five or six lines to an account like the following: 'In the eighteenth and nineteenth centuries there arose men of godliness, zeal, energy, who went abroad through the length and breadth of every land, proclaiming the Gospel of the Son of God, and achieving successes beyond all former precedent in the history of religion after the apostolic age. But these men, though they had zeal enough to gather a great Church, had not wisdom enough to guide it.'"

After an earnest plea against any change, Dr. M'Clintock deprecated the tendency of Young America to set aside the wisdom of the fathers, despise the counsels of age, and make light of the teachings of experience. He read, as a lesson to the point, from the first Book of Kings, twelfth chapter, the account of Rehoboam and his young friends, whose advice he preferred to the counsel of the old men, and thereby divided Israel. His concluding point was to insist that the proposed new law was one for which the Church was not prepared:

> But is it the part of wisdom and prudence to adopt a measure so far in advance of public opinion that it will inevitably defeat itself? One point more, and I have done. Do not the difficulties that have pressed upon all who have attempted to frame a new law for our Church on slavery, at this Conference and for the four years past, show that the time for framing it has not come? A large committee has had the subject in hand for weeks; they have turned the subject over in every shape; yet the law, as they have framed it, hardly satisfies any two men that look at it together. One member of that committee told me, I think, that he had made fifty trials at it without satisfying himself. Is not this, of itself, sir, proof that the time has not come? When the fit time comes there will be no such difficulty. The terms of the law will readily be found when the time for the law arrives. Law is not made; it grows.

Dr. D. W. Clark, of New York Conference, said he deemed the constitution now antislavery. If guilty slave-holders were in the Church they were there by stealth. It was with these views that the New York Conference voted against any change. He protested against the doctrine of Mr. Stevens' speech.

F. G. Hibbard, of East Genesee Conference, did not like the phraseology of the new rule. He did not believe in the right of property in man; wished to vote emphatically against the chattel principle; hesitated, and yet would give his vote in the affirmative on the Majority Report.

H. H. Pearne, of Wyoming Conference, disclaimed

all sympathy for the doctrine that slave-holding was recognized in our organic law.

The discussion thus sketched and abridged occupied the attention of the General Conference almost exclusively for a week, and sometimes for two sessions daily. All who spoke have not been reported. Every distinctive point made on either side of the question has been carefully looked after and presented. Speeches not on the direct line of the argument—or those which were mainly criticisms, or those arguments which, as repetitions, would add nothing to the fund of historic knowledge—are omitted. The number of speakers on each side was about equal. There are more pages occupied with the arguments in favor of antislavery action than of those which give the opposite side of the question. But the friends of the affirmative had necessarily the more extensive field of discussion; and the negative side of the question has not been weakened by any important omission.

The direct vote was taken upon the first resolution of the report only, which was, "That we recommend the several Annual Conferences so to amend our General Rule on slavery as to read: 'The buying, selling, or holding a human being as a slave.'" In favor there were 122 votes; against it, 96. As it required a majority of two thirds, or 149 votes, to adopt it and put it upon its passage through the Annual Conferences, Bishop Waugh announced the result by saying: "The resolution is not adopted, not having two thirds of the votes in its favor."

The second resolution, which proposed a new section on slavery, had been laid on the table during the morning session of May 29. After the vote on the first resolution was announced, Dr. Raymond moved to take up the second; which motion was renewed by Dr. James Floy the next day, appended to one to suspend the order of the day, with a view to offer a substitute.

James Porter, of New England Conference, had said, in support of Dr. Raymond's motion, he was in favor of taking up the resolution, not for a direct vote, but for a substitute to be offered which he had. But if pressed to it—if he must vote for the new section or nothing—he should vote for it. And there were fifty others who sympathized with him, he said. The matter had been carried too far to be dropped here. Let those speeches that have been delivered here go out over the length and breadth of the land, unaccompanied by any antislavery expression of this body, and they will produce results we shall not be able to counteract.

James Floy, in support of his motion, May 30, said:

Difficulties exist in both sections. Brethren must know that there is a North. Our border friends overlook the fact of pressure, almost unbearable, in other parts of our work. This compels us to do something in answer to the question about "extirpation." You ask us to be hushed as death, so that, on our return, when asked, "What did you do?" we shall be obliged to answer, "Nothing at all; only we talked, talked, talked!"

Brethren, we will not be fettered. Would you have us hide our heads in shame when asked, What have you done for the extirpation of slavery? Just now there are peculiar signs of necessity that something must be done. The shed blood of our friends is coming up with strong cries from the Territory of Kansas. Horrible outrages are spread upon the pages of our daily newspapers. What has set fire to Lawrence? Why is that gem of the prairie, that seeks to be consecrated gloriously to freedom, a heap of moldering ashes?

The reasons in favor of suspending the regular order of the day are, first, that some action is needed and expected if we would not disappoint the hopes of our people.

1. It is needed and expected.

There may be exceptions to this. Let not the brethren forget, however, that beyond the border hundreds of thousands are looking for something to be done here.

2. Public sentiment every-where demands it, especially where it is fanned by the aggressions of slavery. The simple question is, On what side is the Methodist Episcopal Church, proslavery or antislavery ?

After other remarks Mr. Floy read the substitute he proposed to offer when the report should have been taken up. It proposed to amend the chapter on slavery by retaining such parts as are found between the quotation marks, and adding what is found in brackets :

1. "We declare we are as much as ever convinced of the great evil of slavery," [and hereby declare that the general rule forbids the traffic in slaves, and is opposed to slave-holding for mercenary or selfish purposes.]

2. "When any traveling preacher," etc., the whole being retained as now.

3. [It is the duty of the Annual Conferences and pastors to apply the General Rules in conformity with these principles.]

The motion to suspend the order of the day was laid on the table by a vote of 124 to 91. The effect of this action, directly or indirectly, was to prevent a vote on the new chapter, and also to prevent the presentation of any substitute or amendment. Besides the substitutes of James Porter and of James Floy, another was in readiness, of which Dr. E. Thomson says : "Dr. Stevens came to us at that General Conference with the following chapter :

Question : What shall be done for the extinction of slavery ?   *Answer :* 1. We are as much as ever convinced of the great evil of slavery. The General Rule forbids the traffic in slaves, and in spirit is opposed to slave-holding for mercenary purposes. 2. It is the duty of the pastors of Churches, in their administration, to apply the General Rule in accordance with these principles."—*Christian Advocate, July* 4, 1861.

" It was drawn," adds Dr. Thomson, " if we mistake not, by Bishop Simpson,* and Dr. Stevens desired that we would offer it as a substitute for the pending report on slavery, or, in case that failed, offer it as an original motion; affirming that if we did he from the East, and Dr. M'Clintock from the center, would support it, and that it might be carried."

The indirect refusal to take up the report on slavery, by laying on the table the preliminary motion to suspend the order of the day, indicated that any further action on that subject was not practicable during that session of the General Conference. A large majority, one hundred and twenty-two, had recorded their names in favor of prohibiting all slaveholding by a change of the General Rule with the concurring vote of the Annual Conferences. Of this number ninety-one were radical Abolitionists, and in favor of partial prohibition by direct and immediate legislation. Comparing the different votes taken by yeas and nays, three classes of voters are recorded— the conservatives, the constitutional Abolitionists, and the radical Abolitionists. The first class, numbering ninety-six, voted against all changes; the second, numbering in all thirty-one, to prevent prohibition of

* This is confirmed by a note from the Bishop, November 22, 1879.

slave-holding by direct legislation, united with the conservatives, and threw the balance of power in favor of postponing further action, as before noted. Final antislavery action was thus deferred rather than defeated.

The sanguine expectations of the Abolitionists in the Church had not been realized. Neither had the forebodings of the Border Conferences proved correct. No new legislation had been enacted. The Rule and the Section on Slavery were not changed; but the moral power of a large majority vote was recorded against slavery, and its death warrant was sealed.

CHAPTER XXV.

ANTISLAVERY RÉGIME.

THE debate and the votes on the subject of slavery at Indianapolis, already noted, were not the whole antislavery action of the General Conference of 1856. A new administration was inaugurated for the publishing and the editorial departments of the Church. James Floy, chairman of the Committee on the Tract Cause, reported "that the Tract Committee, having had under consideration the publication of antislavery literature, recommend for adoption the following resolution: That the Book Agents and the Tract Secretary be, and they hereby are, instructed to publish in book or tract form such antislavery matter as the subject of slavery may demand, including Mr. Wesley's 'Thoughts on Slavery.'"

Efforts were made to leave the matter discretionary, and not make it obligatory by such positive instruction; but that proposition was laid on the table, on motion of R. S. Rust. An effort to postpone indefinitely was defeated; the motion, by W. L. Harris, to take the vote by yeas and nays showing only fifty-three in favor of it. Finally the instructions to publish antislavery literature prevailed by a very large majority.

During the discussion which preceded this action it was stated that three tracts of this class—Wesley's "Thoughts" and Dr. Elliott's "Argument on the Sinfulness of Slavery"—had been published by the

Tract Secretary, Rev. A. Stevens, during the previous quadrennium, which the Executive Committee at New York ordered stricken off the list because their publication was not authorized by them. Mr. Stevens vindicated his action before the General Conference, and insisted that "the circumstances of the case and the condition of the country required it." By the action now taken the possibility of any such conflict of jurisdiction was prevented, and the duty of the incoming administration clearly established, which was promptly and faithfully attended to by the new secretary, Rev. James Floy, who was a radical Abolitionist.

The changes made in the editorial corps by the General Conference were the natural result of, and in harmony with, the decided antislavery views of the majority, yet in no wise proscriptive. Of twelve editors chosen for the ensuing four years, six had voted with the majority in favor of the new rule prohibiting all slave-holding. These were the editors of the "Christian Advocate and Journal," the Sunday-school books, the "National Magazine," the "Western Christian Advocate," the "North-western Christian Advocate," and the "Northern Advocate." The editor of the "Ladies' Repository," D. W. Clark, did not vote with the majority, yet he was fully identified with the general antislavery movement. The editor of the "Quarterly," D. D. Whedon, was not a member of the Conference, and was not recognized as an Abolitionist; but his manly utterances against slavery extension had caused his dismissal from a professorship in the Michigan State University.

The predominance of antislavery sentiment, thus indicated, was manifested in every department of the

Church during the quadrennium commencing with 1856. At this period there were three Methodist bodies at the North, moving in separate columns, on well-defined lines of action, toward the same objective point, against a common enemy—American slavery. These were the Methodist Episcopal Church, the Wesleyan Methodist Connection, and the Northern Conferences of the Methodist Protestant Church. With each the movement had been the work of years. The first two bodies were nearly coetaneous in their antislavery labors; for the organization of the Wesleyans and the newly-awakened antislavery life of the old body dated back then over twenty years. The Protestants of the North took their initiative step November, 1856, and moved into line, fully organized, soon after. And, however separate the path of their respective movements or however·diverse the measure of their power, these three Methodist Churches were now, with accumulated forces, rapidly converging to one grand goal, the overthrow of slavery.

Two of these bodies, the Wesleyans and the Protestants, by withdrawing from the majorities antagonistic to their views, had easily secured a constitutional prohibition of slavery in their discipline; while the Methodist Episcopal Church, doubtless influenced in some measure by their action, and impelled still more by sympathy with the generous civilization of the age and by the benevolence of a common religious faith, had marshaled a vast majority of her communion in active hostility to slavery. And this numerical strength was more than tenfold greater than the united membership of both the other Churches, and was rapidly growing in power equal to the task of enacting a constitutional prohibition of slavery for a Church of a million communicants. The verdict of the General Conference of 1856 was recorded to the effect that slavery was a capital offense against humanity, and worthy of death. The formalities of enacting a constitutional provision delayed the execution of the sentence. But for the law requiring that two thirds should vote in favor of it, such a provision would have been upon its passage at once. As it was, the vote only lacked twenty-seven of being two thirds in a body of two hundred and eighteen.

During the interim between the sentence and its execution, which was deferred for years, there was strong opposition to the extirpating blow, and many fruitless efforts for a reprieve were made by the powerful minority of conservatives, who were probably equal in strength to their representatives in the General Conference, or as ninety-one to one hundred and twenty-four. But the new departure was now inaugurated, and, while it was not as radical as the majority desired it should be, there was no purpose nor probability of retracing the steps taken or going back upon the antislavery record made at Indianapolis.

The " Christian Advocate " at New York, for four years prior to 1856, had been edited by a conservative, whose severe personal criticisms upon Abolitionists, and vigorous resistance to all proposed General Conference action against slavery, were adverse to the prevailing sentiment of the Church, but fully identified, in sympathy and sentiment, with the " Border Conferences " and their conservative friends of the minority. His successor in 1856 was regarded by the radical Abolitionists as a conservative, because of his position and arguments in the General Conference

against an exscinding statutory law, which he opposed
on the ground that slavery was constitutionally intrenched in the Church, and could only be reached by
a change of the constitution. Subsequently, for four
years under the new management, this influential
journal, although less conservative editorially, was
very far behind any aggressive Church action upon
the subject of slavery, and pursued a course agreeing
with the assumption of the editor, "that the limited
margin of slave-holding territory remaining with the
North was so fully provided with the best practical
testimony against slavery by the Churches within its
limits, as to give promise, with due prudence of action
on the part of the North, that the entire field would
be self-redeemed in a few years." But there was a
most extensive antislavery discussion allowed in its
columns, which placed the "Advocate" far in advance of its former position on the question of slavery.

The constitutional right of slave-holders to admission and membership in the Church, so ably argued
by Dr. Stevens at Indianapolis, and for a time largely
accepted by many who were sorry to have it so, was
more positively and successfully challenged after the
General Conference adjourned, by several writers, than
it was even during the debate thereon. A most conclusive argument in support of the proposition that
"Constitutionally we have not been a slave-holding
Church; that the General Rule did not authorize
slave-holding; and that the General Conference was
competent to pass a simple rule of discipline which
would exclude all slave-holders," was prepared by
Professor W. L. Harris, which appeared in the periodical press first, and afterward was published in

book form.   It was entitled "Powers of the General
Conference."   The progress of antislavery sentiment,
and the increasing probability of a statutory prohibition in 1860, was in a great part attributable to the
influence of the line of argument therein furnished,
which maintained the following propositions: The
terms "rules" and "laws" are synonymous; the
General Conference has full powers to make rules for
our Church that do not revoke or change a General
Rule; a statutory rule excluding all slave-holders
from the Church would not revoke or change any
General Rule; the General Rules never did, do not
now, and never can, contain all the terms of membership in the Discipline; there are, and always have
been, and will always continue to be, terms of membership which the General Conference has power to
change, abolish, or re-enact at pleasure; if it had
been the intention to guard the question of slavery by
constitutional provision, it would have been done
when the Church actually did meet to frame a constitution in 1808; but there is not one word on the
subject of slavery, nor was any attempt made to introduce any such restriction; nay, more, such a restriction was deliberately and of design omitted from
the constitution; and, therefore, the General Conference, possessing full power in the premises, may refuse to tolerate slavery any longer, and, by enacting a
statutory rule, exclude all slave-holders from the
Church.

The reception given to this view of the question
very generally may be judged of by the indorsement
of the editor of the "Methodist Quarterly." He
said, in reviewing it: "The large share of this argument by Dr. Harris appeared originally in our Advo-

cates, and its signal ability and apparent conclusiveness attracted general attention. In its present form it is one of the ablest constitutional documents that has ever appeared in our ecclesiastical history, reading very much like one of John Marshall's decisions, leaving nothing further to be said on either side. We trust that every member of the next General Conference will give it a thorough consideration. In its present unanswered condition it is in great danger of settling the opinion of the Church on the topic it discusses." — "*Methodist Quarterly*," *April*, 1860.

There were many of the best men of the Church who fully believed that, if properly construed, the Discipline, without amendment, would exclude all slave-holders. Robert Boyd advocated this view in 1855. James B. Finley argued thus at Indianapolis. Dr. Clark, editor of the "Ladies' Repository," for this alleged reason, did not then vote for a change of the General Rule. "And the Oregon and California Conferences, in 1859, both declined to co-operate in any effort to change the General Rule on slavery, assigning as a reason that, to their understanding, that rule, as it then stood, prohibited all slave-holding."— "*Powers of the General Conference*," p. 48.

In every direction, from various centers, throughout the entire Church, antislavery influences were radiating with accelerating force. The "Sunday-School Advocate" had, in some Methodist schools, been displaced by the "Juvenile Instructor," from the Wesleyan Book Room, at Syracuse, because the latter was an antislavery child's paper. But, after Daniel Wise became editor, in 1856, the first-named paper began to publish "short paragraphs against

slavery and in favor of freedom." This soon called
forth letters of complaint from the "border," without changing the course of the editor, who "persisted
in occasional moderate remarks on the theme." In
the spring of 1858 Mr. Wise informed the writer
that he visited two of the Annual Conferences in that
region. "Several laymen waited" on him, "profess-
ing very high regard for the 'Sunday-School Advocate,' but urging" the editor "to promise to desist
from inserting antislavery remarks, and declaring that
if he would not, they should feel obliged to exclude
it from the Sunday-schools." He declined to make
any such pledge. On the floor of the Conference
he was questioned on the subject, and similar declarations of purpose to ostracize the "Sunday-School
Advocate," were made. His reply was, that "The
Advocate is expected to teach our children the
doctrines and ethics of our Church; that slave-holding is a violation of Christian and Methodist ethics;
that consequently it is my duty to teach the children to think of it as a sin; that so long as I am
editor of the paper I shall firmly, but judiciously,
so instruct them. If the General Conference shall
condemn my course, it can, of course, replace me
with another editor."

The scene in that Conference was one of great excitement. The affair was largely reported in the newspapers. The "Quarterly" for October, 1858, spoke
of it as "a marked discourtesy to a General Conference officer officially present, followed by an elaborate effort to withdraw support from the Church
periodical under his charge because it persisted in
inculcating the holy principles of our Church upon
our children." At another Annual Conference on

the "border," there was an expressed purpose to
repeat the above scene, but as soon as Mr. Wise had
concluded his address, Bishop Ames prevented it by
promptly cutting off replies thereto, and calling very
decidedly for other business. But, directly after, the
Churches along the border began stopping that paper
by hundreds and thousands. The Churches in the
North and West were appealed to, and the response
given thereto increased the subscription list scores of
thousands, but even that did not restore the losses on
the border.

The "Methodist Quarterly Review," when Dr.
Whedon became editor, opened its pages to the general discussion of slavery. An appreciative notice of
Greeley's "History of the Struggle for Slavery Extension," Godwin's "Political Essays," and an oration
by Curtis, in the January "Quarterly" for 1857, was the
occasion for designating this as "a great and permanent question," calling forth these "permanent intel-
lectual efforts," the justification for which was declared to be "the high and exceptional character of
the crisis and the momentous question at stake."

The number for April ensuing furnished an article
by Rev. A. Stevens, "Slavery: The Times," which
proposed for discussion "the latest phase of the question, . . . the very noticeable retrogression of public
sentiment in the South," which was characterized as
"the great American apostasy." As applied "mostly
to the farther South, yet nevertheless to the great
solid mass of the South," Mr. Stevens declared that
"the public bodies, the political guides, the popular
press, the leading theologians, stand almost uniformly
committed to the great apostasy. . . . It is certainly
a startling fact," said he, "that if Washington or

Jefferson could reappear to-day, unrecognized but un-changed, in the midst of the South, avowing the sentiments they once uttered there, they would be swung from the gibbet or die under the lash. . . . This is the condition we have reached in the retro-gression of the Southern public mind."

The "Synopsis of the Quarterlies" for April, 1857, furnishes, from the editor's pen, seven pages of keen analysis of British views of our national affairs, which embrace a compact and complete history of the strug-gle for freedom against domestic despotism in Amer-ica. In conclusion Dr. Whedon adds: "Slavery, though in the South, is not the South. It is only the terrible oppressive nightmare upon the South strug-gling to extend its catalogue of curses over the North. . . . We may call attention to the fact that, in spite of the pro-slavery pretenses to the contrary, the sub-lime and costly act of emancipation by which England abolished slavery in the West Indies has been an ultimate triumph for freedom and humanity."

The last page of the same number sets forth edi-torially what would be the course of the "Quarterly," which in all the years following was faithfully pur-sued. "We have arrived at a crisis in which firm boldness is the true and only conservatism. Pusilla-nimity is destructivism. Avoiding any discussion of changes of our own Church organism on this point, the 'Methodist Quarterly,' as the antislavery organ of an antislavery Church, based upon an antislavery Discipline as it is, will be fearless and free." And the ensuing years of the quadrennium produced able papers from such correspondents as Dr. Thomson and Dr. C. Adams; besides, the "Editorial Parley" and "Quarterly Book Table" often contained antislavery matter of the most effective character, immediately and ultimately.

In addition to those journals authorized by the Church and edited by the appointment of the General Conference, the "Northern Independent," of Auburn, New York, was among the most vigorous and uncompromising antislavery papers in the whole country. The editor, Rev. William Hosmer, had been the editor of the "Northern Christian Advocate" for several years. At the General Conferences of 1848 and 1852 no balloting was necessary in his case. A hand vote only was sufficient, and that was nearly unanimous. But his radical antislavery views and his antagonism of the conservative policy were so intense, that the hitherto invariable usage of choosing the nominee of the patronizing Conferences was repudiated in his case. A unanimous nomination by these was overslaughed by the Conservatives generally, through whose influence another was made editor by a small majority. And thus two antislavery papers were provided for instead of one.

The chagrin of Mr. Hosmer's friends was only appeased after their defeat by the organization of a board of publication which issued the new independent paper of which he was editor during the quadrennium ending with 1860. Although out of his rightful position by unfair dealing, he was yet in the line of a vigorous prosecution of the antislavery enterprise, which had for its objective point the triumph of freedom in the Church and nation.

CHAPTER XXVI.

GENERAL CONFERENCE OF 1860.

THE conflict between the various parties to the discussion about methods of extirpating slavery became intensified after 1856. The attitude of Mr. Stevens in the General Conference of that year, and the apparent inconsistency, thereby indicated, with former deliverances by him as to methods of Church action, were severely criticised by Mr. Wise and others, who were replied to by him through the " Christian Advocate," and also in " Zion's Herald." They favored the prohibition of all slave-holding by statutory legislation. He antagonized it, and insisted on a change of law on slavery by the constitutional proviso, and claimed to be consistent with himself and in harmony with New England Methodists in holding these views.

Subsequently Dr. E. O. Haven, then editor of " Zion's Herald," took issue with Mr. Stevens on the constitutional question, and a warm discussion ensued in their respective papers. A lengthy adverse review of Mr. Stevens' arguments was published by him from the pen of Professor W. L. Harris. Dr. Bond's opinion that " the General Conference is competent to pass a simple rule of discipline which will exclude all slave-holders from the Church without respect to character and circumstances," was quoted by the one party with great satisfaction, and by the other was triumphantly offset with the contradictory opinion of the doctor's, that, " to supplement them (the rules

on slavery) by a statutory provision on the same subject, would be as clearly to violate the Constitution
as to repeal them in part or in whole." Both opinions were from his editorial writings—the first dated
July 5, 1855, and the second dated November 22, of
the same year, in the "Christian Advocate."

For such "a rule of discipline" a host of advocates
was marshaled in every section of the Church north
and west of Maryland. They swarmed through the
press. Solid columns rose to their feet in its favor
at the Annual Conferences of the last year of the
quadrennium. And they included many wise and
reverend men.

Against any action, other than a constitutional
change, not a few of the ablest writers of the Church
were arrayed. But they were earnest in their advocacy of such a change. The antislavery force had
these two wings. Both moved with firm and earnest
steps to the one objective point—the extirpation of
slavery.

A few Conferences were opposed to all antislavery
action. Some opposed it only because they feared a
withdrawal of the Churches on the border more than
they hated slavery. And it was confidently declared,
by leading conservatives, that neither a change of rules
or of the chapter could possibly be effected at the
ensuing General Conference; and to prevent it the
utmost exertion was made by them.

An "Appeal" was addressed to the entire Church
"Concerning what the next General Conference should
do on the Question of Slavery, by Abel Stevens."
It was a 12mo pamphlet of fifty-eight pages, and
favored doing nothing more than giving a declaration
of "the sense of the Church on the whole subject,"

and "a note, put in the margin of the General Rule," declaring, "that the only cases of slave-holding admissible to our communion are such as are consistent with the golden rule." The subject-matter of the "Appeal" was first issued as editorials in the "Advocate."

A reply to these editorials, by Dr. D. D. Whedon, was refused a place in the "Advocate," and therefore first appeared in the "New York Tribune," and afterward in pamphlet form. The reply indicated that "an argument showing its constitutionality can, indeed, be made" in favor "of excluding slave-holders from the Church by a mere majority vote changing our chapter." But the writer preferred "the slow but securely constitutional process of the two-thirds rule," which he advocated with great ability.

A "Ministers' and Laymen's Union" was formed in 1859, at the session of the New York Conference, of which Dr. N. Bangs was president, and Dr. J. H. Perry was put at the head of the executive committee, which, by a circular it issued, proposed a canvass and auxiliary organizations throughout the Church, to effectually protest against the proposed change of the rule on slavery, as an unjust measure, and destructive of the unity of the Church. This called forth a counter-statement by the Antislavery Society of the New York East Conference, from the pen of Dr. Curry, in favor of such a change, which covered the entire ground of the argument, *pro et con*, with marked ability.

Although the moderate expressions proposed by Mr. Stevens, who recognized the necessity for a new testimony and definition of the rule against slavery, were in the interest of the Churches of the "Border Conferences," they met with little favor in that direction. The younger Dr. Bond, editor of the Baltimore "Christian Advocate," whom the Baltimore Conference indorsed unqualifiedly by a unanimous vote afterward, said in his columns, December 3, 1859: "The proposition of Dr. Stevens is as objectionable to us as the Providence resolutions; and the passage of any such declaration will make it necessary for us to consult for the welfare of the Church committed to us. . . . The measure he proposes is 'testimony' to what is abundantly testified — 'definition' of a position already rigorously fixed; law without penalty; discipline without authority; a sop to Cerberus, and a tub to a whale!"

Resolutions in favor of a new rule on slavery were submitted to the various Annual Conferences prior to the General Conference of 1860. They were designated by the name of the Conference which originated them. The New Hampshire Rule, which proposed to make the law forbid "the buying or holding a human being as property," was not presented to the other conferences. The Cincinnati Rule would forbid "the buying or selling of men, women, or children, or holding them, with an intention to use them as slaves." The Providence Rule would have prohibited "slave-holding, the buying or selling of men, women, or children, with an intention to enslave them." The Erie Rule would make the law read, "the buying, selling, holding, or transferring of any human being to be used in slavery."

The official report of votes cast for and against these several propositions in the Annual Conferences, as reported at the General Conference of 1860, at Buffalo, New York, was as follows: On the Cincinnati Rule, 319 votes for, 1,212 votes against it; on the Providence Rule, 1,242 votes for, and 1,329 votes against it; on the Erie Rule, 1,795 votes for, and 1,416 votes against it.

The memorials received on the subject of slavery at the General Conference of 1860 were classified by the committee to which they were referred as "those asking for the extirpation of slavery from the Church," and "those asking that no change be made in the Discipline on the subject of slavery." The results were summed up by a committee of which C. Kingsley was chairman, and Daniel Wise secretary, thus: "Against change, from thirty-two Annual Conferences, one hundred and thirty-seven memorials, signed by 3,999 persons, and forty - seven Quarterly - meeting Conferences. . . . Asking for extirpation, from thirty-three Annual Conferences, eight hundred and eleven memorials, signed by 45,857 persons, and from forty-nine Quarterly-meeting Conferences."

The Committee on Slavery was composed of thirty-two members. A majority and a minority report were presented from this committee. The first elaborately argued against the system of slavery, sketched the antislavery antecedents of the Church, criticised the present Chapter on Slavery, urged a more stringent and unequivocal rule, and closed with recommending: First, "The amendment of the General Rule on Slavery so that it shall read, 'The buying, selling, or holding of men, women, or children with an intention to enslave them.'" Second, "The suspension of the fourth Restrictive Rule for the purpose set forth in the foregoing resolution." Third, "That the following be, and hereby is, substituted in the place of the present seventh chapter on Slavery: '*Question.* What shall be done for the extirpation of the evil of slavery? *Answer.* We declare that we are as much as ever convinced of the great evil of slavery. We believe that the buying, selling, or holding of human beings as chattels is contrary to the laws of God and nature, and inconsistent with the golden rule, and with that rule in our Discipline which requires all who desire to continue among us to "do no harm," and to "avoid evil of every kind." We therefore affectionately admonish all our preachers and people to keep themselves pure from this great evil, and to seek its extirpation by all lawful and Christian means.'" This report was signed by C. Kingsley, Chairman—who had prepared it—and by B. F. Crary, Secretary. The "New-Chapter" section of the report was formulated by Daniel Wise, as he told the writer.

The minority report made no plea for the system of slavery, but affirmed "that slave-holding for mercenary and selfish purposes is wrong." It gave a history of the action of the Church from 1844 onward, tracing the origin of the renewed antislavery agitation, which was attributed to the ministers of the Northern Conferences mainly, who made "a first official effort to change the Discipline" at the General Conference of 1856, "without the support of the membership;" as "out of seven hundred and ninety thousand members not quite five thousand petitioned for a change, and most of these were obtained by the personal efforts of the preachers." And it, moreover, urged that the whole number of petitioners in 186'' was "less than one in twenty of the entire membership." This fact, the want of proper consideration, the best interests of the enslaved, the division and strife inevitable, and the embarrassment to the "Border Conferences" consequent upon any change of the

Discipline, were among the reasons alleged for recommending only a reiteration of the old testimony against slavery, and "that the Committee on the Pastoral Address be instructed to state our position in relation to slavery, and to give such counsel to our Churches as may be suited to the necessities of the case." This report was signed, John S. Porter, chairman ; P. Coomb, secretary.

An interesting and exhaustive debate on the subject matter thus brought forward was participated in by the leading members of the body, and was continued several days. In favor of the majority report elaborate speeches were made by Granville Moody, E. O. Haven, Dr. Edward Thomson, B. F. Crary, P. S. Bennett, R. M. Hatfield, H. M. Schaffer, Dr. Dempster, Prof. C. Kingsley, James Hill, and others. In favor of the minority report the most prominent speakers were P. Coomb, N. Wilson, T. C. Murphy, A. Griffith, J. L. Crane, of Illinois; G. Battelle, S. Y. Monroe, H. Slicer, Thomas Sewall, Dr. Holdich, and Dr. Durbin, with others. The extended report of the discussion in 1856 obviates the necessity for giving this debate in detail ; for the entire argument, *pro* and *con*, is given in the twenty-second, twenty-third, and twenty-fourth chapters of this volume.

The new rule had in its favor 138 votes, with 74 opposed to it, which was less than the two-thirds majority that the Discipline required to put it on its final passage at the ensuing Annual Conferences. When the new chapter was taken up for discussion a proposition was made to refer it to the Annual and Quarterly Conferences for approval. This was lost by a vote of 61 to 150. A motion was made by S. Y. Monroe, in behalf of himself and nineteen others, to adopt the language of the new chapter in the form of a resolution, to be entered on the Journal and inserted in the Pastoral Address, and not to be made a part of the Book of Discipline. Every delegate save one of the Philadelphia Conference voted in favor of the adoption of this resolution. The delegates from the two Baltimore Conferences, with one exception, recorded their names in favor of it. So did the member from Arkansas, both the representatives of the Kentucky Conference, both of the Missourians, and all three of the delegates from the Western Virginia Conference.—" *General Conference Journal*," 1860, p. 256.

" These are the Border Conferences, so called. Twenty - seven out of twenty - nine delegates from these Conferences said, 'The holding of human beings to be used as chattels is inconsistent with the golden rule, and with that rule in our Discipline which requires all who desire to continue among us " to do no harm," and to avoid evil of every kind.' Out of two hundred and twenty-one members who composed the General Conference only two voted against the declaration itself. All but two, apparently, believed it, and wanted to say so somewhere."—" *Christian Advocate and Journal*," *July* 26, 1860. But saying so in this form was voted down by 81 to 132. Another mode was preferred. On the direct vote for adopting the new chapter there were 155 yeas to 58 nays. Subsequently a proposition was made, on motion of G. Hildt and T. B. Sargent, to declare " that this section is understood and meant to be only advisory," which was tabled by a vote of 73 to 131.

In the parliamentary tactics pursued, the minority chose to adopt and promulgate informally the exact

sentiment of the majority on the character of slavery
and in favor of its extirpation.   Dr. T. J. Thompson,
of the Philadelphia Conference, subsequently explained that "the border delegates voted for the substitute of Mr. Monroe as less offensive than putting
the words in the Discipline."—" *Christian Advocate
and Journal*," *August* 9, 1860.   But no one of them
disclaimed the sentiment expressed on the subject of
slavery.

The day following these several votes, on motion of
T. A. Blades and R. Sapp, the General Conference,
by a vote of 175 to 6, declared that:

> *Whereas*, During the pending of the chapter on slavery the
> following amendment was offered as explanatory of the
> chapter: . . . *Provided*, that this section is understood to
> be only advisory; . . .
> *Resolved*, That the said amendment was rejected by this
> body because we regard the chapter itself so clearly declara-
> tive and advisory as not to require any such explanation.

Thirty-nine were absent or did not vote.

The Pastoral Address of 1860, which was signed
by J. P. Durbin, F. G. Hibbard, E. Thomson, M.
Raymond, W. Hunter, H. W. Reed, and Joseph
Brooks, "in behalf and with the approbation of the
General Conference," summed up the action of the
Church to date in the following paragraph :

> 9. The subject of slavery, as related to the Church, has oc-
> cupied her earnest attention for a hundred years, and her
> history on this question shows the difficulty and delicacy of
> the matter.   Her testimony has been uniformly against it as a
> system, and yet she has tolerated the legal relation where cir-
> cumstances have justified toleration.   In the course of half a
> century some doubts have arisen as to the true intent and
> meaning of the Discipline on this subject, and to set this

matter at rest this General Conference has judged it proper to reconstruct the seventh chapter of the Discipline on the subject of slavery, so that it shall be a clear declaration of principles of the Church touching this matter; and to add an affectionate admonition to all our " preachers and people to keep themselves pure from this great evil, and to seek its extirpation by all lawful and Christian means." Thus the General Conference has expressed its judgment by a declaration of principles, and given its godly advice as to the application of these principles by those who may in any way be implicated in this matter, whether as pastors or people; pointing out, in its advice, that in the application of the principles due regard be had to the laws of the States and our duty founded in Christian morals. We sincerely trust that this well-considered action on this vexed question will be accepted by the Church, and that peace and quiet may hereafter reign throughout all our borders.

While the adoption of this Address was under consideration, Mr. J. H. Twombly, of New England, wished to call attention to one or two expressions in the Address which he did not like. " In one place something is said about the extirpation of slavery, and then in another place there is a qualifying phrase thrown in, as though we were afraid we would do too much." He did not think there was the least danger of doing too much, as all past history will show ; but the danger, if any, was that we should do too little." He said :

In another place in the Address there is the expression of a hope that this question of slavery is now settled, and that the Church will accept that settlement; but I have no such hope. I do not like that expression, and I wish it had never been put there, for this is a thing that never can be settled or compromised while slavery exists. I, therefore, move that so much of the Address as has reference to a hope that the question is settled, etc., be stricken out.

Dr. Hibbard understood it to mean simply this: After having carefully and candidly considered the whole matter here, we have come to this conclusion, and for this time have settled the question; and now we hope the Church will accept it, and that we shall have peace. We offer no pledge of silence for the future.

Dr. Harris asked if the word "action" might not be put in the place of the word "settlement;" and by common consent it was inserted, as the Address now reads. ("Daily Christian Advocate," June 5, 1860.)

This was the final disposition of "this vexed question" at that General Conference; and it was authoritatively designated as a reconstruction of the seventh chapter—a clear declaration of principles, an affectionate admonition, clearly declarative and advisory. The opinion expressed that slavery was condemned by God, by nature, by the golden rule, and by the Methodist Discipline, was clear and unequivocal, and it could only be consistently followed by adding, "We, therefore, will not allow our people to practice it." This, however, was not done. They were advised, and they were admonished, but they were not commanded to keep "themselves pure from this great evil."

The new rule, which was very near being successful, did propose to command the preachers and people not to buy, sell, or hold men, women, or children, with an intention to enslave them. And the vote on this rule was the exact measure of the actual antislavery power of the General Conference of 1860. If all the delegates who were elected as friends of the new rule had been true to their constituents and their own avowed principles before their election, the power of that General Conference would have been equal to the enactment of that law within the year ensuing. For this fact, touching personal default, the knowledge of not a few of its members is the voucher, by some of whom this statement was made to the writer. It is not the fault of the Methodist Episcopal Church that a prohibitory law was not formally enacted prior to the civil war. That was the standard of her anti-slavery action, as seen in the votes of the Annual Conferences during the quadrennium of 1856–1860. And it is a palpable error that is perpetrated by many careless journalists when they say the Methodist Episcopal Church waited for the civil government to destroy slavery by proclamation before it dared to prohibit slave-holding by its own legislation. Yet, that Church, by the vote of more than three fifths, if not even in excess of two thirds of its representatives in Annual Conferences assembled, had declared for the prohibition of all slave-holding before the inauguration of President Lincoln. Of forty-seven Conferences, (see "Journal of General Conference," 1860, p. 434,) thirty-one are reported as giving 2,648 votes in the affirmative. Sixteen Conferences are reported as furnishing only 1,212 votes against the form of prohibition proposed by the Cincinnati Rule. The highest number of negative votes is 1,416, which were given against the Erie Rule. But the affirmative votes of the New England and the Genesee Conferences, which are omitted, if counted in, would leave this largest negative vote in a minority of less than one third. As the affirmative votes were not all given for one rule they were not reckoned a legal majority, although the aggregate is unquestionably equal to two thirds, if morally estimated.

The periodicals of the Church were supplied with antislavery editors for the four years following from 1860. An effort was made by the conservative members of the General Conference at Buffalo to displace Daniel Wise, whose radical sentiments on slavery were obnoxious to them; but it failed. A large majority sustained him for the editorship of the "Sunday-School Advocate" and Sunday-school books. Dr. Stevens, the editor of the "Christian Advocate," was sustained by the conservatives, although he publicly declined being a candidate, but he was succeeded by Dr. Edward Thomson, who was elected by nearly a two-thirds vote. Dr. Whedon, whose election as editor of the "Quarterly" in 1856 was only by a small majority, was re-elected by a unanimous hand vote. The vigorous antislavery character of the Conference was thus fully vindicated, and assurance given of a forward movement all along the line. Thereafter the Methodist press was a unit on that subject.

The conservative character of the "Advocate" at New York was changed to that of a decided, yet prudent, representative of the progressive antislavery sentiment of the Church. The distinguished ability and superior culture of Dr. Thomson eminently fitted him to meet the crisis in the nation and in the Church that was now rapidly approaching.

The adjournment of the General Conference found the conservatives unchecked in their hopes of controlling the action of the Church. A new weekly was established in New York devoted to their interests, which obtained extensive patronage, especially in the Border Conferences. A very extensive feeling of disaffection was developed. The course of the great official paper at New York was unsparingly criticised.

Soon after the Conference of 1860 a portion of the "border" assumed a revolutionary attitude. The new statute was repudiated by two Conferences. One demanded its repeal with a threat of separation.

The testimony against slavery which the new chapter gave was clear and strong. The vote in favor of the new rule, that was so near becoming a law against all slave-holding, was a staggering blow to the whole system. And this was all done, notwithstanding the peril to the unity of the Church on the border, as indicated by Conference action and otherwise prior to the General Conference of 1860. The Baltimore Conference, held in March of that year, by a unanimous vote, "determined not to hold connection with any ecclesiastical body that makes non-slaveholding a condition of membership in the Church."

Pursuant to this purpose, yet not in the direct line of consummation, at a preachers' meeting held September 14, 1860, in Wesley Chapel, Washington, a formal complaint was made against the action of the General Conference of 1860 on the subject of slavery, and a plan was proposed for developing and concentrating the conservative element of the whole Church at the next General Conference for a redress of their grievances. The plan included "the repudiation of the new chapter," and demanded that "the control of this question be left with the Annual Conferences." ("Christian Advocate and Journal," Sept. 27, 1860.)

In accord with this action of the preachers' meeting, a convention of laymen from within the bounds of the Baltimore, East Baltimore, Philadelphia, and West Virginia Conferences was held in Baltimore, at the Eutaw-street Church, December 5, 1860. A delegation was present from New York on the evening of the 6th. An address to the Conferences named was adopted, calling upon them to sever their connection with the General Conference. Mr. Fowler presented a minority report opposed to immediate secession. The attendance upon the convention was mainly from within the bounds of the Baltimore Conference. Of its one hundred and sixteen charges, sixty-three were represented.

Respondent to these movements and in sympathy with concerted and contingent separation, "A Card to Methodists" was circulated in the peninsular part of the Philadelphia Conference, suggesting methods of action, which would enable the peninsula to "negotiate with the Baltimore and other Border Conferences in reference to any further action." At the Baltimore Conference for 1861 an earnest discussion was had, looking toward secession, but not reaching any final conclusion. A candidate for elders' orders publicly excepted to the new chapter. For this reason the president, Bishop Scott, said: "I regard myself restrained from ordaining any one who declines to take upon him the ordination vows without qualification or exception. Hence, I cannot ordain Mr. Hedrick."

A convention of laymen was in session at the same time and place with the Baltimore Conference. By a large vote, 91 to 32, the convention adopted a series of resolutions which were recommended to the Conference for adoption. They embraced a declaration that the unconstitutional action of the General Conference had destroyed the unity of the Church, and that the Baltimore Conference does not recognize its jurisdiction; that, nevertheless, if three fourths of all the Annual Conferences would, within the year 1861, agree with it in abrogating the new chapter, and in ignoring the whole subject of slavery in the Discipline, the Baltimore Conference would reunite with them in Church fellowship. When, however, this, or a similar plan, was presented to the Conference, Bishop Scott announced that he could not entertain a motion contemplating a division of the Church. He subsequently allowed the secretary, Rev. J. S. Martin, to put the question on the adoption of a series of propositions, in substance already indicated. When the Bishop resumed the chair, he ordered that the following paper be immediately spread upon the Journal:

> The whole action just had on what is called the "Norval Wilson propositions" is, in my judgment, in violation of the order and discipline of the Methodist Episcopal Church, and therefore is null and void, regarded as Conference action. I, therefore, do not recognize such action as infracting the integrity of this body, and so I shall proceed to finish the business of the present session.   LEVI SCOTT.

The official record shows that the whole number of members was one hundred and seventy-one. Eighty-three voted for the resolution which declared for immediate separation; thirty-nine were absent; two voted nay. As the whole number present was one hundred and thirty-two, the majority was two thirds in the affirmative, whose irregular action was made of no effect by episcopal decision.

The East Baltimore Conference for 1861 adopted * a series of resolutions which demanded the repeal of the new chapter, declared there could be no administration under it, and asked the concurrence of all the

* Rescinded in 1864.

Annual Conferences in a proposition instead, which should give each Conference full power over slavery within its bounds. This proposition was concurred in * by the Philadelphia Conference of the same year by a vote of 174 to 35. But the bolder action of the Baltimore Conference was not concurred in by any of the Conferences. Such was the situation immediately following and consequent upon the doings of the General Conference of 1860.

* Rescinded in 1864.

CHAPTER XXVII.

THE END—SLAVERY VANQUISHED.

THE end of all controversy on slavery drew nigh. In vain were all the great swelling words of unprincipled politicians uttered for slavery. In vain had timid ecclesiastics bated their breath and spoken in whisper tones of slavery. In vain were all the considerate and conservative opinions and measures of religious bodies, which contemplated the possible extinction of slavery by voluntary emancipation, or by inevitable exhaustion, or by miraculous intervention of divine Providence!

The quadrennium following 1860, however, opened with every indication of a continuation of the strife of words about methods of extirpation, forms of condemnation, and lines of discrimination, of slavery. The conservative party in the General Conference at Buffalo promptly established a weekly paper in New York, "The Methodist," which was liberally endowed and ably edited. It antagonized the radical views and radical policy now in the ascendant. Unfortunately, this antagonism lessened the patronage of the "Christian Advocate and Journal," causing temporary financial loss to the Book Concern, alienated personal friendships between prominent ministers and laymen, promoted discord among brethren, and in no wise tended to harmonize the disturbed elements by which a desolating division of the Church was again threatened all along and somewhat above the border.

Meanwhile slavery flourished, grew fat and furious, was more hateful and murderous. It resented the mildest admonition with deadly blows. The martyrdom of Anthony Bewley is in point. A letter from Bishop Morris was published in the " Western Advocate " in November, 1860, relating to it. He was a member of the General Conference of 1860 from the Arkansas Conference—over sixty years of age, small of stature, apparently feeble—a good man, of a meek and quiet spirit, and for thirty years had enjoyed the full confidence and fellowship of his brethren. Falsely charged with a plan of insurrection to make him odious, he left Texas to avoid trouble to himself or others; his enemies pursued him to Missouri and Arkansas, and brought him back by mob violence, and without legal process hung him near Fort Worth, September 13, 1860.* His real offense was that he had refused to be identified with the Church South in 1845, and did unite with the Methodist Episcopal Church in 1848, and thereby became obnoxious to Missouri and Texas slave-holders, whose prejudices and passions were equally unreasonable and lawless.

Events of unusual interest and alarming indications were crowded into the days now passing. The attack of John Brown on Harper's Ferry, October 14, 1859, his capture, and his conviction on the 2d of November, "for murder and other crimes," and his execution on

* The " Central Christian Advocate," in October, 1862, relates that Colonel Chivington, of the First Colorado Volunteers, (late presiding elder of the Rocky Mountain District,) in pursuing the rebel " Texan Rangers," whom he routed and pursued through New Mexico four hundred miles, overtook a gang of twelve, five of whom his men killed, wounding and capturing the other seven. Prisoners already in his hands informed the colonel that those twelve were all present and took part in the murder of Bewley at Fort Worth, Texas.

the 2d day of December following, had profoundly
stirred the nation; and the excitement at the North
was hardly less than it was at the South. The Democratic party sought in vain to fix the responsibility
of John Brown's invasion of slave territory upon
the growing Republican party, whose leaders made
almost frantic efforts to free themselves from the
unjust and damaging suspicion, and with complete
success.

For a year or more radical Abolitionists were very
unpopular, and the meetings of the American Antislavery Society were disturbed by outbreaks of violent
opposition in Boston, Buffalo, Rochester, and Syracuse, in which members of the dominant political
party were active agents, while their Republican
antagonists avoided even the responsibility of protecting Abolitionists in their constitutional rights in
Northern cities. At Syracuse, January 29, 1861, the
Abolitionists were forcibly ejected from their own
hired hall by a mob, which on the following night
crowded the streets with a torch-light procession and
transparent banners with inscriptions such as: "Freedom of speech, but not treason;" "The rights of the
South must be protected;" "Abolitionism no longer
in Syracuse;" and bearing effigies of leading Abolitionists. The latter, amid hootings, mingled
with disgusting profanity and ribaldry, were burned
up in Hanover Square. ("Recollections," S. J.
May, p. 391.)

Below the troubled surface of society, and away
from the persecuted and the persecutors, stood quiet,
thoughtful, earnest men by thousands, pondering in
their hearts the ominous movements and words of
John Brown. Governor Wise said: "He is a man

of clear head, courageous fortitude, and simple ingen-
ousness. He is cool, collected, indomitable, and he
inspires all with great trust in his integrity, and as a
man of truth. They are mistaken who take him for
a madman." And, therefore, Vice-President Wilson
said also, that "his simple and unstudied words, re-
vealing such sublime devotion to principle, such profound sympathy for the poor, lowly, and oppressed,"
such serene trust in God, were seized upon and
hoarded almost as gems from another and better land,
or as the echoes from the heroic age of confessors
and martyrs. His port and bearing, his interviews
with Wise, Mason, Vallandigham, and others, and
his remarks before sentence was passed, produced a
profound impression. "Your people at the South,"
he said, "had better prepare yourselves for a settlement of this question, which will come up sooner
than you are prepared for it. . . . I came to free the
slaves, and only that."—"*Rise and Fall of the Slave
Power*," *Henry Wilson*, vol. ii, pp. 595, 596.

And although John Brown's body had lain moldering in the grave then more than a year, his soul
went marching through the land. In less than a
twelvemonth after the Syracuse jubilee over the
suppression of abolitionism, the John Brown song—
extemporized in Boston harbor—was heard ringing
through the valleys of Virginia and along the banks
of the Potomac.

Slavery had now reached a period of convulsions
which were less ecclesiastical than political. As seen
from a subsequent stand-point, they were premonitory
and prophetic signs of approaching dissolution. The
day of doom drew nigh. The hanging of Brown and
the murder of Bewley were venial sins in comparison

with the fratricidal, wholesale murder that was coolly inaugurated by perjured traitors, when, with fraud and robbery, the political leaders of the South seized the arms of the country and opened a deadly fire upon the national heart and life.

The fearful struggle which ensued involved millions of men and the outlay of thousands of millions of dollars, besides the loss of hundreds of thousands of lives. In the years of bloody strife following, our country entered as never before into " the distress of nations with perplexity." Around and beyond " the sea and the waves roared " dismally. Literally, men's hearts failed them for fear, and for " looking after those things which [seemed] coming on the earth." And yet other men feared not. " In God is our trust," they said. Blood was poured out as water in the field. Wealth was ungrudgingly devoted to the government. Loved ones from thousands of homes were forwarded with benedictions and tears to the camp and fields of battle. These were times that tried men's souls, when they resisted unto blood, striving against the sin of a pro-slavery rebellion. Then it was that the entire antislavery sentiment of the Methodist Episcopal Church, conservative and radical, combined its full power to condemn and destroy slavery by rallying around the national standard heartily. A few Conferences are cited only. Their action is a sample of the many.

The New York East Conference, in April, 1861, on motion of Rev. J. S. Inskip, adopted, unanimously, expressions of unqualified sympathy with and support of the government of the United States in its defense and support of the Constitution and the nation's welfare.

The New York Conference, also, in June of the same year, adopted, by a unanimous vote, Rev. J. B. Wakeley's report on the state of the country, which recited " the formation of the Southern Confederacy ; . . . its seizure of the forts, mints, custom-houses, vessels, and arms of the United States, . . . and unnatural war against the government," as the occasion for declaring that " no treasure is too costly, no sacrifice too great, no time too long, to put down treason and traitors, and to place our Union on a rock so solid that neither enemies abroad nor traitors at home can move it."

The East Baltimore Conference, in March of 1862, on the motion of A. A. Reese and G. D. Chenoweth, expressed their " abhorrence of the rebellion," and said, " We approve and indorse the present wise and patriotic administration ; " affirming, also, that " in the inculcation of loyal principles and sentiments we recognize the pulpit and the press as legitimate instrumentalities." The vote stood 132 yeas, 15 nays ; the negative voters declaring themselves as much in favor of the Union as the others could be.

The Philadelphia Conference, in March of the same year, adopted, by a unanimous vote, the unanimous report of their committee on the state of the country— Charles Cook, chairman—which declared that " we do hereby express our utter abhorrence and opposition to the present rebellion, being the offspring of treason ; . . . and that we pledge our influence to encourage and assist the army and navy, to protect the honor of our flag, the integrity of the Constitution, and the maintenance of our glorious Union."

The New Jersey Conference of the same year, with entire unanimity, adopted an equally patriotic report from its committee—Isaac Winner, chairman—which hailed " with gratification the enthusiastic loyalty of our congregations; " also calling upon the nation " to humble itself before God for its many and grievous sins."

Without a dissenting vote the New York East Conference, in 1862, adopted a report, prepared by James Floy, declaring that " the system of American slavery is evidently, in the good providence of God, destined soon to come to an end," and " that the recent action of our national authorities by which the nation has been unequivocally committed to the cause of freedom, meets with our entire approbation." * And this Conference, with the New York Conference, also, of 1864, memorialized Congress in favor of an amendment to the Constitution which should abolish slavery, twenty-one months before it was achieved. The New England Conference for the same year adopted a report which deserves a larger space, because of its historic statements, as well as its loyal sentiments:

After thirty years of exciting, but healthful, agitation on the subject of slavery, the present aspects of our cause furnish abundant motive for devout thanksgiving to God. The two antagonistic tendencies of public sentiment, existing and increasing in the nation for so many years, have at length reached their legitimate crisis of mutual and final conflict, of which the issue cannot be doubtful. By its own diabolical act [slavery] has been placed in a position where it can claim no constitutional protection, and where there is no

---

* The bill freeing slaves used for insurrectionary purposes was approved August 6, 1861. Another bill forbidding the return of fugitive slaves by persons in the army was approved March 13, 1862. Slavery in the District of Columbia was abolished by Congress April 16, 1862.

prudential motive for its retention; and the voice of the people, which evidently coincides with the voice of God, says, " Let it perish! "

In the Church the progress of the antislavery sentiment has been equally gratifying. Instead of a contemned and meager minority which regarded slavery as a sin, a great majority of the representative assembly of the Church register their solemn verdict of its criminal character, and demand that it shall cease, not only in the ministry, but in the whole membership.

The Black River Conference of 1862 gave a more extended statement of equally important historic truths, and put upon record its judgment that " the signs of the times give evidence that the hitherto dominant and domineering slave-power is rapidly approaching its end, and even now we may witness its horrible death throe. The time is rapidly approaching when the last fetter will be broken and the last bondman be released."

The Central Ohio Conference has the distinguished honor of having adopted resolutions in 1861 contemplating the proclamation of universal freedom as the only solution of the national difficulties. And in 1862, at Greenville, Ohio, September 22, the Conference, by a unanimous vote, adopted a resolution, which was forwarded to President Lincoln, declaring " that we believe the time has fully come that, from a military necessity, for the safety of the country, such a proclamation should be made; and we earnestly beseech the President of the United States to proclaim the emancipation of all slaves held in the United States, paying loyal men a reasonable compensation for their slaves."—" *Christian Advocate*," *Oct.* 9, 1862.

Before this communication reached Washington

the President had already issued his proclamation of freedom, dated September 22, 1862, which was to go into operation one hundred days thereafter, on the first day of January, 1863.

Freedom was not, however, universally secured by the proclamation, which only emancipated "all persons held as slaves within any State, or any designated part of a State, the people whereof shall be in rebellion against the United States on the first day of January, 1863." This qualification was specifically carried out by naming "the States of Arkansas, Texas, Louisiana, Mississippi, Alabama, Florida, Georgia, South Carolina, North Carolina, and Virginia," as the States in which all slaves "henceforward shall be free." But within those States, even, the city of New Orleans, and thirteen parishes or counties of Louisiana, as well as the cities of Norfolk and Portsmouth, with seven counties in Virginia, were excepted in the proclamation, "and," said the President, "for the present left precisely as if this proclamation were not issued." And, besides, the States of Missouri, Kentucky, West Virginia, Tennessee, Delaware. and Maryland, the people whereof were not reckoned as in rebellion against the United States, were entirely exempt from its operation. There were six slave-holding States, three slave-holding cities, and twenty slave-holding counties in the Union after January 1, 1863.

The following year, 1864, in May, the General Conference of the Methodist Episcopal Church met in Philadelphia. The expressions given already from a few of the Annual Conferences, as specimen statements, were fair indications of the almost universal sentiment of the Church at that time on the subject

of slavery. The Conference adopted a new rule on
slavery, by a vote of 207 yeas and 9 nays. The small
minority of dissenters were delegates from within the
then slave-holding States of West Virginia, Maryland, and Kentucky. The delegates from within the
States of Delaware and Missouri, however, were a
unit for the new rule, which forbid "*slave-holding,
the buying or selling slaves.*" So that the Methodist
Episcopal Church alone, of all the Churches in
America within whose communion slave-holding had
been allowed, enacted a prohibitory law abolishing
slavery, even within the States where it was allowed
to continue by President Lincoln's proclamation of
1863.

Moving forward on the same line, in advance of all
the Churches, the same body, already more sweeping
in its prohibition of slavery than the civil authorities,
yet further anticipated the action of the Government
in a formal address to the President. In this address,
after saying, "We honor you for your proclamation
of liberty," they add, "We pray that the time may
speedily come when we shall be truly a republican
and free country, in no part of which, either State or
Territory, shall slavery be known." And this was
followed by declarations, in their report on the state
of the country, in favor of equal rights and compensation to freedmen, and an amendment to the Constitution of the United States which should guarantee
their freedom. The Methodist Episcopal Church in
1864 said: "Justice to those who have been enslaved
requires that in all the privileges of citizenship, as
well as in all the other rights of a common manhood,
there shall be no distinction founded on color. . . .
Provision should be made to give those a share in the

soil who have cultivated it without recompense, and defended it with their blood. . . . We are decidedly in favor of such an amendment to the Constitution, and such legislation on the part of the States, as shall prohibit slavery or involuntary servitude, except for crime, throughout all the States and Territories of the country." These declarations of the Church were soon followed by corresponding national legislation.

A bill prohibiting forever slavery in all the territory of the United States had passed both Houses of Congress, and was approved by the President on the 19th day of June, 1862. Another bill was enacted and approved by the President, on the 25th of June, 1864, providing nearly four thousand colored children in the national capital with the same rights and privileges as white children in the public schools.

A joint resolution, which proposed an amendment of the Constitution prohibiting slavery in all the States forever, after an extended discussion and violent opposition, although successful in the Senate, was defeated in the House, in June, 1864. A bill repealing the Fugitive Slave Act of 1850, and all acts and parts of acts for the rendition of fugitive slaves, was enacted by Congress, and approved by the President on the 28th of June, 1864. An amendment to the Civil Appropriation Bill, which prohibited the coastwise slave-trade forever, became a law, by the approval of the President, on the 2d of July, 1864.

Subsequently the new State of West Virginia adopted a system of gradual emancipation. So did Missouri, but afterward made it immediate in effect. Both became free States without national interference.

The Maryland Convention adopted a free Constitution June 24, 1864. The loyal men of Arkansas and Louisiana framed and adopted free Constitutions, and they of Tennessee had taken steps in the same direction. Kentucky and Delaware stood alone for slavery.

The climax of extirpation was not reached, and the nation swept clean, until the adoption in the House of the joint resolution proposing an amendment to the Constitution, on the 29th of December, 1864. " On the day of the vote the galleries and the approaches thereto were thronged, while senators, judges, cabinet officers, and others, crowded upon the floor. The uncertainty that still hung over the vote, even at the beginning of the roll-call, occasioned the most intense and breathless anxiety and suspense. And when the result was assured, and the Speaker announced that the requisite two-thirds vote (119 to 56) had been given for the amendment, the pent-up feelings of the multitude found expression in the most uproarious demonstrations of delight, in which members on the floor, as well as the crowd in the galleries, took part. After these exhibitions of enthusiasm and gratification had somewhat subsided, Mr. Ingersoll, of Illinois, said : ' In honor of, this immortal and sublime event, I move that the House do now adjourn.' The motion was carried amid similar demonstrations of jubilant and enthusiastic delight. The amendment received the signature of the President, was submitted to the States for ratification, received the vote of the required three fourths of the States, and by public proclamation of Mr. Lincoln, December 18, 1865, the Thirteenth Amendment became a part of the Constitution of the United States of America, and slavery was forever thereafter prohibited by the organic law of the land."—*Henry Wilson's "Rise and Fall of the Slave Power,"* vol. iii, p. 452.

NOTE.—1. *General Conference Reports, on the State of the Country,* 1864.

The Committee have carefully considered the following subject * submitted to them by the General Conference, namely:

"*Whereas,* It is a well-known fact that the Methodist Episcopal Church was the first to tender its allegiance to the government under the Constitution in the days of Washington; and, *whereas,* the fair record of the Church has never been tarnished by disloyalty; and, *whereas,* our ministers and people are deeply in sympathy with the government in its efforts to put down rebellion and set the captives free; therefore,

"*Resolved,* That a committee of five be appointed, whose duty it shall be to proceed to Washington to present to the President of these United States the assurances of our Church, in a suitable address, that we are with him in heart and soul in the present struggle for human rights and free institutions."

The Committee, after further consideration of the subject of the delegation it is proposed to send with an address to the President of the United States, beg leave to report that they have instructed their chairman to present for the approval of the General Conference the address contemplated in the resolution referred for consideration. The Committee still further report that they have nominated as the delegation:

BISHOP EDWARD R. AMES,   REV. GEORGE PECK,
REV. JOSEPH CUMMINGS,   REV. CHARLES ELLIOTT,
REV. GRANVILLE MOODY.

2. *Address to President Lincoln.*

"TO HIS EXCELLENCY ABRAHAM LINCOLN, PRESIDENT OF THE UNITED STATES:

"The General Conference of the Methodist Episcopal Church, now in session in the city of Philadelphia, representing nearly seven thousand ministers, and nearly a million of members, mindful of their duty as Christian citizens, takes the earliest opportunity to express to you the assurance of the loyalty of the Church, her earnest devotion to the

* Adopted on motion of Thomas C. Golden and K. P. Jervis.

interests of the country, and her sympathy with you in the great responsibilities of your high position in this trying hour.

"With exultation we point to the record of our Church as having never been tarnished by disloyalty. She was the first of the Churches to express, by a deputation of her most distinguished ministers, the promise of support to the government in the days of Washington. In her articles of religion she has enjoined loyalty as a duty, and has ever given to the government her most decided support.

"In this present struggle for the nation's life many thousands of her members, and a large number of her ministers, have rushed to arms to maintain the cause of God and humanity. They have sealed their devotion to their country with their blood on every battle-field of this terrible war.

"We regard this dreadful scourge now desolating our land and wasting the nation's life as the result of a most unnatural, utterly unjustifiable rebellion, involving the crime of treason against the best of human governments, and sin against God. It required our government to submit to its own dismemberment and destruction, leaving it no alternative but to preserve the national integrity by the use of the national resources. If the government had failed to use its power to preserve the unity of the nation and maintain its authority it would have been justly exposed to the wrath of heaven, and to the reproach and scorn of the civilized world.

"Our earnest and constant prayer is that this cruel and wicked rebellion may be speedily suppressed; and we pledge you our hearty co-operation in all appropriate means to secure this object.

"Loyal and hopeful in national adversity, in prosperity thankful, we most heartily congratulate you on the glorious victories recently gained, and rejoice in the belief that our complete triumph is near.

"We believe that our national sorrows and calamities have resulted in a great degree from our forgetfulness of God and oppression of our fellow-men. Chastened by affliction, may the nation humbly repent of her sins, lay aside her haughty pride, honor God in all her future legislation, and render justice to all who have been wronged.

"We honor you for your proclamations of liberty, and rejoice in all the acts of the government designed to secure freedom to the enslaved.

"We trust that when military usages and necessities shall justify interference with established institutions, and the removal of wrongs sanctioned by law, the occasion will be improved, not merely to injure our foes and increase the national resources, but also as an opportunity to recognize our obligations to God, and to honor his law. We pray that the time may speedily come when this shall be truly a republican and free country, in no part of which, either State or Territory, shall slavery be known.

"The prayers of millions of Christians, with an earnestness never manifested for rulers before, daily ascend to heaven that you may be endued with all needed wisdom and power. Actuated by the sentiments of the loftiest and purest patriotism, our prayer shall be continually for the preservation of our country undivided, for the triumph of our cause, and for a permanent peace, gained by sacrifice of no moral principles, but founded on the word of God, and securing, in righteousness, liberty and equal rights to all.

"Signed in behalf of the General Conference of the Methodist Episcopal Church,   JOSEPH CUMMINGS, *Chairman.*

"PHILADELPHIA, *May* 14, 1864."

3. *President Lincoln's Reply to the Address.*

"GENTLEMEN: In reply to your address allow me to attest the accuracy of its historical statements, indorse the sentiments it expresses, and thank you in the nation's name for the sure promise it gives.

"Nobly sustained as the government has been by all the Churches, I would utter nothing which might in the least appear invidious against any. Yet without this, it may be fairly said that the Methodist Episcopal Church, not less devoted than the best, is, by its greater numbers, the most important of all. It is no fault in others that the Methodist Church sends more soldiers to the field, more nurses to the hospitals, and more prayers to heaven, than any. God bless the Methodist Church! Bless all the Churches! And blessed be God! who in this our great trial giveth us the Churches!

"A. LINCOLN."

CHAPTER XXVIII.

TROPHIES OF THE TRIUMPH.

THE close of the war, by the success of the Union army, gave to the nation substantial trophies of the triumph of freedom; and the overthrow of slavery by national legislation throughout all the land opened the way for our Church to prosecute its legitimate work in the Southern States, from which it had been excluded for more than twenty years.

During the interim previous to the General Conference of 1868 the Bishops of the Methodist Episcopal Church, at their meeting held June 14, 1865, in Erie, Pa., were addressed by a minister of one of the non-episcopal Methodist bodies, through Bishop Simpson. He said:

Within twenty-five years past the antislavery agitation culminated in the Wesleyan Methodist Connection in 1843. The pro-slavery principle was embodied in the great secession of 1844, and organized the Methodist Episcopal Church, South. As a sequence of these facts, and more or less remotely related thereto, came the terrible Rebellion. By a singularly happy coincidence, now soon occurs the Centenary of American Methodism, at a time when the national heart is throbbing with gratitude to God for victory, liberty, and union. Surely this is the fit time for the fragments of Methodism to be gathered into one. And who should initiate a movement for union? With either of the smaller Methodist bodies it would be presumption. With the Methodist Episcopal Church it would be magnanimous. — "*Reunion Defended*," 1868, p. 12.

The writer had only anticipated the purpose of the Bishops. Their unanimous, well-considered action was a trophy that signalized the defeat of slavery and the dawning of a new era. A series of resolutions were put upon record and published. They said:

1. As Bishops of the Methodist Episcopal Church, we rejoice at the overthrow of the terrible Rebellion which threatened our national existence; and we render thanksgiving to Almighty God for his signal mercies to our country.

4. In the removal of the great evil of slavery from among us, we consider that the great cause which led to the separation from us of both the Wesleyan Methodists of this country and of the Methodist Episcopal Church, South, has passed away; and we trust the day is not far distant when there shall be but one organization, which shall embrace the whole Methodist family in the United States.

5. Especially would we rejoice if there could be a general union of all Methodists who agree in doctrine, and who are loyal to the general government, and who are opposed to the evil of slavery, in the approaching centenary of Methodism, which occurs in 1866.

8. We will occupy, so far as practicable, those fields in the Southern States which may be opened to us, and which give promise of success, and our mission shall be alike to the white and colored population.—" *Christian Advocate*," *June* 29, 1865.

The extension of its jurisdiction into all the Southern States opened a door for the return of thousands of Methodists to the communion of the Methodist Episcopal Church, from which they had been forcibly separated by the Southern secession. And it afforded a new field for missionary work by which many other thousands were gathered into the Church, so that in the general Minutes of the Church for 1876 there was reported 16 Annual Conferences, 1,266 traveling preachers, and 210,846 members, including 32,533 probationers, where it had no members ten years before.

"The Church property owned by colored members of the Methodist Episcopal Church in the South, consisting of 1,751 plain, comfortable houses of worship, valued at $1,793,483, and 162 humble parsonages, valued at $75,105, aggregating $1,868,588."— *"Eleventh Annual Report of the Freedmen's Aid Society," by Dr. Rust.*

The organization of the Freedmen's Aid Society in 1866, and the energetic administration thereof in securing and disbursing more than three quarters of a million of dollars in eleven years, for establishing and supporting educational institutions in the South, has been, perhaps, the most remarkable agency in multiplying trophies of the great triumph of freedom.

From the Eleventh Annual Report of this Society the following summary of facts is compiled for the current year, 1878. Says Dr. Rust, the veteran and indefatigable secretary:

The Society has aided in the establishment and support of chartered institutions at Nashville, Tenn.; Atlanta, Ga.; Orangeburgh, S. C.; New Orleans, La.; and Holly Springs, Miss. Theological schools are organized at Orangeburgh, S. C.; Baltimore, Md., and New Orleans, La. Medical colleges are established at Nashville and at New Orleans. Institutions are aided which are not chartered, at Greensborough, N. C.; Jacksonville, Fla.; Waynesborough, Ga.; La Grange, Ga.; La Teche, La.; Meridian, Miss.; Huntsville, Ala.; Marshall, Texas; Little Rock, Ark.; and Mason, Tenn.

In these institutions the number of pupils taught during the year is classified as follows: Biblical, 400; Law, 25; Medical, 50; Collegiate, 75; Academic, 275; Normal, 1,000; Intermediate, 510; Primary, 605: total, 2,940. Our teachers are unanimous in the judgment that colored pupils learn as

rapidly as the white pupils, and that they are far more enthusiastic in their studies. A few, commencing with the al-
phabet and spelling book, passing through the elementary
branches, taking Algebra, Geometry, Physiology, Chemistry,
Latin, Greek, French, and the whole curriculum of college
studies, have graduated with honor and have entered with
enthusiasm upon the work of elevating and saving their race.

By the financial statement submitted it will be seen that we
have collected and disbursed this year $63,402 85. We have
sustained in the field seventy teachers. We have now a quarter of a million dollars' worth of school property in the South.
One hundred thousand have been taught by those educated
in our schools.

Said Bishop Haven at this anniversary meeting,
after referring to an elegant steel engraving of the
General Conference of the Church South, which was
held at Nashville in 1858, the colored servitor of
which is engraved with water-pitcher in his hand,
who afterward became a minister of marked ability
in our Church in New Orleans:

Turn now to another picture, drawn not yet on a steel plate
by an engraver's tool, but drawn on the retina of many a
grateful eye—a picture from life in the same city. It is in
1878, twenty years exactly after the first assembly had met.
It is not at the capital, but on a high street in the south part
of town. A plat of ground, some thousand feet in length and
several hundred feet deep, is covered by four brick buildings.
The first is the original mansion where the gentleman of the
estate resided, and where his servants served him—a spacious
edifice, with large halls, lofty parlors, and long corridors.
Next to that is a chapel bearing on its front the honored
name of Bishop Thomson; next to that a building for recita-
tion rooms and dormitories; and next to that a tall edifice
containing a dissecting room, philosophical and library rooms,
and dormitories. The whole four are the property of the Society whose anniversary we are met to celebrate, and are
known as the buildings of the Central Tennessee College. In
that chapel is gathered a large audience, met to hear the

graduating exercises of the Meharry Medical School. On the platform are seated the leading physicians of the city, who have been employed as lecturers to the students. The president of the school, a Northern gentleman, is a graduate of the School of Medicine of Vanderbilt University. Three young men present their theses on medical subjects and receive their diplomas. The Dean gives an address, and these doctors of the city utter their congratulations. The crowded house, all well-dressed, the stirring music, the delight flashing from every eye—these are the accessories to the central figures—colored doctors receiving the diplomas which give them social and professional equality with every other physician in the State, receiving them with the approval of distinguished white representatives of that most sensitive and scrutinizing of professions.

What a change from the one who was born thrall, and expected all his days and all the days of his children and children's children to remain thrall, pouring water for his owners or their ecclesiastical representatives, and these youth going out to minister to the health of the community, the accredited equals of every citizen. And all this in twenty years! That is the Freedmen's Aid Society of the Methodist Episcopal Church in one illustration! That is her work, her claim, her purpose. The past is prophetic of the future.

I need not lead you up the slow steps that have reached the summit. Slow as they have appeared, they have landed us, in less than half a generation, on the loftiest table-lands of humanity. That land may stretch out farther, and may slope up higher, but it is the same plateau. The physician of to-day may know more than Galen and Hippocrates, but he does not rank his profession higher. So the graduate of Meharry, a decade hence, may excel in attainments him of yesterday, but he can never cease to respect the earliest students of his school.

This twenty years should be reduced by one third, if not one half. It was not until three years after the picture of 1858 that the opening gun of the new civilization was fired in Charleston, and heard round the world. It was not until seven years after that the first school was established. That school I visited in the fall of 1866. It was located in a building that had been used as a gun factory by the Confederate forces and confiscated by the national government. On rough benches sat rougher people—youth, children, men, and women—in rags of linsey-woolsey and jeans, patched like Joseph's coat, not through pride and plenty, but through poverty, bootless and shoeless and stockingless, knowledgeless certainly, most would have said brainless. They were Israelites without the Egyptian spoils, Israelites in their original brick-kiln degradation, Israelites despised by the Egyptians, from whom they had escaped by other arms than their own, and despised by those who had, from their own motives of self-preservation, delivered them. There they sat, crouching over their primers, spelling with difficulty the easiest words, answering stammeringly the simplest questions, strong only in the gift of song and the faith of their teachers.

In twelve years they have passed on and up through primary and grammar school, and seminary and college, into and out of the professional school, the capstone of culture, recognized as such through all the world and all the ages. Shall we not exultingly exclaim, What hath God wrought! He hath holpen his servant Israel. To those who sat in darkness and the shadow of death light hath sprung up—light on the inner and the innermost eye; light for a people that were not a people, but are now the people of God; light henceforward and forever.

Equally distinguished, as one of a new series of great events, was the monumental action of the General Conference of 1868. To unshackle the limbs of a slave is well. To recognize his manhood is better. But to repudiate the discrimination made against American citizens of African descent hitherto, by according them equality before the law and at the ballot-box, is a superlative enfranchisement, which has not yet been fully achieved and guaranteed by the nation at large. But such was the effect of the action of the Methodist Episcopal Church assembled at Chicago. Ever afterward, before her ecclesiastical courts, with the elective franchise, and in their eligibility to office, no distinctions were allowed on account of nationality, color, or previous condition.

Among many, who were active and influential in promoting and securing their logical climax of freedom in the Church, Gilbert Haven was the most positive, persistent, and conscientious advocate. As a popular journalist generally—but especially as editor of "Zion's Herald"—for the years coetaneous with and following the war of rebellion, when the great national crisis was reached, his pen was in perpetual motion on behalf of equal and exact justice for the African, because he was a man among men, and a brother among Christians.

His first appearance in the General Conference of the Church—of which he was, four years afterward, chosen one of the honored Bishops—was in 1868, at the most opportune period in her history for achieving grand triumphs for divine truths and human rights. The General Conference of 1864 had authorized the Bishops to organize the preachers of African descent into Mission Conferences. And at the Conference of 1868 their delegates were, after a careful discussion and with great unanimity, recognized and admitted to membership upon terms of entire equality. The vote was two hundred and nine for admission, and only twenty-one against it. And this minority would probably have been much smaller had not the motion to admit included also several other Mission Conferences which were represented by white preachers.

The presence of Benjamin Brown, of the Washington Conference, and John P. Bowser, his alternate; James Davis, of the Delaware Conference, and An-

thony Ross, the alternate of Dr. J. P. Newman, of
the Mississippi Conference, was a token of the permanent establishment of equal ecclesiastical rights.
And they became, personally, trophies of a triumph
of such magnitude as to warrant the record of their
names in this connection. For they were heralds of
a new era, which, however, had been foreshadowed
by the General Conference of the American Wesleyan Connection which met at Cleveland, O., in 1844,
and enrolled promptly Lewis Woodson, of African
descent, who was the superior, in some respects, of
not a few of his associates.

Following this precedent, it was further determined, unanimously, to extend the usual courtesies
to ecclesiastical bodies irrespective of color, and a
telegraphic inquiry from the General Conference of
the African Methodist Episcopal Zion Church, then
in session at Washington City, presented through
Gilbert Haven, was responded to at once, on motion
of Daniel Curry, by the following resolution:

1. That we will cordially welcome a delegation
from the General Conference (named above) for con-
sultation and ultimate union of that Church with
our own.

The following day, May 19, a reply was received,
stating that Rev. Bishop Singleton T. Jones would
leave Washington on the 20th as a delegate to the General Conference at Chicago, in the interest of affiliation
and union with the Methodist Episcopal Church. On
the 22d of May Bishop Jones appeared, was introduced to the body, and addressed them with marked
ability on the subject of Methodist unity. A committee was appointed to consider the subject, and
afterward a commission of eight, with the Bishops,

was appointed, and instructed "to confer with a like commission from the African Methodist Episcopal Zion Church for the union of that body with our own;" and also were "empowered to treat with a similar commission from any other Methodist Church that may desire a like union."

No organic union resulted from this action, but a fraternal intercourse followed, which ultimately embraced also the African Methodist Episcopal Church, and the Methodist Episcopal Church, South, whose representatives were received and heard on the platform of the General Conference at Baltimore, in 1876. At the same session fraternal delegates were ordered to be appointed by the Bishops to nine Methodist bodies in America. ("Journal," 1876, p. 381.)

The action of the General Conference of 1836, at Cincinnati, (see Chapter IX,) which "disapproved, in the most unqualified sense, the conduct of the two members of the General Conference, who are reported to have lectured in this city recently, upon and in favor of Modern Abolitionism;" and which also declared that the Conference was "decidedly opposed to modern abolitionism, and wholly disclaim any right, wish, or intention to interfere in the civil and political relation between master and slave, as it exists in the slave-holding States of this Union," was brought to the attention of the General Conference of 1868, at Chicago, by a memorial from Elkton, Maryland, which I. Cunningham presented May 9. The matter was referred to the Committee on the State of the Church, which reported, May 28:

Believing that the object sought by the memorial from Elkton, Maryland, signed by Rev. L. C. Matlack and fifteen of his official members, is just and desirable, we recommend

to this body the adoption of the following resolutions:
1. That this Conference does not approve the action of the
General Conference of 1836 in censuring certain of its members for publicly speaking against the great evil of slavery;
and that we hereby rescind and pronounce void the aforesaid
preamble and resolutions.   2. That the preceding preamble
and resolutions be placed on the "Journal of the General Conference."   And, on motion of Gilbert Haven, the Secretary
was instructed to transmit to the parties concerned, [Rev.
Samuel Norris and Rev. George Storrs,] if living, and if not
to their families, certified copies of this action, rescinding
the action of the General Conference of 1836.

The resolutions now rescinded and pronounced void
had consummated a triumph over the Abolitionists
by a vote of 120 to 14, which remained unchallenged
for thirty-two years.   The reversal of this action by
almost unanimous consent was a signal trophy of the
triumph over slavery.   Such an instance of official
renunciation of wrong action, and of the *amende
honorable*, cannot be found on record in all Christian
history.   It was unqualifiedly doing "works for repentance," to salvation that needed not to be repented
of.   An equally interesting instance of Annual-Con-
ference action deserves mention and may fitly be
given, of a later date.

The action of the New York Conference in 1838,
censuring and degrading Paul R. Brown, is recorded
in the tenth chapter of this history.   The cause of
that action, with its reversal and the complete vindication of his career, is found recorded in the Journal
of that Conference for 1873.   It reads thus:

Whereas, Our esteemed brother, Paul R. Brown, after forty-
five years of uninterrupted service in the Christian ministry,
is about to retire from the effective ranks, we feel this a
fitting occasion to express our high official esteem of his

character as a man, a Christian, and a minister; of his marked fidelity and efficiency in the discharge of his duty in the pastorate, the presiding eldership, and in the various councils of the Church; and especially and emphatically of his noble, dignified, unflinching devotion to the great principles of human liberty and equality when such devotion was costly; and,

Whereas, This Conference in 1838, under the influence of mistaken judgment, as we now believe, though with the purest intention, did, by vote, censure and publicly reprimand our brother for no other cause than his advocacy of antislavery sentiments; therefore,

Resolved, That we rejoice with him in the triumph of the principles which he so fearlessly maintained for conscience' sake; and that we hereby revoke the vote of 1838, and honor him as one of the pioneers of a holy cause.

Resolved, That we tender to Brother Brown our profound regard, assure him that we shall not forget him in his retirement, but that we will ever pray that the evening of his days may be peaceful and his end triumphant.

Adopted by a unanimous vote.

Besides these adjustments on the one hand with the antislavery men of the former days, there were others in the opposite extreme of the old controversy with whom an adjustment seemed desirable. Between the two great families of Methodism in America a great gulf of non-intercourse had become fixed and apparently impassable for more than twenty years. With the downfall of slavery and the new life of a reconstructed North and South following the terrible struggle of civil war, that became possible which otherwise would have been forever impossible, "formal fraternity."

The primary step in that direction had been taken by the General Conference of the Methodist Episcopal Church, South, in 1846, by appointing Dr. Lovick Pierce a delegate to the General Conference of the

Methodist Episcopal Church, which met in Pittsburgh, May 1, 1848, to tender to that body their Christian regards and salutations. But Dr. Pierce was not received in that capacity for the alleged reason that "there are serious questions and difficulties existing between the two bodies," and, therefore, the Conference at Pittsburgh did "not consider it proper at present to enter into fraternal relations with the Methodist Episcopal Church, South." Personal courtesy was extended to Dr. Pierce, which he declined to receive; and departed, with the assurance respectfully made, that the Church he represented "can never renew the offer of fraternal relations between the two great bodies of Wesleyan Methodists in the United States. But the proposition can be renewed at any time, either now or hereafter, by the Methodist Episcopal Church."

The Erie meeting of the Bishops of the Methodist Episcopal Church, in 1865, was the first occasion of an expression of desire for friendly relations with the Church South, which is already noted at the opening of this chapter. That was followed by the Commission of 1868, which was appointed by the Chicago General Conference specifically to treat with the African Methodist Episcopal Church, and "with a similar commission from any other Methodist Church" desiring a union of Methodist Churches. On this ground the Board of Bishops, at their meeting in Meadville, Pa., April 23, 1869, appointed Bishops Morris, Janes, and Simpson, a commission to confer with the College of Bishops of the Church South at St. Louis, on "the propriety, practicability, and method of reunion." A communication was made to them expressing the opinion, "that should your approaching General Conference (1870) see proper to appoint a similar commission, they will be promptly met by our commission, who, we doubt not, will be happy to treat with them, and to report the result to our next General Conference," (1872.)

The reply to this embodied a dignified and regretful reference to the mission of Dr. Pierce, and its rejection; a disclaimer that slavery was "in any proper sense the cause of the separation," which they attribute to "certain constructions of the constitutional power and prerogatives of the General Conference, assumed and acted upon, which" were "considered oppressive and destructive of the rights of the minority;" a suggestion that fraternal feelings and relations must first be established between the two Churches; and finally a disclaimer of any authority to determine "the propriety, practicability, and methods of reunion."

This did not deter our commission, at a meeting held at Philadelphia, November 23, 1869, from a formal indorsement of the proffer made by our Bishops; and the appointment of Bishop Janes and Dr. W. L. Harris a deputation to bear a communication to the General Conference of the Church South, (in session at Memphis, Tenn., 1870,) which asked them to appoint a similar Commission. Their reply was in substance "the full indorsement" of the action and opinions of their College of Bishops in reply to ours at St. Louis—a doubt as to the authority of the Commission to make proposals of union to the Church South—which union, moreover, in their judgment, the "true interests of the Church of Christ" did not require nor demand. They, however, expressed their "sincere desire that the day may soon come when proper Christian sentiments and fraternal relations between the two great branches of Northern and Southern Methodism shall be permanently established."

Responsive to this desire our General Conference of 1872, at Brooklyn, N. Y., "*Resolved*, To appoint a delegation, consisting of two ministers and one layman, to convey our fraternal greetings to the General Conference of the Methodist Episcopal Church, South, at the next ensuing session," which met in Louisville, Ky., May 6, 1874. Rev. Albert S. Hunt, D.D., Rev. Charles H. Fowler, D.D., and General Clinton B. Fisk were selected by the Bishops, and all of them were in attendance.

Their reception was hearty, generous, brotherly. A cordial Christian greeting was promptly extended to them; and their addresses were so wisely conceived and eloquently uttered as to awaken deep emotion and elicit applause, with tears and shouts of praise. The Committee on Fraternity at Louisville, said: "Their utterances warmed our hearts. Their touching allusions to the common heritage of Methodist history stirred within us precious memories. . . . Every transaction and utterance of our past history pledges us to regard favorably and to meet promptly this initial response to our long-expressed desire." And it was responded to by the appointment of delegates to bear Christian salutations to the General Conference of the Methodist Episcopal Church, which met in Baltimore, May 1, 1876; also, commissioners to adjust all existing difficulties between the two bodies. The delegates were, Lovick Pierce, D.D., James A. Duncan, D.D., Landon C. Garland, LL.D. The commissioners were: E. H. Meyers, D.D.,

R. K. Hargrove, D.D.; Thomas M. Finney, D.D.; General Robert B. Vance, and Hon. David Klopton.

The American centennial year, with its grand monumental exhibition and demonstrations, accompanied with universal rejoicings over the prevailing peace, prosperity, and unity of the nation, was happily the occasion for consummating, officially, formal fraternity between the North and the South, through the representatives, jointly, of more than two million three hundred and fifty thousand Methodists, at the General Conference in Baltimore.

The addresses of Drs. Duncan and Garland, and the communication from Dr. Lovick Pierce, whose venerable character and loving words achieved as much as their eloquent voices, were followed by appropriate action, and by the appointment of a commission to meet with the commission of the Church South, above named. Morris D'C. Crawford, D.D.; Hon. Enoch L. Fancher, LL.D.; Erasmus Q. Fuller, D.D.; Gen. Clinton B. Fisk, and John P. Newman, D.D., were appointed the commissioners.

The climax of these brotherly negotiations was reached when, at Cape May, N. J., May 17, 1876, the commissioners of both boards, by a unanimous vote, adopted the following "Declaration and Basis of Fraternity" between said Churches, namely: Status of the Methodist Episcopal Church, and of the Methodist Episcopal Church, South, and their co-ordinate relation as legitimate branches of episcopal Methodism:

Each of said Churches is a legitimate branch of Episcopal Methodism in the United States, having a common origin in the Methodist Episcopal Church, organized in 1784. Since the organization of the Methodist Episcopal Church, South, was consummated, in 1845, by the voluntary exercise of the right of the Southern Annual Conferences, ministers, and members, to adhere to that communion, it has been an evangelical Church, reared on scriptural foundations, and her ministers and members, with those of the Methodist Episcopal Church, have constituted one Methodist family, though in distinct ecclesiastical connections.

The triumph, as a great fact, is abundantly vouched for by these historic memorials. They belong to a new stage of Christian civilization, which will advance evermore. They are monumental, and mark the opening of the grandest volume of American history.

23

CHAPTER XXIX.

A GLANCE AT OTHER CHURCHES.

THE varied action of the Methodist Episcopal Church on the subject of slavery for over half a century has been under review in these pages. What difficulties were encountered before accomplishing the work providentially assigned to it, what influences were antagonized, what conflicts were endured, and what temptations to inaction were continually resisted, cannot now be fully known. Other Churches were embarrassed in the same manner. A glance at their efforts, and their inaction as well, will more fully explain the situation.

The Protestant Episcopal Church did not allow slavery a place among the questions to be dealt with by ecclesiastical bodies. No testimonies are to be found in the proceedings of its General Conventions. "She has remained a mute and careless spectator of this great conflict," said Hon. John Jay.

The Baptist Churches recognize no central body holding general jurisdiction. Their antislavery testimony was given by local Churches. It involved no great struggle as a denomination; but a separate Antislavery Missionary Board was sustained liberally for many years. The Free-Will Baptists refused fellowship to all slaveholders as early as 1839. Having no membership at the South, they had no occasion for an antislavery struggle such as the Methodist Episcopal Church had.

The Methodist Protestant Church at its organization, in 1830, could not get "Southern co-operation in conventional action until their slave-holding laws were as strongly guarded by the constitution against the action of all ecclesiastical bodies as the morality of the Holy Scriptures."—*Bassett*, p. 104. Their General Conference of 1834 took no action on the subject of slavery, but in 1838, 1842, 1846, 1850, and 1854, a majority vote disclaimed all authority to act thereon, and referred it to the Annual Conferences. Earnest discussions were had, and a large minority at each session sought to secure antislavery action and to expunge from their Discipline the word "white," which qualified and limited the privilege of suffrage, but without success. The utmost achieved at any time was a declaration, in 1846, "that the holding of slaves is, under many circumstances, a sin against God, and in such cases should be condemned by the Methodist Protestant Church. Nevertheless, it is our opinion that under some circumstances it is not sinful." But this declaration was defeated in 1854.

A delegated convention from fifteen Northern Annual Conferences was held at Cincinnati, November, 1857, which memorialized the General Conference of 1858, asking antislavery action, stipulating, as the inevitable alternative, withdrawal from that body. Their petition was not granted, and these Conferences organized a separate body, which was thoroughly antislavery in character and action. But no antislavery expression has ever been adopted by any General Conference of the old Methodist Protestant Church, except the very mild utterance of 1846, which was canceled by the vote in 1854, so leaving slavery unimpeached.

The Presbyterian Church, in the Synod of New York and Pennsylvania, 1774, took up the subject of negro slavery. But they deferred " the affair to.the next meeting." In 1787 they recommended, " in the warmest terms, to every member of the body, and to all the Churches and families under their care, to do every thing in their power, consistent with the civil rights of society, to promote the abolition of slavery." This was reaffirmed in 1793.

The General Assembly in 1795 assured " all the Churches under their care that they view with the deepest concern any vestiges of slavery which may exist in our country," and refer to the deliverances, 1787 and 1793, as their present views. The Assembly, in 1815, reaffirm their old testimonies, and add that " they consider the buying and selling of slaves by way of traffic inconsistent with the spirit of the Gospel." And in 1818, after much discussion, the system of slavery was condemned, as " inconsistent with the law of God, . . . irreconcilable with the spirit and principles of the Gospel of Christ," and a " blot on our holy religion ; " and they urged speedy efforts " to obtain the complete abolition of slavery throughouth Cristendom and the world."

At Pittsburgh, in 1836, the subject was indefinitely postponed by a vote of 154 to 87. Before the next action was taken against slavery two Assemblies were in operation—the Old School and the New School bodies.

The New School General Assembly in 1839 referred the subject to the lower judicatories. In 1840, after requesting certain presbyteries to rescind resolutions which excluded slave-holders from their pulpits and communion tables, the question was indefinitely postponed. In 1843 they did "not think it for the edification of the Church to take any action on the subject." But in 1846 the system of slavery was condemned as "intrinsically unrighteous and oppressive," while slave-holders are yet deemed worthy of "ecclesiastical and Christian fellowship."

In 1849 there were memorials from four synods and thirteen presbyteries asking the Assembly to "free the Church from all participation and connection with slave-holding." They responded by re-affirming the testimonies of 1815, 1818, and 1846. And in 1850, by a vote of 87 to 16, resolutions were adopted deploring the evils of slavery, and declaring slave-holding a disciplinary offense, except when "it is unavoidable, by the laws of the State, the obligation of guardianship, or the demands of humanity." The next two years this action was indorsed informally; and in 1853, after condemning the institution of slavery as "injurious to the highest and best interests of all concerned in it," measures were adopted for securing the statistics of slavery among their Churches. This was never accomplished.

In 1855 the system was condemned, the intemperateness of word and action exhibited by its opponents was regretted, and antislavery action was recommended. This was followed in 1856 by a statement that the constitutional power of the Assembly was limited to reproof, warning, testimony, and recommending reformation; which was exercised in 1857 toward the Presbytery of Lexington, South. They had given official notice that many ministers, ruling elders, and members there "held slaves from principle and of choice, believing it to be, according to the Bible, right." The Assembly said: "We do hereby call on that Presbytery to review and rectify their position. Such doctrines and practices cannot be permanently tolerated in the Presbyterian Church."

After the separation the Old School Assembly, in 1845, replied to certain memorialists as follows: "The question is this, Do the Scriptures teach that the holding of slaves without regard to circumstances, is sin, the renunciation of which should be made a condition of membership in the Church of Christ?" To this an extended answer is given, and then summed up thus: "The Assembly intend simply to say, that since Christ and his inspired apostles did not make the holding of slaves a bar to communion, we, as a court of Christ, have no authority to do so: since they did not attempt to remove it from the Church by legislation, we have no authority to legislate on the subject." Adopted: yeas 168, nays 13. As this was construed to be a rescinding of the previous testimonies of the Assembly, a disclaimer was adopted in 1846, and further action was declared not needed. This declaration was repeated in 1849, and in 1850 the subject of slavery was laid on the table until the slave-holders' Rebellion was inaugurated.

At the General Assembly of 1861 there was an intense, angry, and lengthy debate on the following resolution, in which nothing was said about slavery, although it pointed in that direction: "*Resolved*, That in the judgment of this Assembly it is the duty of the ministers and Churches under its care to do all in their power to promote and perpetuate the integrity of these United States, and to strengthen, uphold, and encourage the Federal Government in the just exercise of all its functions under our noble Constitution." This was met by a counter resolution, "That the General Assembly think it inexpedient at this time to give any formal expression of opinion touching the existing crisis, and that consequently the whole subject be indefinitely postponed."

In 1862, however, the "Deliverance" of the Assembly, which was adopted by a vote of 199 to 20, declared that "the system that makes, or proposes to make, the relation of master and slave hereditary, perpetual, and absolute, must be wrong, as it is a negation of the principles and precepts of the Gospel, and of the very idea of civil liberty and of inalienable rights."

The New School Assembly took its last action, prior to the great Rebellion in 1860, by a vote refusing "to instruct their Church Extension Society not to aid any Church that has in its communion one or more slave-holders;" giving as reasons, that no Presbyterian Church was sustaining or fortifying the institution of slavery; and they would not withhold from slave-holders the bread of life; and that no instructions were needed by the committee. But in 1863 the Assembly, in session at Philadelphia, adopted a report on the state of the country, presented by Albert Barnes, which declared that the system of human bondage as practiced in the South is in direct violation of human rights and the teachings of our better natures, therefore they gave the strongest support to the President's proclamation. And in 1865 the same body unanimously adopted a memorial demanding the right of franchise for the colored men.

The Congregationalists of this country, mainly occupying the New England States, or other Northern States, without any connectional bond, and only indi-

rectly implicated in slavery, were yet slow to become
antislavery in sentiment, and that was without disciplinary power, except when adopted by local independent Churches.   There can be no comparison historically, therefore, between them and Methodism in
its struggle and triumph.

With the other Churches already noted—of much
less extended territory and numerical strength, however—the comparison of records is largely in favor
of the Methodist Episcopal Church.   Forty years of
unqualified condemnation of slavery, alternated by
twenty years of indifference or toleration, is succeeded by twenty other years of antislavery conflict which
ultimate in extirpation.   Slavery always called a great
evil—the traffic in slaves ever forbidden—slave-holding never allowed in the traveling ministry—and no
word of apology or vindication of slavery on Scripture
grounds ever uttered by the General Conference; it
was a becoming climax, too long delayed and too
gradually developed, which that Church reached in
1864.   Note the mile-stones, as indicated by the action
of successive General Conferences :

1844. It is the sense of this General Conference that he
(Bishop Andrew) desist from the exercise of his office so long
as this impediment (holding slaves) remains.

1856. We recommend the Annual Conferences so to amend
our General Rule on Slavery as to read (forbid) "the buying,
selling, or holding a human being as a slave." (Yeas, 122;
nays, 96.)

1860. We believe that the buying, selling, or holding of
human beings as chattels is contrary to the laws of God and
nature; inconsistent with the golden rule, and with that rule
in our Discipline which requires all who desire to remain
among us to do no harm, and to avoid evil of every kind.
We therefore affectionately admonish all our preachers and

people to keep themselves pure from this great evil, and to seek its extirpation by all lawful and Christian means. (Yeas, 155; nays, 58.)

We recommend the amendment of the General Rule on Slavery, that it shall read (forbid) "the buying, selling, or holding of men, women, or children with an intention to enslave them." (Yeas, 138; nays, 74.)

1864. The proposed New Rule is an expression of a long conviction entertained by the majority of the Church—the utterance of an edict which conscience dictates and the teaching of God's word approves. . . . So far as we are concerned, then, the question, What shall be done for the extirpation of slavery? shall be answered by a rule uprooting it and forbidding it forever. . . . Relying on the promise and mercy of God as far as we can, we "proclaim liberty throughout all the land to all the inhabitants thereof." *Resolved*, by the delegates of the several Annual Conferences in General Conference assembled, That we recommend the amendment of the General Rule on Slavery, so that it shall read (forbid) "slave-holding, buying or selling slaves."

The vote was 207 yeas, and 9 nays. The concurrent vote of the Annual Conferences showed that the majority of traveling preachers was equally large for the New Rule. One Conference only gave a majority against it. Many of the largest Conferences were unanimous in its support, and of the others a few only gave any negative votes. And the formal record of a foregone conclusion was in a few months on the Annual Conference Journals, from which it was transcribed into the Discipline as one of the laws of the General Conference of 1864.

The comparative energy and fidelity displayed needs no comment. The facts speak plainly and fully. The amount of effort required to carry forward successfully the great revolution of public sentiment in the Methodist Episcopal Church, on the question of slavery, can only be known to those who were witnesses and active agents therein. These efforts were begun by a few in 1835, and brought to a close in 1860. The culminating point was reached in twenty-five years. Then the position of the Methodist Episcopal Church was definitely settled. All slave-holding thereafter was prohibited. The practice became a fraud.

CHAPTER XXX.

RETROSPECTIVE.

WHAT hath God wrought! One hundred years ago the American nation, then at the beginning of its history, was cursed with a system of chattel slavery which at that time was two hundred years old. For with the earliest provincial settlements of the sixteenth century in America slavery was practiced. And so deeply rooted and wide spread was its development during the century just passed, that the propagandists of slavery deemed it merely a question of time when its prevalence, in practice or toleration, would extend to the utmost limits of the continent. Between the Northern Lakes and the Gulf of Mexico, and from ocean to ocean, the hunters of men were confident that they and their assigns would pursue and seize their prey at their own pleasure, and at the cost of the national treasury, to the end of time.

Thirty years ago Rev. Daniel Worth, when traveling on the Ohio River, was introduced by the captain of the boat to a slave-holder, thus: "My friend Mr. Worth is an Abolitionist, but a good fellow." "This gentleman is one of the best of good slave-holders." And they were at once mutually acquainted, and engaged in earnest conversation.

"I should like to know, Mr. Worth," said the slave-holder, "if you really believe that slavery will ever be abolished?" "I do most certainly believe that slavery must die." "Well, Mr. Worth, I believe that slavery will live forever. I have not a doubt of it. But I should like to hear one good reason for your notion that slavery will ever die." "There is," said Mr. Worth, "one all-sufficient reason why slavery must die." "Let me hear it, if you please," said the other. "It may not satisfy you," he replied; "although with me it is the ground of an unwavering faith." Then rising to his full height—over six feet, a stalwart man of commanding presence, and full of the sublime thought that struggled for utterance—he thundered in reply, "Sir, slavery must die because God Almighty lives!"

Whatever of human agency was employed, the life of God was the pulse of antislavery power. The human instrumentality was often marked with the weakness of prejudice, and even passion. Not wholly unselfish, nor entirely submissive to the divine Will, were the purposes of many who, nevertheless, were doing God's work. There were, however, many instances in which self-sacrificing Methodists and others, for conscience' sake, and because they loved their neighbor as themselves, had freed their slaves, or pleaded for freedom, and became thereby mighty, through God, in pulling down this stronghold of Satan. An entire generation of these have passed from earth, and are unknown to fame, having no place in history as recorded by human hands. But God has their names in his "Book of Remembrance."

It was a grand discipline which our fathers passed through, although heavy burdens were borne by them, apparently almost in vain, while slavery grew and spread its baneful influences in Church and State. And it was a noble strife that a portion of their successors of the present generation bravely sustained against fearful odds for a quarter of a century, which, moreover, culminated in a final triumph. Yet never was it more appropriate than it is now to say, " Not unto us, O Lord, not unto us, but unto thy name give glory, for thy mercy, and for thy truth's sake." (Psalm cxv. 1.)

There is a sad and fearful aspect to this great triumph of freedom. Not for his mercy's sake alone was this accomplished. " By terrible things in righteousness wilt thou answer us," is the declaration of the psalmist. And God's answer to the reckless indifference, as well as the haughty defiance, exhibited toward his poor and toward himself, was terrible indeed, in the agencies employed to bear the message of his providential will. What might have been, is perhaps indicated by the history of West India emancipation, and the relation of the English Wesleyans thereto.

Our American Methodism was too far away from the land of Wesley, and too early and too closely associated with powerful influences which weakened and demoralized its antislavery sentiment, to maintain unflinchingly to the bitter end the primitive ground on that question. Therefore the contrast between English Wesleyanism and the Methodist Episcopal Church in their respective relations to Abolitionism, which is now briefly recalled.

The Wesleyan Methodists of England were first and foremost and untiring in their co-operation with the friends of emancipation. They were a unit in their unqualified antagonism to slavery. All their chapels were open for antislavery meetings. Every gathering of the English Conference, for several years, was the occasion for antislavery declarations.

Memorials against slavery and for emancipation were universally circulated by the Wesleyans, and tens of thousands of signatures thereto were forwarded to Parliament. The Missionary Secretary and the Presidents of conferences hesitated not to antagonize the movements of the Colonial Government for slavery, and held them at bay bravely in behalf of the Wesleyan missionaries among the West India slaves.

With such a support outside, the Christian statesmen of Great Britain within the government were made strong and valiant. We will look in vain for a parallel to Sir Thomas Fowell Buxton among our American statesmen of a similar period in our history. Writing to his daughter on the subject of a division in the House of Commons, in the conflict for West Indian emancipation, he says: "If ever there was a subject which occupied our prayers it was this. Do you remember how we desired that God would give me his Spirit in that emergency; how we quoted the promise, 'He that lacketh wisdom, let him ask it of the Lord, and it shall be given him;' and how I kept open that passage in the Old Testament in which it is said, 'We have no might against this great company that cometh against us, neither know we what to do, but our eyes are upon Thee;' the Spirit of the Lord replying, 'Be not afraid nor dismayed by reason of this great multitude, for the battle is not yours, but God's.' If you want to see the passage, open my Bible, it will turn of itself to the place. I sincerely believe that prayer was the cause of division. The course we took appeared to be right, and we followed it blindly."—"*The Still Hour,*" *A. Phelps,* p. 51.

Thus, with a solid Wesleyan communion, untiring in its zeal, joined with lesser religious forces, led by

Bible-reading statesmen, who believed God's word and sought to do God's will, it is no marvel that a peaceful emancipation was achieved in a few years, at the moderate outlay by the British government of twenty millions of money.

Unfortunately for our reputation as a people, and unhappily for the cause of humanity and of religion, the attitude of the Methodist Episcopal Church was not like that of the English Wesleyan body, nor were our lines of action parallel to theirs.

Nor indeed were our statesmen of the Bible-reading class, and prayerfully reliant on the promises of God, after the pattern of Sir Thomas Fowell Buxton. When William H. Seward, as a politician merely, suggested in the American Senate the fact that there was a higher law than the Constitution of the United States, the Christian statesmen of our Senate laughed him to scorn, and "the higher law" became a hissing and a by-word. And there was no lack of Christian ministers, so-called, who rebuked the doctrine of a higher law as a fanatical dogma. And what followed?

In the absence of the American Churches from their rightful original position of practical antagonism to slavery, and by their reverse action, which continued for an entire generation; by the sanction, extension, and support of slavery through the national government for three quarters of a century of legislation, the providential necessity was developed for an earthquake of rebellion, and the hot thunderbolts of war, in order to break loose the shackles which Church and State had forged and fastened on four million pair of hands. Aye, and more fearful yet was the bloody sacrifice that immolated as many lives of armed men in battle as there were shackled men set free! It is a little thing to add that the treasury of the nation was exhausted by a war-debt equal to fifteen hundred dollars for each of the four million souls set free! "Terrible things in righteousness" were the answers from God!

The closing words of this retrospect may seem unhistoric; yet they are written. The preceding pages may appear delinquent. With a careful endeavor to use all the information at command, it may yet seem that some persons and many facts have not been noticed as they deserved. In some instances there was a lack of authentic knowledge, notwithstanding special efforts to secure it. In many other cases there was an entire absence of information. If occasion shall arise for a revised edition, opportunity may be afforded for supplementing the record in these respects.

For material aid afforded in compiling this history the writer is indebted largely to Thomas W. Price, of Philadelphia, whose valuable library and personal influence in securing volumes of special value from the Mercantile Library Association have been at my command.

Not less valuable service has been rendered by Bishop W. L. Harris in allowing the use of nine large folio scrap-books containing the discussion of the subject of slavery in the Church for several of the most exciting years prior to 1860, which he had compiled from the Methodist press and carefully indexed. I had not known of these folios, nor would it have been possible to obtain the information they contain but for his mentioning and generously offering them to me as "just the thing you need."

The Book Agents at New York furnished the bound volumes of the "Christian Advocate" for the memorable period including 1859–1868, covering the close of the conservative and the inauguration of the radical *régime*, which brought the Church to the Asburian theory and practice on the subject of "African liberty."

The bound volumes of the "Methodist Quarterly," from the library of Dr. Whedon, who maintained the position so bravely of the antislavery editor of "an antislavery organ of an antislavery Church," were of great value, and are used freely.

This brief retrospect of information furnished, with a grateful recognition of its sources, individually considered, is preliminary to a recall of the field passed over and the struggle participated in personally for more than forty years now past.

The conclusion reached is amazing. The memories awakened are thrilling. The contrasts of personal positions and personal relations are almost sufficient to suggest the suspicion of possible deception. "It is as a dream when one awaketh."

Fifty-four years ago I stood gazing sadly in my native city, Baltimore, upon chained gangs of men and women, followed by wagons laden with infant children, moving off from George Woolfolks' slave pens, on Pratt-street, toward the great national mart of the domestic slave-trade, Washington, the capital of "the land of the free and the home of the brave."

Forty-four years ago, yet a minor, I was secretary of the Wesleyan Antislavery Society of the Methodist Episcopal Church, at Philadelphia, with eleven others; Henry J. Pepper, president. Soon afterward my name was before the Philadelphia Annual Conference, a candidate for admission, but rejected by a unanimous vote, because—secretary of an antislavery society and "a modern abolitionist." A unanimous rejection was repeated the following year by the same body for the same reason. This was followed by my expulsion from the Local Preachers' Association of Philadelphia because unacceptable as an abolitionist; also by a refusal, in 1839, to renew my license to preach at the Quarterly Conference of Union Church, and by a threat of expulsion afterward from my pastor for preaching without a license; and, finally, by fleeing for refuge to Lowell, Massachusetts, under the protection and patronage of Orange Scott and the New England Conference. This was in 1840. There my itinerant life began.

Twenty-one years were occupied in New England, New York, and the West, in active co-operation with the "modern" Abolitionists. The pulpit, the press, and the ballot-box were all none too capacious for a zeal, perhaps without knowledge at times, which owed its main inspiration to the scenes witnessed in the streets and fields of Baltimore, joined with the thrilling tales of slavery from the lips of a Quaker-Methodist mother, made indelible by reading the "Genius of Universal Emancipation," edited by Benjamin Lundy and William Lloyd Garrison at Baltimore.

Three years were spent in camp and field life; first as a chaplain for less than a year; then, in the crisis following M'Clellan's Peninsular Campaign, much of the following year was spent in giving military addresses in the State of Illinois, enrolling volunteers, and finally returning to the army a field-officer of cavalry. Thenceforward, until after the Rebellion was put down, two years were filled up as a subordinate officer; sometimes in command of post, or at the head of the regiment, and not unfrequently heading a charge of cavalry in line of battle; and, finally, as Provost-Marshal of St. Louis city and twenty-two counties, with the administration of justice committed to my hands, embracing all matters involving the relations of the soldier with the citizen, or servants and their masters, and landlords and soldier families who were tenants. The "code" of law to be administered was my own sense of equity alone.

Fifteen other years have elapsed. The preacher unanimously rejected two years successively by the Philadelphia Conference (in 1837 and 1838) was received by the same body in 1867 with perfect unanimity and hearty greetings when fifty years old. The thirteen years following, and reaching to 1880, have been spent in the pastorate of the Methodist Episcopal Church, and distributed in the States of Pennsylvania, Maryland, Louisiana, and Delaware. Three times I have been allowed to represent my brethren in the General Conference. To-day is closed gladly the record of an eventful history. "The lines have fallen to me in pleasant places. I have a goodly heritage. Surely goodness and mercy have followed me all the days of my life; and I shall dwell in the house of the Lord forever."

ANTISLAVERY BIBLIOGRAPHY.

———◆———

American Slavery as It Is: Testimony of a Thousand Witnesses. Small 8vo. New York: American Antislavery Society. 1839.

Debates of the General Conference of 1844. 8vo. Reported by MATLACK and LEE. New York: O. Scott, Publisher. 1845.

Prison Life and Reflections. One volume, 12mo. By GEORGE THOMPSON. Oberlin: Printed by James M. Fitch. 1874.

Methodism and Slavery. 12mo. By L. C. MATLACK. New York: Wesleyan Methodist Book Room. 1848.

Life of Orange Scott. 12mo. By L. C. MATLACK. New York: Wesleyan Methodist Book Room; C. Prindle, Agent. 1848.

Sinfulness of American Slavery. Two volumes. By Rev. CHARLES ELLIOTT, D.D. Cincinnati: L. Swormstedt and J. H. Power. 1851.

The Great Secession. One volume, 8vo. By Rev. CHARLES ELLIOTT, D.D. As above.

American Slave Code. One volume, 12mo. By WILLIAM GOODELL. New York: American and Foreign Antislavery Society. 1853.

Antislavery Measures of the XXXVIIth and XXXVIIIth Congresses, (1861–1864.) One volume, 12mo. By HENRY WILSON. Boston: Walker, Wise & Co. 1864.

History of Slavery in Massachusetts. By GEORGE H. MOORE. New York: Published by the Appletons. 1866.

Recollections of our Antislavery Conflict. One volume, 12mo. By SAMUEL J. MAY. Boston: Fields, Osgood & Co. 1864.

The Underground Railroad. One volume, 8vo. BY WILLIAM STELL. Philadelphia: Porter & Coates. 1872.

Rise and Fall of the Slave Power in America. Three volumes, 8vo. By HENRY WILSON. Boston: James R. Osgood & Co. 1872, 1875, 1877.

Life of Rev. Adam Crooks. One volume, 12mo. By Mrs. E. W. CROOKS. Syracuse: Wesleyan Methodist Book Room. 1875.

Life and Times of Rev. George Pegler. An Autobiography. Syracuse: Published for the Author, at the Wesleyan Book Room. 1875.

Abraham Lincoln and the Abolition of Slavery. One volume, 12mo. By CHARLES GODFREY LELAND. New York: G. P. Putnam's Sons. 1879.

William Lloyd Garrison and His Times. One volume, 12mo. By OLIVER JOHNSON. Boston: B. B. Russell & Co. 1880.

INDEX.

Indians enslaved, 36.
Indian slaves massacred, 27.
Indictment, Christian Advocate, 187.
Inskip, John S., 327.

Janes, Bishop, 180, 349.
Jefferson *versus* Slave-trade, 32.
Jones, Bishop, 345.
Jury trial, fugitives, 38.

Kentucky Conference, organized 1852, 212.
Kingsley's Compensation Plan, 213, 218.

Lay Conventions, 1860, Baltimore Conference, 319, 320.
La Roy Sunderland, 85, 86, 110, 122, 130.
Las Casas, 26.
Lay Union, 308.
Lee, Luther, 113, 122, 126.
Legislation for freedom, 333.
Legislatures *versus* Abolitionists, 83.
Levings, Noah, 94.
Lewis, Judge, Louisiana, 107.
Liberty Party candidates, 203, 206.
Light, G. C., 94.
Lincoln, Address to, 335.
Lincoln's Proclamation, 330.
Lincoln to the Methodist Episcopal Church, 337.
Literary institutions, South, 340.
Longstreet, A. B., 161.
Lord, Rev. W., of the Abolitionists, 98.
Louisville Convention, 177.
Lowell Convention, 127.
Luckey, Samuel, 92, 122.
Lundy, Benjamin, 199.
Luther, for slavery, 28.

Mansfield's, Lord, decision, 35.
Marshall, Chief Justice, 57.
Maryland Emancipation, 333.
Maryland Methodists aroused, 149.
Mason, Senator, 38.
Massachusetts slavery, 37.
Mattison, Hiram, 238.
M'Clintock, John, 288.
M'Ferrin, J. B., 175.
Meadville, meeting of Bishops, 349.
Matthews, Judge, on Slavery, 36.
Medical graduates, African, 300.
Memorials (1860) classified, 310.
Merrill, Abram D., 86.
Merrill, Joseph A., 91.
Merritt, Timothy, 110, 113, 122, 126, 127.
Methodism, introduction of, 47.
Methodist antislavery bodies, 297.
Methodist Antislavery Societies, 85.
Methodist Episcopal Church, in the South, 339.
Methodist Episcopal Church, South, 177.
Methodist Episcopal Church *versus* Slavery, 58.
Methodist Protestant Church, 355.
Michigan Conference, 83.

Miller, Col. J. P., 39.
Ministerial and Lay Union, address, 308.
Ministerial and Lay Union, reply thereto, Curry, 308.
Missions, West Indies, 75.
Mob law, 1860, 325.
Modern Abolitionism, argument, 122, 125.
Monroe, Samuel Y., 208, 312.
Moody, Granville, 312.
Moravians for slavery, 31.
Morris, Bishop, 100, 120, 129, 324.
Murphy, T. C., 312.

New Chapter, 1860, 311.
New Chapter, advisory, 314.
New Chapter, repudiation of, 319.
New Chapter, vote on, 313.
New England and secession, 152, 160, 172.
New England Antislavery Society, 80.
New England Conference, 85, 109, 129, 329.
New Hampshire Conference, 86, 109, 129.
New Jersey Conference, 328.
Newman, Dr. J. P., 345.
New Rule, (1839,) New England Conference, 133.
New Rule, (1856,) vote on analyzed, 290.
New Rule, (1860,) Annual Conference vote on, 309, 317.
New Rule, (1860,) General Conference vote on, 312.
New Rule enacted, 1864, 331.
New Rules proposed, 309.
New York Conference, 82, 112, 347.
New York East Conference, 327, 329.
New York memorial, 1840, 135.
New York Mills Convention, 125.
New York Preachers, *versus* Fugitive Law, 207.
Norris, Samuel, 93, 95, 304.
North Bennet-street Church, 85.
North Carolina Conference memorial, 52.
Northern Advocate, 217, 220.
Northern Independent, 305.
North-Western Advocate, 221.
Nullification, 226, 319.

Oglethorpe, Governor, 30.
Ohio Conference, 1835, 82.
Olin, Stephen, 158.
Oneida Conference, 111, 184.
Ordination of colored men, 1800, 73.
Outlaw system, slavery, 34.

Pastoral Address, Slavery, 102, 137, 314.
Pastoral Letter, Hedding and Emory, 90.
Pastoral Letter (1800) on Slavery, 65.
Parkersburgh mob, 187.
Patriotic Conference action, 327, 330.
Payne, Robert, 94, 175, 176.
Pearne, W. H., 280.